To fellow Veteran -

Dick Ayesh

THROUGH BLUE SKIES TO HELL

Through BLUE SKIES to HELL

America's "Bloody 100th" in the Air War Over Germany

By
EDWARD M. SION

Philadelphia & Newbury

Published in the United States of America in 2007 by
CASEMATE
1016 Warrior Road, Drexel Hill, PA 19026

and in Great Britain by
CASEMATE
17 Cheap Street, Newbury RG20 5DD

ISBN 978-1-932033-67-0

Cataloging-in-publication data is available from the Library of Congress
and the British Library.

Printed and Bound in the United States of America.

For a complete list of Casemate titles please contact:

CASEMATE PUBLISHERS
Telephone (610) 853-9131, Fax (610) 853-9146
E-mail: casemate@casematepublishing.com

CASEMATE PUBLISHERS
Telephone (01635) 231091, Fax (01635) 41619
E-mail: casemate-uk@casematepublishing.co.uk

CONTENTS

ACKNOWLEDGMENTS		vii
PREFACE		xi
1.	GROWING UP IN THE AIR CAPITAL	1
2.	THE MAKING OF AN AIRMAN	5
3.	THE BOMBARDIER'S ARSENAL	13
4.	TOP SECRET BOMBSIGHT	21
5.	BOMBER FORMATIONS & FIGHTER TACTICS	27
6.	BLIND BOMBING, RADARS AND PFF	37
7.	HEADING TO COMBAT	49
8.	WELCOME TO THORPE ABBOTTS	53
9.	LEGEND OF THE BLOODY HUNDREDTH	65
10.	SITUATION GROUND WAR, POST D-DAY	69
11.	SITUATION AIR WAR, FALL 1944	79
12.	THE NERVE CENTER AT HIGH WYCOMBE	83
13.	THE AIR WAR ON SYNTHETIC OIL	97
14.	GERMAN DEFENSES AGAINST BOMBERS	107
15.	EVE OF COMBAT	117
16.	MISSION BY MISSION (I)	123
17.	LONDON ENCOUNTERS	143
18.	MISSION BY MISSION (II)	151
19.	THE LUCKY BASTARDS HEADING HOME	175
20.	THE IMPACT OF STRATEGIC BOMBING ON FINAL VICTORY	179
21.	20TH CENTURY MORAL ISSUES AND 21ST CENTURY IMPLICATIONS	187
NOTES		195
BIBLIOGRAPHY		205
INDEX		211

This book is dedicated to my dear Mother,
Mrs. R. Rae Sion (1916–2003),
who inspired and encouraged me to write it,
and
to my Father and Uncles who served our nation in the
Armed Forces during World War II:
Michael E. Sion
(US Army Corps of Engineers, Aleutians Campaign, North Pacific)
Edward G. Sion, MD
(US Army Medical Corps, Combat Surgeon, Western Europe)
Richard R. Ayesh
(US Army Air Corps, Western Europe)
Fred J. Ayesh
(US Army Air Corps, Guam, South Pacific)
William A. Ayesh
(US Army Air Corps, Guam, South Pacific)

ACKNOWLEDGMENTS

In course of this project I was assisted by numerous individuals who generously devoted their time and shared their insights on the air war with me. First and foremost, I thank my Uncle, Richard R. Ayesh. Without his combat diary, expertise, advice and guidance, this book would never have been written. I am deeply grateful to Gene Jensen, the pilot of my Uncle's crew, who kindly and generously made available his unpublished memoirs ("The Chronicles of Gene") relating his war experiences and stories of the many close calls experienced by his crew. I would also like to thank co-pilot Jim Millet for his interest and shared insights on life at Thorpe Abbotts as well as reminiscences of the missions.

I am profoundly grateful to my publisher David Farnsworth and to my editor Steven Smith for their decision to publish the book and for their enthusiastic interest, patience, support and guidance during the entire process. I also thank Ms. Tara Lichterman of Casemate Publishing for her always cheerful assistance.

I am deeply indebted to my friend Jason Homer, illustrator and computer graphics expert who was responsible for many of the maps and illustrations in the book, and to his wife, Jackie Zavodnick, MD, for her unceasing encouragement and patience during the time-consuming effort required to complete the work.

In the United Kingdom, I owe an immense debt of gratitude to Ron and Carol Batley, the curators of the 100th Bomb Group Memorial Museum at Thorpe Abbotts for their kind hospitality and insights during my visit to Thorpe Abbotts. It is a pleasure to gratefully acknowledge the extensive help of Mr. Tom Oakley, a volunteer at the Museum, who generously and enthusiastically shared his insights, vast store of knowledge and local anecdotes about the 100th Bomb Group, war-time civilian life in the UK generally and in East Anglia specifically (including his own) and many details of the always dangerous assembly into formation off the English coast, as well as wartime incidents at the base.

In the United States, many friends and colleagues have assisted me in the completion of this book.

First, I am pleased to extend my deepest gratitude to Michael Faley, Official Archivist and Historian of the 100th Bomb Group Memorial, and Mr. Jack O'Leary for sharing their encyclopedic knowledge of the air war and every aspect of the 100th Bomb Group. They have both given unselfishly of their time to help make this book a reality. I am indebted to Ms. Jan Riddling, archivist and historian of the 100th Bomb Group for providing her insights and expertise, especially on ground crews and for her willingness to serve as a reviewer. I am deeply grateful to Ms. Susan Whitney for her expert advice on writing, organization, and early editorial assistance.

It is a pleasure to thank my colleagues who shared their book publishing experiences and offered much encouragement and insight, usually within local establishments consuming various libations. Among these individuals are Professors William Wagner, and Lawrence Stepelevich, and Dr. Robert Stokes at Villanova University and Dr. Jay Holberg at the University of Arizona. I thank Mr. Jon Seal and Mr. Andreas Parsch for their kind permission to quote their unpublished material. I am indebted to Mr. Fred Preller for making available his expertise on the air war and pointing me to much useful and rare material on operational activities at High Wycombe. I thank the personnel at the National Archives Still Photo Division in College Park, Maryland, especially Rutha Beamon, for their kind assistance with archival photographic materials.

Last but not least, I thank my loving and supportive family who encouraged me every step of the way. I thank my daughter Melanie, a medical student at Georgetown University, who digitized my uncle's diary from beginning to end, remarking along the way, "Dad, going through this diary is like watching a movie." I thank my son Michael, an MBA student at Penn's Wharton School, for his continual interest and his expert assistance with formatting, organization and the intricacies of Microsoft Word. My wife Miriam has been an unswerving source of encouragement and advice throughout the process and helped compile the endnotes.

PREFACE

How did a research scientist and professor who never served in the military manage to write a book on the air war over Europe in World War II? Well, I was a born and reared in Wichita, Kansas, where it was commonplace to cont [illegible] After all, Wichita was the [illegible] pro-duction facilities, fro [illegible] oeing plant and McConnell [illegible]

Wichita,

But a key event t [illegible] intel-lectual life occurred [illegible] New Jersey just after I was born and my father had been discharged from the Army (where he served in the Aleutians campaign). He commuted to work in Philadelphia while my parents cared for my great uncle, Rev. Paul Sion, who had retired from the Catholic Priesthood and lived in the house next door. One day, my parents bought a set of encyclopedias from a door to door salesman published by The Grolier Society and called "The Book of Knowledge." These books absolutely ignited an unrelenting passion for both science and history that has stayed with me to this day.

Moving back to Wichita when I was six years old, I grew up hearing my Mother often telling me of my Uncle Richard's wartime experiences—of the time he was missing in action, of the anxiety the family went through, and of the horrible things he witnessed but never talked about. My Mother told me never to bring it up to him and I never had the nerve to do so until the year 2000, 55 years after the war's end, when the whole country seemed to awaken to the sacrifices and courageous deeds of the Greatest Generation, the one that saved the world. At that time, I sent him an e-mail containing a long list of questions about his service as a bombardier on a B-17 bomber in the 349th Bomb Squadron, 100th Bombardment Group, 13th Combat Wing, 3rd Air Division of the Eighth Air Force. He told me about a diary he had kept right after each combat mission and let me photocopy it as well as many of his wartime photographs and documents.

It was then, with my Mother's inspiration and encouragement that I decided to write a book with his war diary as the centerpiece. However, I was too much of an academic not to realize that staring at me was an opportunity to share the knowledge I was acquiring with others and to accumulate and convey that knowledge from first principles. I wanted to produce a book that was both in-depth and comprehensive—a mini-textbook if you will—on the air war, with a special focus on the time of his service during the crucial final year of the war, 1944–45. Therefore, when I began the research for this book my plan was to address every aspect of the air war in the form of specific chapters devoted to each separate topic as background material for a deeper understanding of the content of the diary. This was a fairly radical departure from the approach of most books on the air war, where brief but personal accounts of the combat experiences of many airmen as well as explanations of their equipment and of technology are intermingled and scattered throughout the book. If my plan has succeeded with readers only time will tell.

To many, the year 1944-45 in the European theater seemed like the beginning of the end of the Third Reich and a period of relief from the war's unbearable tensions, incessant anxiety, uncertainty, unprecedented bloodshed and human suffering. This growing air of optimism sprang out of many encouraging developments: Allied air superiority had been established over Western Europe just prior to D-Day; the advancing Red Army was rapidly pushing into Eastern Europe and Reich territories; the Allied armies were engaged in a broad assault on the vaunted Siegfried Line and approaching the Rhine following their breakout from the Normandy beachheads; and widening Allied operations in Southern Europe following the invasions of Mediterranean France and Italy yielded new ports, supply lines and staging bases for Allied air strikes from Italy.

The boundaries of Nazi-occupied Europe were gradually shrinking and German transportation sectors, war production factories and synthetic oil facilities were being decimated by round-the-clock strategic bombing by the RAF (at night) and the USAAF (during daylight). The combined bomber offensive dropped a greater tonnage of bombs during this final year of the war than the combined total in all the previous war years put together. For the heavy bomber air crews of the Eighth Air Force, the Allied air superiority and long-range fighter escort services of the superb P-51 Mustangs led to a decline in the mortality rate of bomber crews from one of every two lost to one of every three and the concomitant increase in the number of missions required of a crew from 25 to 35 missions in 1944–45.

Richard R. Ayesh, whose unaltered combat diary is the centerpiece of this book, would be among the first to point out that the real heroes of the air war were the guys who served in the bloodiest years of 1942 to early 1944 when loss rates of bomber crews were staggering, when the Luftwaffe was at maximum strength, and before long-range fighter escorts were available to help protect them. These guys had it much tougher.

They faced the most fearful odds of survival compared with later crews who flew with fighter escorts against a "weakened" Luftwaffe. Among the earlier crews of the 100th Bomb Group were airmen who made the Bloody Hundredth legendary, including figures like Bierne Lay, Bucky Eagan, Harry Crosby, Rosie Rosenthal, Big Frank Valesh, Buck Cleven, "Cowboy" Roane, "Handle Bar" Hank Lyster, Lucky Luckadoo and others. However, the bomber crews in the final year of the war went through their own living hell, facing great peril and poor odds of survival. This was because underlying the rosy veneer of optimism and imminent victory described in the previous paragraph were troubling technological and industrial developments perceived acutely by the Allied high command at Supreme Headquarters Allied Expeditionary Force (SHAEF). The war was far from over.

The reality was that Germany was becoming a cornered state under siege with millions of Wehrmacht troops still under arms and with production of war materials, weapons, armor and especially aircraft, including jet aircraft, proceeding at an alarming rate despite the heavy Allied bombing.

In the fall of 1944, these sources of anxiety for Allied commanders were multi-fold: the disaster of the British-led Operation Market Garden; the unexpected German counter-offensive in the Ardennes, with the worry that the Germans would re-capture Antwerp, the finest port in Europe, thus extending the duration of the war; strong suspicion of Stalin's intentions on the Eastern Front; the possible new appearance of miracle weapons developed with German ingenuity; and a resurgence of German aircraft production which reached an all-time high in the summer and fall of 1944. As Dr. Richard G. Davis points out in his Ph.D dissertation "Carl Spaatz and the Air War in Europe," Spaatz's chief concern and alarm (shared by Doolittle and others) was the possible resurgence of the Luftwaffe. In only two oil-targeting missions on September 11 and 12, 1944, the Eighth lost 75 bombers to Luftwaffe fighters.

Adding to the peril for Eighth bomber crews was the increased concentration of anti-aircraft flak artillery, especially the deadly "Acht-Acht" 88mm guns, due to the redeployment of guns and munitions from the lost territories and the introduction into combat by the Germans of the world's first operational jet fighter, the Messerschmitt 262. The Allies had no aircraft which could oppose this lethal fighter. By the fall of 1944, German aircraft production had been largely dispersed and moved underground as much as possible. There remained frequent attacks on the United Kingdom by V-1 flying bombs and V-2 missiles, each carrying a 1,000-lb. warhead. There was increased deployment of improved snorkel-equipped U-boats which could remain submerged, while the emergence of Sturmgruppe (up-armored Focke Wulf 190 fighters with rapid-firing 30mm cannon) using new tactics, destroyed 28 of 37 bombers in one bomb group on one day.

Adding to the anxiety of the Allied command was the weather factor. In the fall of 1944, the weather in central Europe was worse than it had been since the beginning of the century. Clearly, under the besieged Nazi regime, there was a fanatical determination to preserve the Reich, defend the Fatherland at all costs and push for an armistice favorable to Germany. All of these matters must have weighed heavily on the minds of Carl Spaatz, Jimmy Doolittle and other Allied air commanders. The air of pessimism was real.

While I have attempted to maximize the coverage of all topics on the air war in 1944–45 from the perspective of the 100th Bomb Group and the Eighth Air Force in general, it is obvious that no single book can encompass all aspects of relevance. There are many areas not covered here, including POWs, mercy and cargo operations after the official end of strategic air combat missions, and the operations of VIII Fighter Command. Nonetheless, I have tried to include several topics which have received little or no coverage in books on the air war in general and the Eighth Air Force in particular, such as target selection decision-making, photoreconnaissance, operations and layout at High Wycombe, the headquarters of the Eighth Air Force Bomber Command (code-named PINETREE), radar bombing, and details of munitions and ordnance.

The unaltered diary contained in these pages was written by Lt. Richard Ayesh immediately after each mission and hence is free of any post-war embellishments, distortions or inaccuracies due to faded memories. After most of the diary entries, I have added clarifying annotations and tried to provide non-technical explanations of the technology, tactics and weaponry used during the air war. In this way I hope the readers will gain an incisive, more comprehensive picture of the final year of the air war and in doing so achieve a deeper awareness of the sacrifices, horrors and tragedy these air crews experienced on behalf of us all during World War II.

THROUGH BLUE SKIES TO HELL

1

GROWING UP IN THE AIR CAPITAL

The story of Dick Ayesh's service in the United States Army Air Corps began the same way it did for hundreds of thousands of other loyal, brave Americans of the Greatest Generation. He was born of immigrant parents in Wichita, Kansas who barely spoke English and arrived on our shores in 1910 to seek a better life and the fulfillment of the American Dream. His birthplace was a two room house on the west side of town, the son of Samuel and Mabel Ayesh, both immigrants from the Christian town of Marjayoun in what is now Lebanon, five kilometers from the border with Israel, in southern Lebanon.

The west side of Wichita was the least affluent area of town and developed from an area on the west side of the Big Arkansas River called Delano during the old days of frontier Wichita. This area once conta [illegible] uring the wild rough and t [illegible] yatt Earp, nearby US Cava [illegible] as so-named after the Mini [illegible] nistration, Columbus Dela [illegible] a lived on the east side of th [illegible]

Delano

The area in which I live.

As with any immigrants to America, his parents wished to bask in all of the freedoms and opportunities for prosperity their new country offered. Among the first generation of Lebanese immigrants in Wichita, the grocery, merchandizing and peddling enterprises were one of the easiest ways to get started and make a living. For some, there was also help available from the earliest immigrants who arrived in the 1890s. After beginning in the peddling business, Sam and Mabel had five children, four boys and a girl. Dick was the second youngest child.

Like immigrants of any nationality to a new country, life in Wichita was not easy in these early years when the immigrant families were not always made to feel welcome. The boys, Ralph, Fred, Dick and Bill and their sister Rae all worked at a variety of jobs to help support the family through very lean times. During the awful struggles of the depression years, any jobs were grabbed up immediately including selling newspapers, babysitting, laundry, shoe shining and working in grocery stores. In these times wages of 10 cents a night or 25 to 35 cents on a weekend was a good wage. Other jobs included holding a ladder for a sign painter (Kansas law required it), walking peoples' dogs, carrying out groceries and meeting teachers (during teaching conventions) at the train station or their hotels and carrying their luggage. For the entire family, it was a struggle for survival financially. However, much needed comfort and encouragement were provided by strong family bonds and the moral and spiritual support and sense of community provided by the two Greek Orthodox Churches in town, St. George and St. Mary, each church having members who first immigrated to the States from separate regions of southern Lebanon. The community remains close knit to this day. Dick, his brothers and sister attended the McCormick Elementary School (now listed on the National Historical Register), a few blocks from his home, Allison Junior High School and Wichita North High School in the Riverside section of the city.

During Dick's childhood, the aircraft industry began to blossom in Wichita. The industry flourished because of the proximity of affordable labor, manpower, petroleum (beginning with the discovery of the Eldorado field), railroads and the central location of Wichita in the nation, all of which made the area attractive to aviation pioneers such as Clyde Cessna, Walter Beech, Lloyd Stearman and others. This same era saw the emergence of pilot heroes like Eddie Rickenbacker, Charles Lindbergh, Jimmy Doolittle, Amelia Earhart (a Kansan), Howard Hughes and flying circuses, carry overs from the flying circuses which sprang up after World War I. It was little wonder that any American child, not least one growing up in Wichita, might be attracted to flying at a very early age. Dick began building model airplanes at age 5 and his very first flying experience came at age 6 while playing with a childhood friend on the west side of town.

In a dry flat field of clover and alfalfa at Seneca and Harry streets, the Inman Brothers Flying Circus had come to town and were giving rides in their Ford Tri-Motor for $1. Dick's friend's mother took them to the field and paid for a plane ride for each of them. Among the friends and classmates with whom he grew up, there were a number of future aviators like Colonel Jimmy Jabara who would fly P-51 Mustangs in World War II and later became America's first jet ace in the Korean war, Tommy McConnell (after whom McConnell Air Force Base in Wichita was named) who flew in the Pacific, and Dick's closest friend, Bob Tate, who flew with the Royal Canadian Air Force and, after Pearl Harbor, was transferred to the USAAF and was later killed in action in the Pacific flying a P-38 fighter over New Guinea.

2

THE MAKING OF AN AIRMAN

Before the war began, jobs were plentiful in the rapidly growing air industry in Wichita. Aircraft companies such as Cessna, Beech, Stearman and Boeing were producing both military and commercial aircraft. Wichitans of all ages found employment in this industry and Dick was no exception. Upon graduating from Wichita North High School in 1940 and with college unaffordable, he worked in a grocery store before getting a job at Cessna Aircraft in April 1941, first in the machine shop and then in final assembly. While at Cessna, Dick married a woman whom he had met through a close boyhood friend, his first wife, Mary Kay.

Then arrived the Day of Infamy, December 7th, 1941.

The nation was shocked and enraged by the sneak attack on Pearl Harbor, and the entire country was galvanized in support of all-out war against Japan. However, prior to the Japanese attack and before Germany declared war on the US, the case for war against Hitler's Germany was not as clear-cut, even with the formation of the Berlin-Tokyo-Rome Tripartite Axis. A significant fraction of the American populace was made up of individuals with isolationist attitudes toward foreign entanglements and people of German stock who were among the earliest American immigrants.

Indeed, public opinion polls taken in the months preceding Pearl Harbor revealed that 80% of the public opposed war with Germany. Some German-Americans and Americans in general organized themselves into groups supporting accommodation with Germany and a non-aggression pact with Hitler. Leading Americans such as Henry

Ford, Senator Alf Landon and Charles Lindbergh spoke out strongly against war with Germany. However, it did not take long for Americans to become familiar with the racial overtones underlying the expansionist ambitions of Hitler's regime. The Nazi ideas of racial superiority and racial purity as well as "Lebensraum" and the victimization of the Jews, despite Hitler's enmity toward Bolshevism and the USSR, left little doubt in people's minds that the Nazis were the enemy of America. Nazi doctrines could not have been more inimical to the very foundations of America and American thought. After Pearl Harbor, the American public was firmly in favor of fighting the Germans and Italians as well as Japan.

Dick was nineteen years old when he heard about Pearl Harbor. He had just seen a movie at the Palace Theater on Sunday afternoon, December 7th when he saw a newsstand with a special edition of the Wichita Eagle showing a huge headline. Everyone was shocked, angry and suddenly felt vulnerable, not unlike the reactions of Americans and much of the world to the horror of 9/11. The armed services were quickly overwhelmed by enraged Americans who volunteered to get revenge on the "Japs." Prior to the attack, a peacetime draft had already been created when President Franklin Roosevelt signed the Selective Training and Service Act of 1940 into law and formally established the Selective Service System as an independent Federal agency. Each male was given a classification of either 1A, 1B, 3A, 3B or 4F, the latter meaning an individual was physically unable to serve. Deferments were granted for flat feet or other disqualifying physical conditions (4F), a defense job (3A) or being married (3B).

While patriotism and the fervor to get even had only intensified among our fighting men, the reality gradually settled in that America had embarked on a long-term, highly costly, two-front global war with casualties that would utterly dwarf our losses in World War I.

At the beginning of the war, Dick was not drafted and he tried to enlist but was told to continue working in the vital aircraft industry at Cessna, helping to build trainer aircraft for the Royal Canadian Air Force. He also could not get into the Air Corps due to the requirement of two years of college. During this time, Canadian air force officers visited Wichita to pick up newly built trainers and used the opportunity to recruit Americans for service in the RAF and the RCAF. A number of American pilots voluntarily served in both the Canadian and in the British Royal Air Force during the Battle of Britain. Among them was Dick's best friend throughout junior high school and high school, Bob Tate, who later would return to the States and serve as a US fighter pilot in the Pacific theater in 1944. While working at Cessna during these times, Dick's dream of flying in the service only intensified.

In his own words:

> I was employed at Cessna Aircraft from April 1941 to January 1943. I actually built Cessna twin engine trainers (bomber trainers) for the US Army Air Corps and the Royal Canadian Air Forces.
>
> Right **after** Pearl Harbor, I knew I wanted to join the Army Air Corp. The problem was you had to have two years of college. As a kid, that was what I always had wanted to do but the 2 yrs of college was always in the way. In April of 1942 they dropped the 2 year college requirement and I tried to enlist here in Wichita but because I was in a defense job they wouldn't listen. My Dad had to sign my application (parental consent) because I was only 19. I also had to have 3 letters of recommendation which I still have! Finally in May, Kansas City accepted my application and ordered me up there for my entrance exam. (It was sort of like a college entrance exam-you had to have some level of intelligence or you couldn't get in).
>
> I passed that and I was sent to Ft. Leavenworth for my physical (which was quite rigid) and sent home. A few weeks later they sent me a postcard that I had been accepted. I still have that card! We were told they would let me know when and where to report. Finally in January of 1943 I was ordered to Jefferson Barracks in St Louis, Mo for Basic Training (that was to learn Army life I guess, i.e., drilling, marching and all that).
>
> It was pretty demeaning, as an example, the latrine had about 20 toilet stools with no partitions between them. I guess it was to break down any embarrassment you might have. We

lived in wooden huts. We had a very severe winter and that's why it was called "Pneumonia Gulch" because so many got sick. I knew my dad's brother lived in St. Louis so on my first "pass" to town I looked him up (after I had a "good steak" at a restaurant). He was employed at a rope factory and glad to see me. He had not seen my Dad since they left Lebanon.

Anyway, after that I was sent to Oshkosh State Teachers College in Oshkosh Wisconsin for what the Army called "College Training Detachment" or CDT. They crammed 2 years of college into us in 3 months, i.e. physics, mathematics, trig, geometry and other college courses. The only good thing about it was we were the first detachment at that college and the townspeople treated us like heroes. We put on a parade for them every Saturday afternoon and they would invite us to stay with them on weekends.

In May 1943 I was sent to the Aviation Cadet Training Center in Santa Ana, California for more testing and evaluation. We were quarantined for four weeks before being classified. I qualified for all three positions (pilot, navigator, bombardier) but they had enough pilots and Navs already so they classified me as a bombardier. If you didn't accept that, they "washed you out." I don't know if this was really true but the rumor was out there and it was effective. If you questioned your classification, you were washed out. Nobody dared question their classification. I thought about not accepting it because I wanted pilot training but they said I could always go to pilot school after I had done my tour overseas. Besides, the psychologist who interviewed me said I shouldn't care what I was doing as long as I was "fighting for my country." He previously had asked me why I had enlisted and I had said "to fight for my country."

At Santa Ana, airmen in training had to develop a range of skills, all of which were essential to every officer in the bomber crews.

The several levels of training included gunnery training, bombing, survival exercises, parachute jumping, fundamentals of navigation, radio operation and actual training flights. The Army Air Corps expected its airmen to achieve proficiency in a whole array of in-flight skills. Among the tests to qualify bombardiers was skill in identifying features such as cities, rivers and mountains on topographic maps and photographs as well as manual dexterity in performing multiple tasks. For example, a cadet would be timed while manipulating pins from one side of a magazine-sized board, while having a stick in his right hand, seated facing a chair with his feet on rudder pedals. The board was arranged much like the red and black squares of a checker board. This tested manual (digital) dexterity by timing how fast, for example, a cadet could remove the square-headed pins from round holes and place them on the other side of the board into perfectly fitted square holes when the machine was on.

Another exercise used oppositely spinning metallic saucers on turntables on which a cadet would, with both hands simultaneously, try to keep a stylus fixed onto the same point on both saucers with his performance measured much like an electronic blood pressure machine. In still another test, a cadet would face what looked like a chair with the seat, arms and legs removed and the top, bottom and middle (spine) of the chair covered with a line of red lights. Wherever a red light illuminated, a maneuver had to be made to match a green light under the red light. This would test coordination in banking turns and manipulating a control stick by having the cadet follow a red light much like in today's video games. Cadets would also be seated on highly elevated chairs, 12 feet off the ground, as they trained a bombsight on moving electrical targets.

Finally after being classified a bombardier, Dick was sent to gunnery school in Kingman, Arizona for gunnery training for two months. He learned how to fire .50-caliber machine guns from every position on the bomber and also submachine guns and pistols. In order to assess accuracy during air-to-air gunnery practice, cadets were assigned different colored shells for their gunnery practice with 50-cal. machine guns. Each shell was color-coded to within about a half inch from the shell tip. Dick's color was blue. As a plane towed a bed sheet-sized target, each trainee's color-coded shells would register hits. He recalled being very pleased with the number of blue marks on the target. Trainees were taught how to lead a target by firing with shotguns from the back of a pickup truck at randomly launched targets shaped like Frisbees. The back of the pickup had a wooden frame three to four feet high which would anchor the trainees while their truck followed a winding track. The targets were launched from eight to ten different positions and distances from the moving truck, much like skeet shooting.

After that it was to Deming, New Mexico for bombardier training. He flew in AT-11's, trainers that were made by Beechcraft. They looked something like miniature B-24 Liberators with a plexiglass nose.

They practiced forming up as a group and learning how to use the highly secret Norden bombsight. The practice target on the bombing range was a 20 by 20-foot "shack," a wooden structure. The bomb contained white powder. In his own words, "on my first practice bomb run, with my instructor sitting next to me on my right, I made all of the settings to the bombsight and released the bomb but saw nothing of the impact below. He shouted "you got a shack"! I learned that I had hit the shack dead center, which is why I saw nothing. Hell, I felt like I had gotten a hole-in-one in golf. It felt exactly like that when you hit a shack dead center." The CE (circle of error) on these practice bombings was 200 feet. A memorable character to all of the bombardier cadets was their chief instructor, an officer who always warned them of the consequence of misbehaving or screwing up training: "Yous guys ain't gonna get no furloughs!"

Dick was now officially a newly minted bombardier and he could take heart in the expressed feelings of other "pilot-wannabe" American bombardiers, one of whom brashly pointed out "Bombardiers are the sharpest, smartest, best-trained member of any bomber crew—and often the best-looking too!"[2] Later, they could all take pride in the fact that the first airman in the Eighth Air Force to be awarded the Congressional Medal of Honor was a bombardier, Lt. Jack Mathis, of the 303rd Bomb Group. Dick's classification as a bombardier was the next best thing to being a pilot and, with a deep sense of pride, he took the Bombardier's oath:

> Mindful of the secret trust about to be placed in me by my Commander in Chief, the President of the United States, by whose direction I have been chosen for bombardier training

. . . and mindful of the fact that I am to become guardian of one of my country's most priceless military assets, the American bombsight . . . I do here, in the presence of Almighty God, swear by the Bombardier's Code of Honor to keep inviolate the secrecy of any and all confidential information revealed to me, and further to uphold the honor and integrity of the Army Air Forces, if need be, with my life itself.

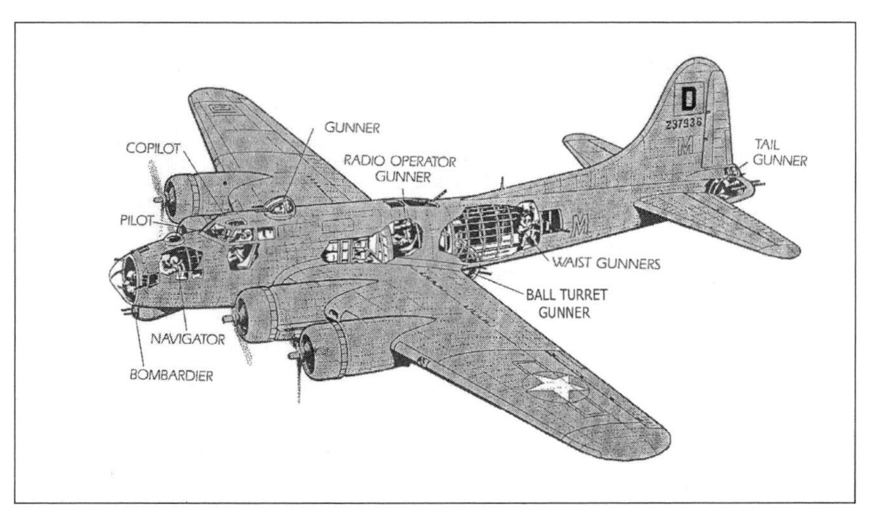

Cutaway drawing of a Boeing B-17G heavy bomber with crew positions. (Courtesy of Harold (Diz) Kronenberg, 390th Bomb Group)

He was fascinated by the B-17 Flying Fortress, a four-engine heavy bomber with a crew of ten which was actually built partly at Boeing Wichita. Boeing oversaw the production of 12,730 B-17s, the vast majority of which were used in high-altitude strategic bombing missions over Europe.

To Dick and countless other airmen, the B-17 was a beautiful aircraft that was known by most to be both easy and enjoyable to fly. Prospective pilots were given the opportunity to learn every detail of the electrical, fuel and hydraulic systems on the B-17, and to disassemble (and reassemble) one of the big radial engines. Their training included longer day and night practice cross country missions and they had to master instrument flying. Half of the crew members occupied the area forward of the bomb bay and the other half the area rearward of the bomb bay.

The B-17 had an empty weight of 33,000-lbs. and a maximum loaded weight of 65,000 pounds, and was powered with four 1,200 horsepower Wright R-1820-97 nine cylinder air-cooled single radial engines. It also had General Electric Type B-22 exhaust-driven turbo-superchargers, installed under engine nacelles. It had a wing span of 103 ft. 9 in., a length of 74 feet 9 in., and a height of 19 feet 1 inch. It had a theoretical ceiling of 35,000 ft., a range of 4,400 miles and a maximum speed of 295 mph at 25,000 feet which was also its optimum bombing altitude. The B-17G, with a normal bomb and fuel load flew at 160 mph on a typical mission. Many B-17s were fitted with extra internal wing tanks, known as Tokyo tanks, to extend their range.[3]

It could carry a bomb load of 2,200 to 8,000-lbs with the largest bomb type carried being a 2,000 pounder. A 4,000-pound bomb load was typical for long missions, though the B-17 could carry up to 8,000 pounds internally for shorter distances at lower altitudes. By using external bomb racks beneath the wings, an even larger bomb load was possible. These increased bomb loads proved to be highly effective against German oil and airplane production facilities. The B-17G's armament consisted of thirteen .50-caliber machine guns which were mounted in turrets in the upper fuselage, belly, and tail. All but the tail turret were power-operated. In each turret was mounted a pair of .50-caliber machine guns. In addition, there were single .50-caliber machine guns on flexible mounts firing from hatches in the sides of the fuselage, one on each side and one .50-caliber machine gun at the overhead opening in the radio room. This last machine gun was discarded late in 1944 when crews were reduced from ten to nine men and the radio operator took over a waist gun position during fighter attacks.

The B-17G was fitted with a chin turret under the nose in which the bombardier could operate twin .50-caliber machine guns if the need arose from a head-on attack. In short, the B-17, bristling with machine guns, was aptly nicknamed the "Flying Fortress."[4]

3

THE BOMBARDIER'S ARSENAL: Munitions and Bombs

There are many categories of bombs dropped from planes, but most all of them have in common a container, usually aerodynamically shaped, a fuse, explosive material or filler, and a stabilizing device. The most commonly used munition was the general purpose (GP) bomb which could have nearly a third to a half the total weight of the bomb as explosive charge (the charge to weight ratio or CWR). Upon ignition of the filler inside the container, pressures of hundreds of tons per square inch and temperatures of several thousand degrees were instantaneously reached, with roughly half the explosion energy fragmenting the container and ejecting the fragments at high velocity (5,000 to 10,000 feet per second), the other half of the energy supersonically compressing the surrounding air, yielding the destructive blast that destroys structures.

As Dick relates, "The bomb sizes were determined by the amount of destruction and the target. A 2,000-lb. bomb would do more damage. It depended on the target. We could carry twelve 1,000-lb. bombs or six 2,000-lb. bombs. Twelve 1,000 pounders would cover a larger area. RDX bombs had the plastic explosives which were very efficient. Fragmentation bombs were used on ground troops because they broke into little pieces of shrapnel. Incendiary bombs were packaged in clusters that broke apart upon release and could burn through 12 inches of steel." They were filled with highly combustible chemicals such as magnesium, phosphorus or petroleum jelly (napalm), in clusters over a specific target. These were generally used against troop concentrations in the field or in marshalling yards. However, as discussed later, incendiary bombs, if dropped in large number from low altitude over a city center with many buildings could ignite a firestorm, a fate which befell Hamburg and Dresden.

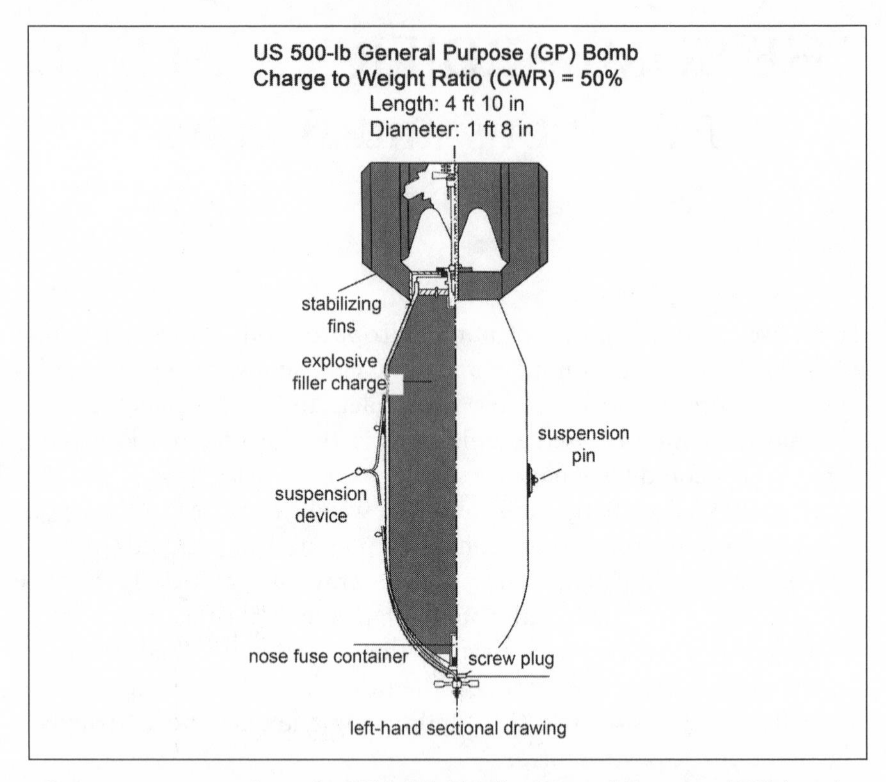

Cutaway cross-section of a USAAF 500-lb. General Purpose (GP) bomb. The M-64 500-lb. GP bomb was used extensively by the Eighth Air Force in the final year of its operations.
(From *The Air War* by Janucz Piekelkiewicz, Octopus Publishing Group)

As stated earlier, GP (General Purpose) bombs typically had a CWR of 30–50%, meaning that most of the weight of these bombs consisted of metal casing, not the explosive material. The thinner the metal casing, the more the blast effect of the impacting bomb. It became clear that the weight of the bomb casing could not be avoided, only minimized. Thus, new, heavier, weapons were developed such as the 4,000-lb. high capacity ('Block Buster') which greatly increased the destructive power.[5]

MC (Medium Capacity) bombs had a CWR of 40–50% while HC (High Capacity) weapons had a CWR of 75–80%. These explosives, used mostly by the RAF but also by the Eighth Air Force, were essentially explosive-packed metal drums. Aerodynamic shaping and streamlining were unnecessary since these bombs were carried internally. As already mentioned, the 4,000-lb. "Block Buster" or "Cookie" was a very effective weapon in this class, and after its introduction rapidly became a mainstay of the Allies.[6]

For incendiary bombs, both sides at the beginning of the war depended upon thermite (a mixture of aluminum and rust), and magnesium-filled bombs. These bombs did not destroy from explosion but rather when ignited, as in the case of magnesium, burned very intensely at extremely high temperatures. An array of incendiary bombs were used by the USAAF, for example, the 100-lb. M-47A1, using phosphorus, the 4-lb. M-50 using magnesium, the 2-lb. M-52 using magnesium, the M-17 using magnesium and consisting of a 500-lb. cluster of M-50s. The incendiary bombs used most often in Europe by bomb groups like Dick's in the Eighth Air Force were the M-17 Incendiary bombs. Most of the other incendiaries cited above were used extensively against Japan.

The M-69 incendiary, developed for the USAAF by the Esso research component of the Standard Oil Development Co. (New Jersey), consisted of a 6.5-lb., 19-in. length of six-sided pipe (resembling a long tin can) filled with gasoline which was thickened to the consistency of sticky, raspberry-pink jelly by the addition of a still-secret powder.

This jellied oil (napalm) bomb generated almost twice as much heat in proportion to weight as a magnesium incendiary and spread its devastation much more rapidly. If dropped in loose clusters of 14, or "aimable" clusters of 38 for greater accuracy, these finless jellied oil-bombs when released over a target would break apart at about 2000 feet altitude. Each M-69 would eject a long strip of cloth to help orient itself and strike the ground nose-first. The payload of napalm was ignited by a time fuse four or five seconds after impact when each M-69 becomes a miniature burning gas jet or flamethrower that hurls cheesecloth "socks" full of furiously burning jelly out the tail of the bomb for roughly 30 to 300 feet depending upon conditions. Anything in contact with these burning socks was enveloped by sticky, fiery pancakes, each spreading very rapidly to more than a yard in diameter. When dropped in a cluster of such M-69 bomblets, the number of fires overwhelms any firefighting efforts.[7] It proved to be especially effective in bombing missions against Japanese cities, which were largely made of wood and paper. For use in Europe, the Allies adopted the M-19 incendiary bomb which used jellied oil and consisted of a 220-lb. cluster of 36 M-69s.

A few other bombs had very special or unusual characteristics. For example, a cluster of five 12-pound bomblets were strapped together in a hexagon shape. Every bomb had a safety wire which kept the bomb from arming. A little key fit into a brace (hook) on the strap that kept the incendiary from coming apart in the plane.

Bombs from the bomb dump at each base were loaded on long, low, flat trailers hauled to the planes by tractors, hoisted into the

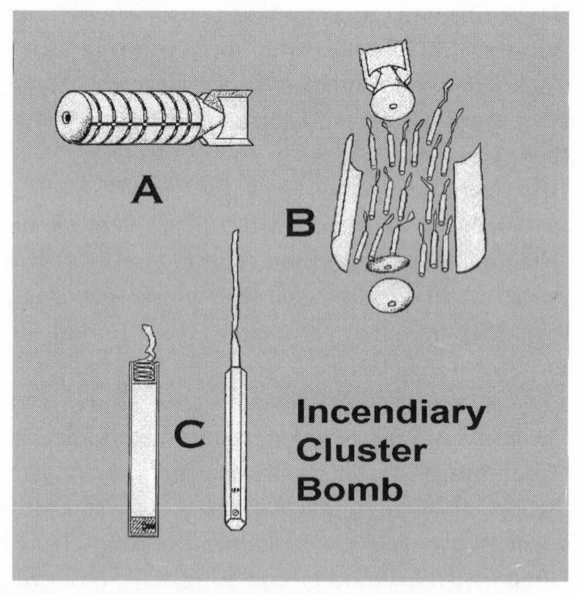

Incendiary cluster bomb consisting of a cluster of M-69 bomblets, each filled with jellied oil. (From a post-war US Government Report on bomb damage, 1946). The incendiary used most often in Europe during the final year of Eighth Air Force operations was the 500-lb. M-17 aimable cluster bomb consisting of 110 M-50A1 magnesium-filled bomblets.

bomb bays with hand-operated winches and hung on horizontal racks called shackles in the bomb bay. The number of shackles varied, depending upon the bomb load for a given mission. Armorers inserted the fuses, and attached a cotter pin to the fuse mechanism of each bomb, as a safety measure to prevent premature detonation on board. The cotter pin stopped the propeller in its tail from spinning, as it would do while dropping.

Overall, no less than three safety devices prevented premature detonation of a bomb: the cotter pin had to be removed by hand from the fuse mechanism of each bomb; an arming wire had to pull out of the fuse assembly when the bomb fell from the plane; and an impellor had to spin off the fuse assembly from the action of the wind during the descent of the bomb. All these devices were safety measures, but if any one of them remained in place, then the bomb would not explode on impact because the striker pin would be restricted from igniting the explosion at the instant of impact with the ground. The result would be a "dud," thousands of which were found across Europe during and after the war, and continue to be unearthed by farmers and construction crews to this day.

In the air war over Europe there were early versions of "smart bombs." These efforts could be regarded as an initial rudimentary stage in the evolution of the cruise missile. The Azon, regarded by many as the first smart bomb, was a 1,000-lb. bomb with a radio-steerable tail that a bombardier could control with a joystick. This could be used for smaller targets that needed greater bombing accuracy. In July 1944, as part of a project called Aphrodite, a blind-bombing terror weapon was made from used or damaged B-17s or B-24s, sometimes carrying 20,000 lbs. of explosives and turned into flying bombs. This weapon was given the Department of Defense designation BQ-7.[8,9]

Ideally, the plan was for a two-man crew to make the take off and to get the plane pointed in the right direction. Afterward, the BQ-7 would be handed over to radio control by an accompanying B-17, and the crew would arm the warhead and then leave the aircraft by parachute while still over England. A Lockheed P-38 fighter would be standing by to destroy the BQ-7 in case something went wrong. The controlling B-17 would then direct the BQ-7 to the target area over continental Europe and lock its controls into a crash course into the target before turning to escape. This particular project was code-named "Castor" or sometimes "Perilous."[10]

In practice, the plane was put on autopilot, the crew bailed out and the plane was to hit something when it ran out of fuel. President John F. Kennedy's oldest brother Joe Kennedy Jr. was killed while on an Aphrodite mission. The plane in which he perished was a converted Consolidated PB4Y-1 that was a Navy version of the B-24 Liberator. The Liberators converted for Aphrodite missions were intended primarily for use in the Pacific theater and were designated BQ-8. In total, approximately 25 Fortresses (mainly B-17Fs) were converted into radio-controlled flying bombs under the designation BQ-7. They were designed to be used against heavily-defended German positions or against German submarine pens or deep fortifications that had resisted conventional bombing.[11]

The BQ-7 conversions were made at US bases in England. The B-17s selected for the project were stripped of their normal military equipment and packed with up to 9 tons of Torpex high-explosive and fitted with an impact fuse. During their take-off and initial climb, the BQ-7 was manned by only a pilot and an engineer. After reaching cruise altitude, the crew pointed the aircraft toward the general direction of the target, activated the remote-control equipment, armed the fuse and parachuted to the ground. To facilitate bail-out, the B-17's canopy was removed, and the cockpit converted to an open one with a windshield only. The BQ-7 was then controlled from either another B-17, modified to CQ-4 configuration, or a P-38 fighter which accompanied the BQ-7 on its way to the target.[12] A B-17 named Mugwump, from the 100th Bomb Group, was one of the planes used for this purpose.

A total of fifteen BQ-7s were launched against German targets between August 4, 1944 and January 1, 1945. Follow-up intelligence revealed that the results were largely disappointing, since the BQ-7 was essentially a low-yield weapon with very little penetrating power and was limited to a thirty-degree slant descent. Moreover, the BQ-7 was as dangerous to the Allied side as it was to the Germans. In August of 1944, a crewless BQ-7 went out of control and crashed into an East Anglian forest, blasting a crater about a hundred feet across.

Another crewless BQ-7 went out of control shortly after launch and began to circle a British industrial area on its own initiative before it luckily crashed into the sea. Due to these and other serious friendly incidents as well as the generally disappointing results, the Castor project was abandoned as being just too dangerous for practical use.[13]

4

TOP SECRET BOMBSIGHT: Hitting the Pickle Barrel

To achieve the objectives of strategic daytime bombing, the Eighth Air Force used the most sophisticated aiming device in the world, the Norden bombsight. It was invented by C.L. Norden, a Dutch civilian inventor, to actually fly the aircraft during a bomb run.

He had originally developed the device in 1931 for sea-based aircraft, intending its use primarily for coastal defense. The Navy carried out testing for two years, after which the Army adopted it for use in bombers and ordered 90,000 units at roughly $10,000 per unit for an eventual cost of $1.5 billion. This staggering amount in 1930s' dollars comprised 65% of the entire cost of the Manhattan Project.[14]

The USAAF placed the Norden into service in March 1943. It was so cloaked in secrecy that when it was carried outside of a secure sight, an armed guard was required to accompany the airman carrying it. It even had a self-detonating charge that enabled the crew to destroy it rather than having it captured. In reality, unbeknownst to the Allies, the Germans knew about this bombsight as early as 1943, as it had been captured.

Even earlier, an American worker with pro-German sympathies at a plant manufacturing Nordens provided technical details of the bombsight to the Nazis. The Norden consisted of a gyroscopically stabilized telescopic sight coupled to an electromechanical computer into which the bombardier fed inputs for altitude, atmospheric conditions, airspeed, ground speed, ballistics, trail and drift. During the bomb run, the sight was slaved to the automatic pilot to guide the aircraft to the precise release point. In the hands of a skilled bombardier, the

Norden was a remarkably accurate sight. If the bombs failed to hit the target, it was due to a variation in course or of the data that was fed in, not the Norden.[15] According to Dick, "The Norden was truly that accurate if all of the conditions were just right. This was not hype."

Essentially the Norden was an airborne computer. It gave the bombardier unprecedented precision. But it was very complicated to use and required a large number of input factors whose uncertainty affected the precision of the drop. Input parameters such as air density, wind force and direction, the height, air and ground speed of the aircraft, drift, bomb configuration (aerodynamics of the bomb load) and other readings had to be entered into the bombsight computer (Lt. Charles Hudson, lead bombardier).

An appreciation of its complexity is provided by the noted historian and author, Robin Neillands, who once asked a USAF Major in one of the bomb groups to explain in simple terms the operation of the Norden bombsight. The steps between lining up the bombsight and pressing the bomb release took four pages (!) and involved the use of gyroscopes, bubble levels, tachometers, course knobs, rate knobs, arming triggers and an intervalometer to vary the spacing of the bombs on the target so that bombers behind the lead bomber would release their bombs more accurately on the target. All of this was to happen while requiring an accurate forecast of wind direction and speed, accurate ground speed, perfect aircraft trim, perfect preset of bombsight data and for the crosshairs to stay on the aiming point once the plane is flying straight and level with the pilot direction indicator on center.[16] In other words, while on the bomb run, the aircraft could take absolutely no evasive action since the platform had to be level in order for the stabilized crosshairs to stay on the target.

The basic structure of the Norden consisted of two parts, a top unit and a base unit. The base unit was a box-shaped device called the stabilizer, fixed to the floor directly below the nose. The top unit was the actual bombsight which was roughly cylindrical in shape with an optical eyepiece and all of the adjustment controls. The pilot had to trim the aircraft for a precise altitude and air speed at the Initial Point (IP) and strictly maintain that during the bomb run. If pilot skill was sloppy, the result was an inaccurate drop regardless of how precisely the bombardier had set up the sight.

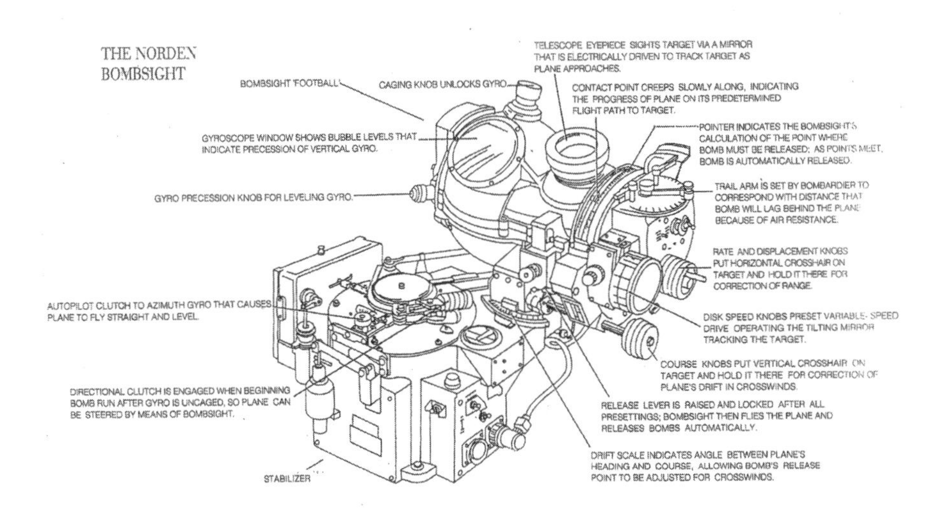

Schematic diagram of the Norden Bombsight.
(Courtesy of Philip Kaplan, from *Round the Clock* by Philip Kaplan and Jack Currie, Random House, 1993)

In practice, the B-17, with its huge, dome-like plexiglass window in the nose, gave its bombardier a field of visibility that was expansive, enabling him to see out to very great distances. This was the most magnificent view in the aircraft if a war was not raging. It was also the most exposed position in the plane to enemy fire and flak. The bombardier was seated on a low, fixed armour-backed seat behind the Norden bombsight at the lip of the B-17's nose. He would first locate the target visually by looking over the Norden and through the plexiglass nosepiece. Once he saw the target, he would attempt to line it up in the small telescope on the Norden. There was a reticle in the eyepiece of the telescope with two crosshairs, one to show drift to the left or right of the target, the other crosshair to establish the rate of closure, with both crosshairs being centered on the target. On the right side of the small telescope were two indices, one showing the bombing angle determined by the bombardier, the other the "rate" index. This would move the first index in synchrony with the forward speed of the B-17. When these two indices met, the bombs were automatically released.[17]

The disadvantages of the Norden were primarily (1) that in order for it to be most effective, the bombardier had to be able to see the target (often difficult over Europe at high altitude with flak, clouds and fighter-infested skies) and fly the aircraft under the most hazardous conditions, straight and level over the target; (2) the Norden would cause individual bombers to drift somewhat in the sky once the target was located and locked into the crosshairs. This heightened the risk of collision with other B-17s and, for bomber formations, it tended to loosen the defensive closeness posture of the formation against fighter attack, making individual bombers easy prey.[18, 19]

In any event, the need to keep such tight defensive formations over Europe compromised the accuracy of the Norden bombsight, since individual bomb runs were not possible without breaking formation. Whole bomber formations had to drop their loads on the lead bombardier's command while the plane had to be kept as level and steady as possible. Unfortunately, this was not always possible due to the inevitable small differences in timing and heading, complicated by things which would go wrong, such as turbulence, nearby flak bursts, sudden evasive action by pilots, malfunctions and jammed equipment. All of this led to dispersed bomb patterns.

Formations of B-17s proved unable to fight their way unescorted to targets deep inside Germany in the face of determined fighter opposition without incurring excessive losses. Deep raids were called off in mid-October 1943 and were not resumed until February 1944, when long-range escort fighters, notably the P-51 Mustang, became available in significant numbers.

As a bombardier, Dick knew that his single most important role, and the ultimate purpose of the crew and plane, was accurate and effective bombing using the Norden bombsight to destroy targets. He was in personal charge of typically 5,000 lbs of high explosives. To fulfill this role, he had to master every detail of every kind of bomb, be able to fuse them, understand bombing probabilities, the source of bombing errors, and the various conditions which affect the bomb dropped from the plane. These included altitude and true airspeed, both of which were controlled by the pilot; bomb ballistics, that is, the size, shape and density of a bomb which determined the air resistance during its fall; the trail, that is, how far horizontally behind the plane the bomb was located at the moment of impact; the actual amount of time of the bomb's fall from release to impact; the groundspeed of the plane which affects the trail of the bomb; and the drift of the bomb which is determined by the direction and velocity of the wind.[20]

He knew he had to remain very calm and focused as he entered all the data into the Norden on ground speed, rate of closure, wind drift, estimated air resistance and time of fall. In the event of a frontal attack, he was also responsible for the firing of the chin turret guns, two .50-caliber machine guns, as well as a .50-caliber machine gun on his left if the need arose.

5

BOMBER FORMATIONS AND FIGHTER TACTICS

The firepower from tight formations of B-17s theoretically was to spell doom to an approaching enemy fighter. B-17s flew in tightly stacked defensive formations, bringing to bear maximum firepower on Luftwaffe fighters. The basic squadron formation of B-17s was a squadron "box" of 9 or 12 aircraft; three squadron boxes staggered vertically and horizontally formed a group; and three groups in trail formed a combat wing.

This tightly packed formation was intended to maximize defensive firepower and better concentrate the bomb load to the target. This basic concept of a combat box was developed in large part by then Colonel Curtis E. LeMay. As the war progressed, these formations were increased from 18 bombers to 21, 36, or 63 B-17s. When it was first introduced at the end of 1942, the 18-aircraft formation, known as the Group Javelin Down, was made up of high, middle and low six-plane squadrons stepped diagonally downward toward the sun.[21]

The USAAF was initially confident that tight, self-defending formations of B-17s, flying fast and at high altitude, could penetrate enemy air space by day without fighter escort.

After all, a combat wing of 63 B-17G aircraft in 1944, each carrying 9,000 rounds of ammunition, could bring to bear 819 .50-caliber machine guns firing 14 rounds a second over an effective range of 600 yards. A .50-caliber machine gun had a firing pattern 600 yards across at a distance of 1,000 yards. Even the 18-plane formation could deliver the devastating firepower of 234 .50-caliber machine guns mounted in the 18 B-17s flying against attacking enemy fighters. The hope was that this number of guns would produce an unassailable wall of fire around the formation. However, reality set in soon enough. Despite this seemingly impenetrable wall of fire around the formation, losses suffered by B-17 bomb groups continued to mount.

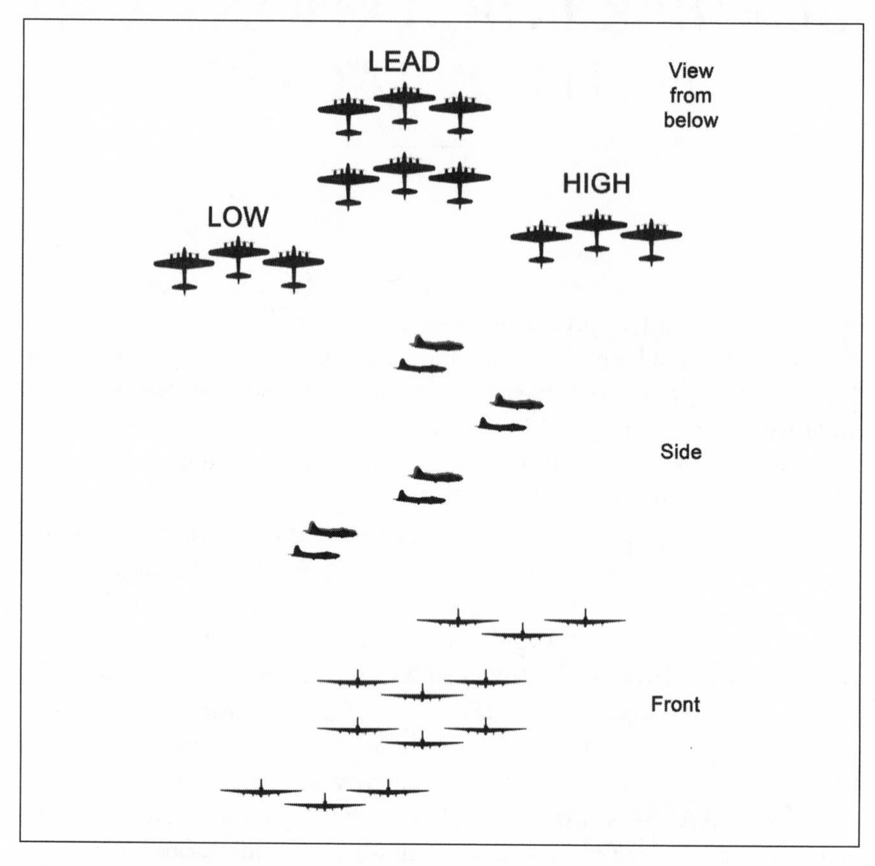

Three views of a typical B-17 squadron formation during the final year of Eighth Air Force operations, viewed from the side, bottom and front. (Note that in the side view four B-17s are partially obscured.)

As the Eighth Air Force began to make deeper and deeper penetrations into Germany from the spring of 1943, it sustained increasingly heavy losses at the hands of German fighters. By the autumn of 1943, German fighters, alerted by radar and deployed in depth, were destroying Eighth Air Force bombers and crews more quickly than they could be replaced. This continued until, at last, long-range fighter escorts, specifically the P-51 Mustang, entered the war. By December of 1943, bombing missions were protected by long-range fighter escorts. Having these escorts to and from the target made an immense difference.[22, 23]

The principal fighter escorts for the USAAF in Europe in 1942–43 were the P-38 Lightning and the P-47 Thunderbolt. The P-38 Lightning was used heavily early in the air war in Europe to attack marshalling yards, troop concentrations and to escort Eighth Air Force bombers in raids over France in preparation for the D-Day invasion. It added a new dimension to American fighters in that its design was a radical departure from other fighter aircraft because it had two engines. With a second engine, the P-38 was less vulnerable to flak and to damage from attacks by enemy aircraft because the loss of, or damage to, one engine did not necessarily mean the aircraft was going down. The multi-engine configuration reduced the Lightning loss-rate to anti-aircraft gunfire during ground attack missions. However, the downside was that the P-38's limited range made it unsuitable for long range bomber escort.

The Lockheed P-38L Lightning had a wingspan of 52 feet, a length of 37 feet 10 inches, a height of 12 feet 10 inches and an operational weight of 17,500-lbs. It had a maximum speed of 390 mph, a service ceiling of 40,000 feet, a range of 900 miles at 30,000 feet, and was powered by two Allison V-1710-111/113 liquid cooled engines giving it 1,425 horsepower. Its armament consisted of one 20mm cannon and four .50-caliber Browning machine guns, an external bomb load of 4,000-lbs or ten 5-inch rockets.[24,25,26] The P-38 also played a vital role in its conversion to a photo-reconnaissance aircraft.

One of the most famous multi-purpose escort fighters was the Republic P-47 Thunderbolt, known as the Jug due to the shape of its fuselage. It weighed more than six tons, was more than 14 feet high, 36 feet long and had a wingspan of 41 feet. It was powered by an 18-cylinder Pratt and Whitney R28 radial engine that produced 2,300 horsepower. Like the B-17s it escorted, it was equipped with a turbo-supercharger for efficient engine performance above 20,000 feet. It had a range of 1,100 miles with an auxiliary fuel tank and a service ceiling of 40,000 feet. Its armament consisted of eight .50-caliber machine guns and ten 5-inch rockets or 1,500-lbs of bombs. This very large, heavy fighter, with a top speed of 433 mph, was virtually unmatched in aerial combat by any other prop-driven Allied aircraft until the appearance of the P-51 in December 1943. A total of 15,600 P-47 Thunderbolts were produced by Republic Aviation during the war. Like the B-17s themselves, the P-47s could absorb a lot of damage and still keep flying.[27,28,29]

It was considered one of the vital protectors of the bomber stream. As it turned out, the P-47 was also a devastating low-level fighter bomber which strafed, bombed and rocketed German airfields, railroads and troop concentrations. When attacking German Tiger tanks at low altitude, a P-47 could overcome their heavy armor by ricocheting rounds off the autobahn to hit the tank's vulnerable underbelly.[30]

Unfortunately, even when an extra belly fuel tank was added to the P-47, its effective range limited it to escort duty only as far as the Rhine, not far enough to stay with a bomber stream all the way to a target deep inside Germany. It was not until the North American P-51 Mustang was introduced that long-range fighter escort protection could be provided to and from targets deep into Germany and Eastern Europe.

The P-51D, of which 9,602 were built during the war, had a length of 32 feet, a wing span of 37.04 feet, a normal takeoff weight of 10,100-lbs., and a Rolls Royce Merlin 68 engine with a normal takeoff horsepower of 1,490. It had a maximum speed of 439 mph at 25,000 feet and a service ceiling of 41,900 feet, giving it a range, with drop tanks, of 2,055 miles. Its armaments included six .50-caliber machine guns with 1,260 rounds, two 1,000-lb. bombs or ten 5-inch rockets. While in service during the air war, the P-51 was credited with 4,950 air kills, 4,131 ground kills and 230 kills of the V-1 buzz bombs. This aircraft made all the difference to the strategic bombing effort by providing escort protection to bombers deep into Germany during daylight precision bombing.[31,32,33]

A problem to be overcome by the fighter escorts was their high speed relative to the slower bombers because they had to stay with the bomber stream to offer protection. The problem was solved by having the fighters meander side to side and above and below the bombers, always keeping up combat air speed in case of enemy fighters but staying with the bombers through these maneuvers. Typically, the fighter group came in from the rear of the stream but about 3000 feet higher than the bombers. When the group was directly above the bombers, they would split into three squadrons, usually of 16 planes each. The squadrons would fly in flights of four planes lying astern of the bombers and two or more flights in line abreast. One squadron remained above the stream to provide top cover for the bombers and the other two squadrons fanned out to the flanks. Eventually, and quite gradually, the fighters would pull out in front of the bombers but then another fighter group would feed in from the rear.[34]

These escort aircraft were known affectionately to the bomber crews as their "Little Friends." As Dick saw it, bomber crews were also a little envious of the fighter pilots. As he recalls, "You'd see young fighter pilots talking up a storm at the bar about their exploits. They could have the run of whatever they wanted, and from tailors, many had red satin lining in their jackets. They were really hot shots, a pretty cocky bunch. Hell, they'd sleep until eight or nine, then shoot over there catching up with the bomber stream for escort. They could go 400 mph and didn't have to form up like we did. These guys got credit for a kill whether destroyed in the air or on the ground." Dick recalled it was always impressive to see their drop tanks fall when enemy fighters appeared in the area. The P-51s would then be lighter, more maneuverable and faster climbing.

For the fighter pilots of both the Luftwaffe and the USAAF, these large bomber formations posed many difficult challenges on the attack and on the defense, respectively. This was because the bomber formations themselves, the Luftwaffe attack strategy and the combat range of the escort planes all continually evolved over time. For German fighter pilots, the task of attacking massive streams of bombers flying in ever tighter, coordinated formations and escorted by fighters with increasing combat capability and range was a highly formidable one.[35]

For American fighter pilots to adequately protect the bomber stream, they had to remain very close, within 50–75 feet, of the much slower moving B-17s. But by remaining so close, this proximity restricted their natural advantage of altitude and speed. On the other hand, it also presented them with opportunities to dive on enemy fighters below the formation. By early 1944, thanks to a momentous decision made by the newly appointed commander of the Eighth Air Force, Lt. General James Doolittle, American escort pilots were given more flexibility of movement, and flew escort further out to the sides and the front of the formation but always above the formation.[36] As we shall see, this change in tactics was a key factor in the Allies gaining air superiority in Western Europe prior to D-Day because for the first time, the escort fighters were given the freedom to go after the Luftwaffe away from the bomber stream, on the ground as well as in the air.

A typical tactic for three fighter escort squadrons in the fighter group escorting the B-17 combat box was as follows.[37] One squadron would overtake the bombers and position itself above the stream, dividing into two sections, one some miles ahead of the other. A second squadron, also divided into two sections, positioned itself above and about a mile laterally outward from the bombers on each side of their box. The third squadron positioned itself about 4,000 feet above the bomber stream, one section directly above and the other about ten miles ahead towards the sun where it would be ready to intercept any attacks from this "blind spot."[38]

Thus, by increasing the spacing of the fighter escorts from the bomber stream in essentially this manner, the fighter escorts were better capable of detecting impending attacks before visual detection was made by the bomber crews. Therefore, the fighter escorts had a jump on the Germans. They could attack Luftwaffe fighters before they could form up for a coordinated attack against the bomber stream. However, caution had to be exercised in over-committing escort fighters at the expense of the safety of the stream, since a seeming attack by enemy fighters from a certain direction might be a feint intended to draw away escort fighters, leaving the bomber stream vulnerable to attack from different direction.[39,40]

The danger the stream itself posed to the Luftwaffe attackers must have created overwhelming fear. As stated earlier, the combat box formation, depending upon how many squadrons were in the formation, bristled with as many as 200 to 700 .50-caliber heavy machine guns. It is well-documented that B-17 gunners aboard the bombers shot down far more enemy fighters than is credited to their fighter escorts.

On the other hand, German fighters employed a frontal approach to the low and lead squadrons while menacing the high element from the rear. The more experienced German pilots appeared to slow the rate of closure (which could be as high as 600 mph) to increase their accuracy and seemed to time their attacks to whenever they saw the top and ball-turret gunners occupied with firing to rear and side attackers. If German fighters approached to within 250 yards to try to improve their marksmanship, they became point-blank targets for the B-17 gunners. As one might expect, only the less experienced pilots would tend do this. Usually German fighters would speed ahead by about three miles past the formation, then, swinging their yellow noses around in a wide U-turn turn, 180 degrees, and approach the bomber stream head-on to minimize their exposure to the B-17 gunners. They would often attack from out of the sun at 12 o'clock high and approach a formation in pairs and fours, aiming their wing cannon at the heavy bombers' cockpits.

However, there was a price to be paid for this tactic. It could backfire because the further ahead the enemy fighter flew before turning, the more fuel the plane expended. Furthermore, the 18–21 plane formation of a squadron was generally about a thousand feet deep and 300 feet wide, with from eleven to thirteen .50-caliber machine guns aimed at any German pilot daring to penetrate the formation.[41,42]

Still, the frontal attack promised the German pilots their best chance of survival. Occasionally, they would fly so close to the bombers that they had to climb steeply at the last second to avoid the protruding tail of the B-17. A two-gun chin turret was added to the B-17G model, operated, when needed, by the bombardier, specifically to counter head-on attacks.

On the other hand, if enemy fighters attacked the formation from the rear, they tried to concentrate the attack by sending successive four-plane (Schwarm) formations, one after another, at the bombers, quickly firing, and then climbing over the formation. Whether attacking from in front or behind, the German fighters often finished their attack with a split-S, while taking fire from the bombers' waist, tail and belly guns, to open up as much distance from the American gunners, as quickly as possible.[43]

Other Luftwaffe tactics and tricks made life difficult for the American escort fighters. For example, as Michael Spick notes in

Luftwaffe Fighter Aces, "One flight of FW-190s would be sent down through the formation as a decoy; the remainder stayed above to fall on the USAAF fighter escorts when they dove after the sacrificial flight."[44]

Ultimately, while German weaponry and tactics improved, the Luftwaffe fighter force was being seriously depleted by a shortage of pilots, with fewer and fewer experienced pilots left to lead the attack against the bombers. This difficulty was soon matched by severe shortages of fuel in the spring and summer of 1944 and as the USAAF attacks on fuel supplies and synthetic oil facilities intensified. Thus, the hours of training flight time available to new German pilots was severely limited and they entered combat poorly trained or inexperienced. While it was tactically effective for Me-110s and FW-190s armed with rockets and cannon, accompanied by Me-109s flying top cover, to break up bomber formations and fall on the stragglers like killer sharks, it was ultimately the heavy losses and the lack of sufficient fuel (a direct result of Eighth Air Force bombing) that sealed the fate of the Luftwaffe. The Allies had the overwhelming advantage that they could quickly replace their lost planes and crews due to their combination of industrial productivity and virtually a limitless supply of fresh, well-trained pilots. This disparity in a war of attrition ultimately decided the long and deadly air war over Europe.

Since so many B-17s were lost over Europe, it comes as no surprise that a few Flying Fortresses fell into Nazi hands, either by being forced to land on German airfields or by the Germans piecing together flyable examples from the fragments of crashed aircraft. By various means, the Germans were able to make about forty such Fortresses airborne, an amazing number which were employed for deception, training and surveillance.

For example, while most of these captured B-17s were given high visibility Nazi insignia and used for the training of fighter pilots in the development of effective combat tactics against USAAF-operated Fortresses, some were flown in their original USAAF markings for deceptive purposes such as sneak penetrations of Allied territory, the dropping of enemy spies, supplying secret bases and providing data on the altitude and positions of the bomber stream during USAAF attacks.

There is plenty of eyewitness-confirmed evidence, including in Dick's diary, that there was often a captured Allied fighter or bomber piloted by Germans, flying as inconspicuously as possible off to the side of the bomber stream, transmitting back to ground stations the altitude and air speed of the formation. Lt. Charles Alling, a pilot in the 34th Bombardment Group[45] also described captured B-17s used stealthily by the Luftwaffe as decoys. They would also follow returning USAAF B-17 formations, pretending to be a crippled straggler, hoping to draw a B-17 out of the formation to cover it against fighter attack during the flight home. Once the protective B-17 closed in, the decoy would fire at it with its own guns or would call in German fighters to finish it off. This practice was enough of a threat that USAAF bomber formations would often fire upon an approaching straggler that could not be positively identified.

There was also a clandestine Luftwaffe unit, I/KG 200, that used captured B-17s which were assigned the cover designation "Dornier Do 200." For example, they used captured Allied aircraft for the construction and maintenance of a series of secret airstrips and fuel dumps. Moreover, a captured Fortress was used to parachute agents into Jordan in October of 1944.[46,47]

6

BLIND BOMBING: Radars and PFF

The rudiments of early radar can be described as a sending station or antenna which transmits continuous light waves, each wave peak separated from the next or previous wave peak by the radar wavelength. As the antenna rotates at a constant speed, the radar (light) waves are spread over a large circular area. When the radar light waves intercept a stationary or moving target, an image appears on a glass screen or scope. This basic principle underlies the radar systems used by all sides during World War II. The RAF's bombing missions early in the war relied on "blind bombing" using a new ground-based radar navigational device called "GEE" (derived from "Grid" or "Ground Electronic Equipment") which transmitted radar waves from three widely separated transmitting stations to enable a navigator to locate his bomber's position in the sky relative to the target.

Thus, GEE was the first radar navigational aid. The three ground transmitters were located 96 miles apart on British soil. This created a grid of radio beams that extended over part of Europe with a range of about 400 miles. The receivers aboard an aircraft could calculate the impulse frequencies coming from the three transmitters which enabled the navigator to fix the location of nearby aircraft precisely up to a distance of six miles.[48] The GEE Box was essentially a cathode ray tube. The time to take a fix was approximately fifteen seconds. The GEE Box measurements of the time difference in the arrival of signal from the ground stations were in millionths of a second while the accuracy of the fix was approximately twenty-five feet at sea level.[49]

In principle, GEE, along with pathfinder marking, claimed a

bombing accuracy of one-tenth of a mile. The bombers utilized the most skilled pilots, bombardiers and navigators to fly in the pathfinder units ahead of the bombers. These pathfinder units were aircraft which located the area target and marked the area by dropping flares. For example, the RAF pathfinder procedures included the following.

The pathfinder aircraft were either "finders" or "lighters." Nine miles before reaching the target, the pathfinder "finder" would begin to drop flares every thirty seconds over the flying lane the bombers were to follow. Then the lighters circled the target area where first they dropped flares (sometimes called Christmas trees) followed by incendiary bombs. Then the finders would fly a criss-cross pattern across the marked line, dropping more flares. The point where the two lines of flares intersected marked the bombing zone where the main bomber force would release its main payload of bombs. A second pathfinder squadron would fly along ahead of the bomber stream to drop additional flares if needed. This procedure resulted in reduced amounts of time over the heavily defended target zone and thus decreased the number of bombers lost due to increased time of exposure to enemy fire.[50]

Among the problems encountered by the RAF were that the pathfinder flares often burned out before the bomber force arrived at the target and that the Germans made effective use of decoy fires which diverted many bombers. But the most serious problem with GEE was its vulnerability to jamming by the Germans.

The GEE Box was not only a critical tool in fixing the location of a target during blind bombing. It was also the absolutely essential instrument needed to confine each bomb group and combat wing within its allotted air space during the complex, simultaneous assembly of thousands of aircraft competing for air space over England at the beginning of a mission.

It became clear to both sides that night bombing and "blind" daylight bombing would become effective only with the development of better radars: OBOE and H2S on the Allied side and systems such as Wurzburg-Reissen and Lichtenstein on the German side. For both the Germans and the Allies, there was always an underlying reluctance to implement a new system due to the risk of it being captured and subsequently used against themselves. This applied to ground radars, airborne radars and even jamming methods.

OBOE, an acronym for "observer bombing over enemy" was a precise electronic bombing system developed by the British that emitted a bass tone to guide bombers to their target using this continuous beacon. Bombers tuned into ground stations which emitted a continuous signal allowing navigators to plot their positions in the sky relative to a pre-determined bomb release point.[51]

This was an improvement over GEE which, as mentioned earlier, was easily jammed. OBOE was actually a further development of the German "blind bombing" system known as Knickebein that they used during the Battle of Britain. OBOE used two ground transmitting stations, the "cat" and the "mouse," to lead an aircraft to a target on the shortest possible path. For example, a bomber would be guided toward a target along a circular path whose radius was the bomber's fixed distance from one radar station while a second radar station tracked the same bomber to a pre-arranged distance at the target where the bombs would be released. Therefore, OBOE made it possible for a bomber to hit its target from high altitude without visually seeing the target, in other words "blind bombing."

The range of OBOE radar was restricted to 270 miles, imposed by the curvature of the earth; nonetheless, this range allowed raids on the Ruhr Valley as far east as Dortmund. Bombers and lighter aircraft (that is, the pathfinders) would mark the target area with colored markers on the ground to guide the main bomber force to the target area. This technique of bombing proved successful against the vital Krupp works, which covered hundreds of acres located in the center of Essen, an effort that culminated in the RAF attack on July 25–26, 1943.

With fog, rain and generally bad weather either grounding the bombers or preventing visual bombing as the year wore on, the USAAF began its own radar bombing with the few available OBOE sets. OBOE had been introduced in October 1943 and first used on a USAAF mission in early November when five pathfinder aircraft equipped with Mark 1 OBOE sets led a force of 374 B-17s to raid the iron foundry and marshalling yards at Gelsenkirchen. Unfortunately, the lead planes encountered problems with OBOE and the bombing was off target.[52] Problems with the reliability of OBOE continued to plague the Eighth Air Force throughout November.

A major development in increasing the range of bombers carrying out blind bombing missions was a radar system that could operate independently of ground transmitters. British scientists had developed just such a new airborne radar instrument called H2S in 1940 to locate targets through thick overcast. The name H2S was rumored to have been chosen because a British officer, while visiting a manufacturing facility for the radar, noted that the room smelled like rotten eggs, hence H2S or Hydrogen Sulfide.[53]

To some, another source of the name was "home sweet home". Pathfinder planes equipped with H2S scanned the ground and transmitted a picture of land and sea contrast on cathode ray tubes located inside the pathfinder planes. A flat surface like water would return few echoes, a hilly terrain would return more, while a city with buildings would return strong echoes and the radar reflection would appear very bright on radar screens. While H2S had a range that was greater than OBOE, it was not as precise and the amount of H2S equipment was initially very limited. Target maps were constructed to simulate how the target would appear on the cathode ray tubes of H2S. But these maps had to be up-to-date, otherwise what appeared on the tube would not correspond to the target map. This air to ground radar soon appeared in a new, improved American version called H2X.

In H2X, referred to as "Mickey" by American airmen, a high frequency electrical impulse was sent downward through a revolving antenna underneath or in the nose of the bomber and this beam of energy scanned the earth's surface. The reflected signals picked up by the antenna produced the same crude map-like image on a cathode ray tube or oscilloscope as in H2S. Thus water appeared as dark areas, ground appeared as light areas, and cities appeared as bright areas.

When the target was sighted, special pathfinder planes dropped sky marker flares for the rest of the bomber stream. When the Mickey ship dropped its bombs, the rest dropped theirs.[54] On November 3, 1943, 555 B-17s were led by several pathfinders equipped with H2X sets to raid Wilhelmshaven. Since at this stage the H2X radar sets were scarce, only 12 of the bombers were equipped with the radar scanner, which was nose-mounted at this early stage. By the fall of 1944, more B-17 lead ships had been fitted out as PFF platforms with H2X

Mickey sets placed in a retractable opaque dome called the radome on the B-17 which replaced the ball turret.

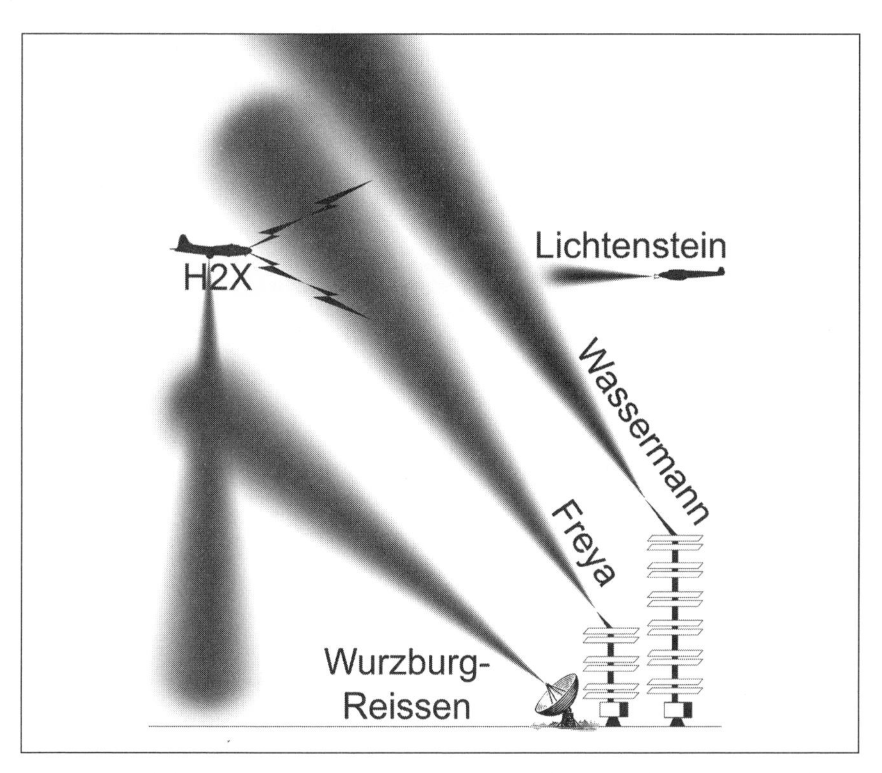

A notional illustration of the radio noise and H2X airborne radar of an approaching B-17, picked up by principal German ground (Wurzburg-Reissen, Freya, Wassermann) and airborne (Lichtenstein) radar defenses.

It is clear that without "blind" radar bombing or bombing through overcast with H2X, the generally poor weather over the continent during the Fall and Winter of 1944–45 would have severely limited operations to only a few visual bombing missions per month, thus grossly under-utilizing a bomber force the size of the Eighth and doing minimal damage to German war production, oil and transportation targets. Unfortunately, the radar resolution of H2X (i.e. the minimum target size that would give an identifiable return on the radar screen) was so poor that it could only locate a target roughly the size of a city.

Moreover, the Germans placed high priority facilities like synthetic oil plants away from urban areas. Nevertheless, if conditions allowed visual bombing in combination with H2X the accuracy improved substantially. If a target was located in a coastal region, then H2X bombing accuracy was greatly enhanced. For example, H2X tactical bombing early in the morning of D-Day was carried out quite successfully through 100% undercast.[55]

A considerably more accurate "blind" bombing technique than H2X alone, called Gee-H, utilized an airborne transmitter and two ground beacons (called the Cat and Mouse as in GEE) to fix a target's location. The range of Gee-H was 300 miles. When used in combination with H2X, radar bombing accuracy was improved substantially.[56]

Another major development in bombardment tactics was the introduction of "air scouts" which were P-51 Mustangs sent out ahead of the bomber stream to report on the weather over the targets, enemy fighter activity and any other useful information.

This program was the brainchild of Colonel Budd Peaslee, commander of the 348th Bomb Group, and was implemented by General Doolittle with the formation of the 1st Scouting Force.[57] The air scout planes were the "seeing eyes" of the heavies.

They were piloted by experienced bomber pilots who were retrained on single-engine planes. The air scouts would advise the wing and division commanders by VHF radio transmissions on the best course and altitude for the bomber formation to take to avoid abortive weather conditions. They also proved helpful in assisting large formations attempting the always dangerous assembly during thick overcast. The air scout program was driven by the frequent difference between weather on the continent versus what was predicted by air corps meteorologists, causing massive recalls of bomber formations already en route to their targets. This mismatch between forecasts and actual weather necessitated having secondary targets and hence increasing the time that bombers had to spend over hostile enemy territory. The air scouts program proved to be very successful.[58]

On the German side, a long-range, ground-based radar called Freya and a shorter range one called Wurzburg-Reissen permitted the early detection of incoming bombers and the vectoring of fighters as well as searchlights and flak artillery onto them. This system involved fighter control stations and the deployment of fighters in a so-called "box" or Himmelbet, the "four poster bed" defense system.[59]

The Himmelbet defense system utilized a network of radar stations stretching from the Baltic Sea through Holland and France to Switzerland and to Berlin, called the Kammhuber Line, named after its designer, Lieutenant General Josef Kammhuber. It was continually expanded as Allied planes found ways to avoid detection by flying around it.[60] The system was, in reality, a comprehensive, fully integrated, network of a nocturnal defense force, searchlights, radars, flak guns and night fighter stations.

The German night fighters utilized a short-range radar set in the fighter aircraft and a longer range radar set on the ground carefully tuned by a ground controller who would vector the fighter toward an approaching Allied bomber. The aircraft most commonly used as night fighters by the Germans were the Junkers-88, the Me-110s and the Me-410s. A ground controller could bring a Junkers-88 to within 3 miles of an intruding bomber before the radar set on the night fighter would pick up the enemy bomber.[61]

Each Himmelbett station was equipped not only with Wurzburg-Reissen radar but also with the older Freya radar to guide one German interceptor to its intruder (enemy bomber) target. German Freya radar was a long-range radar system with a maximum range of 78 miles which could pick up even radio communications between bombers taking off and their control towers. The role of Freya was primarily to give early warning. The Freya sets were made up if a series of horizontal antennae mounted in an array vertically upward along a tall pole.[62]

The Wurzburg-Reissen sets utilized giant radar antennae or dishes and could detect incoming planes out to a range of 48 miles. It was a more localized but more precise radar typically with 20-foot parabolic dishes. This was intended to track individual bombers by providing the height and speed of bombers for the searchlights and flak guns and to guide the night fighters onto them so that the fighters' airborne radar, code-named "Emil-Emil," could lock onto it and close in for the kill (see below). An even longer range radar was developed by German scientists in order to increase the range of the Freya. They equipped it with a taller, highly focusing antenna. This new radar facility was called Wassermann and had a range of 180 miles (300km) over twice the range of Freya.[63]

In a daring paratrooper raid on a Wurzburg installation at Bruneval, France, the British were able to capture a number of intact components as well as a German technician. British scientists under R.V. Jones dismantled the radar, learning the dipole and frequency setting parts of the Wurzburg set.[64] They found that once the set had been jammed at one frequency, it could not be switched to another. By using simple tin foil strips (chaff or "window") dropped from Allied aircraft to swamp German radar with false signals, the Allies and Germans both realized that they could jam each other's radar by releasing these metallic strips which produced spurious electromagnetic transmissions onto monitoring radar screens, thus giving the appearance of a bomber aircraft. It was found that the jamming strips were most effective when they were cut to a length about one-half of the wavelength of the Allied or German radar device being fooled.

Intelligence coups on both sides yielded new avenues for countermeasures and technology advances. The Allies had jamming devices codenamed Mandrel, Carpet and Shiver, which were airborne radio transmitters specifically designed to jam and swamp German ground radar such as Freya and Wurzburg. There were also radio transmissions from the bombers codenamed Tinsel and Jostle which could drown out radio communications between German fighters and their controllers. Counter-measures, codenamed Cigar and Corona, utilized German-speaking RAF operators assigned to transmit false and confusing directions to German fighters.[65]

Eventually, German scientists developed early versions of air interception radar, which would aid in locating and attacking approaching bombers, including one named Lichtenstein. This airborne radar was fitted to German night fighters to allow them to detect Allied bombers. It had an effective range of 2 miles and led German night fighters to within range of enemy bombers located by Freya and Wurzburg radar by homing in on the emissions of H2S (H2X to the Eighth Air Force) radar sets and radio transmissions of the bombers.

The Lichtenstein system operated even under poor weather conditions. The problem was that only one bomber could be tracked at a time. Unfortunately for the Germans, it is apparent that the

Kammhuber system erected against the RAF ultimately backfired because its deployment was one important factor which forced the RAF to give up daylight bombing and switch to area bombing at night, causing vastly more German civilian casualties.[66] Of course, other reasons for British night bombing were that they lacked the precision Norden bombsight and the long-range fighter escorts needed for accurate daylight bombing without unacceptably high losses of crews and aircraft.

This German Freya and Wurzburg target-locator systems were revealed to the British through radio monitoring of communications between German ground controllers and night fighters. The British crews discovered that the German radar operated at a frequency of 490 megahertz. On the other hand, the Germans downed a British Stirling pathfinder plane which carried a 330-pound device they found in the wreckage of the rear lower fuselage. What they had fortuitously discovered was an H2S panorama airborne radar that worked independently of ground station transmitters and under conditions of poor visibility. Most importantly, they found that the H2S unit operated with a wavelength of 8.7 cm.[67]

Soon the Germans also employed a Spanner infrared target designator. The night fighter boxes could be saturated by a large bomber stream and many bombers would get through. Any bombers that strayed from the stream would be picked up by the Wurzburg sets and attacked by night fighters. Day fighters, like the Me-109 and its variants, lacked range because the wing space for extra fuel tank capacity was insufficient. For night fighting, the Focke-Wulfe was more versatile and stronger. The first night fighters were bomber-type planes like the Dornier, Do-17 and Do-217. They had about six hours' flight endurance. The Heinkel-219, the Junker-88 and its variants were the most versatile night fighters. The Me-110 G-4, and by the fall of 1944, the first jet fighter, the Me-262, were also highly effective. A favorite tactic was to have a Ju-88 with its cockpit lights on followed by a trailing Ju-88 blacked out which would open fire behind it.[68]

The susceptibility of the Himmelbett system to jamming led the Germans to introduce a new fighter plane tactic known as Wilde Sau and Zahme Sau (Wild Boar and Tame Boar). Instead of being guided to enemy bombers by radar, Luftwaffe night fighters no longer relied on radar but detected brightly lit targets visually rather than by radar and therefore were immune to Allied jamming. For example, parachute flares could be dropped by German planes above the bomber stream to illuminate it for night fighter attack. The disadvantages to German fighters using Wilde Sau tactics was that the fighters could be hit by their own flak and, if with single engines, could stay airborne for only a limited time.[69] The Zahme Sau system infiltrated large numbers of fighters into the bomber stream in a given zone when the bomber stream was making its approach.

Later, German night fighters were fitted with the newest wide angle FuG-20 airborne radar made by the Telefunken Company and called Lichtenstein SN-2, known as SN-2 for short.

This radar, also known as Flensburg and Naxos (FuG-227 and FuG-350, respectively), was fitted to German fighters to permit them to home onto radio transmissions from the bombers' H2S or H2X transmissions. SN-2 radar and other new German airborne radar developments were revealed to the British by the capture of the new German night fighter, the Junker-88 G-1 on 13 July, 1944. SN-2 could locate Allied bombers in absolute darkness within a range of four miles, thus allowing the night fighters to locate and destroy them. SN-2 operated on a frequency of 85 Megahertz and could not be jammed with chaff or window.

Chaff (window) could be dropped by the Allied bombers to jam German radar and disable the German Himmelbett defensive system, but the British were reluctant to use it because they feared the Germans would then use it against them by jamming the radar of British night fighters when the Germans raided Britain. The SN-2 radar was also immune to the Seratte airborne radar radio receiver carried by British night fighters which originally had been able to detect the transmitted waves from German airborne radar and track and attack the German night fighters. Now the Germans had a counter-measure in the form of SN-2

The capture of the Ju-88 G-1, mentioned above, also revealed a major surprise to the British. Their Monica radar, used to warn bomber crews of approaching German night fighters, had been compromised. It turned out that since the beginning of 1943 the British Monica had been leading German night fighters right into the RAF bombers.(69) The German radar Naxos had also permitted German night fighters to intercept the H2S signals and thus locate bomber streams from a distance of 90 miles. Obviously, the British responded by removing Monica radar warning devices from all aircraft, and thereafter H2S radar systems were to be switched on only after the bombers were within the range of German ground radar stations. Allied bombers also had on-board equipment code-named Boozer that, like Monica and Fishpond, warned bomber crews when they were being tracked by German radar and warned of approaching German fighters.[70]

7

HEADING TO COMBAT: Crew FE-350-FA

Once Dick Ayesh's bombardier training was completed in Deming, New Mexico, he was ordered to report to the air base at Lincoln, Nebraska to join up with the crew to which he was assigned. He met his fellow air crew for the first time at this base. They were Gene Jensen, pilot, Jim Millet, copilot: John Gonda, navigator; Floyd Thomasson, flight engineer; Jim Roberts, radio operator; and Bob Bird, Joe Latiolait, Henry Sublett and Elmer Adams as gunners. They were ordered to proceed to the air base at Sioux City, Iowa for three months of combat crew training, which included simulated fighter attacks and gunnery practice (over the Black Hills of South Dakota). This training was designed to teach each crew member to perform his duty under combat conditions and to function as a team.

They flew practice bombing runs, flew long cross-country flights (sometimes in very adverse weather), logged instrument time, and were introduced to formation flying. They had to be at the base before daylight and would not be home until late in the afternoon or early evening. As Dick recalls, "There were some enjoyable places to eat, drink and be entertained in Sioux City whenever we had some free time to go into town. I also remember that when we approached the base in Sioux City to land on any clear, warm day, we would fly over these apartment buildings with girls on the rooftops sunbathing in the nude!"

Again there were training accidents. During Dick's time at the base, two B-17's collided on a formation flight. All crew members, ten on each plane, died. There had been many fatal accidents in Primary,

Basic and Advanced flight schools, but never one in Dick's experience that took the lives of so many classmates. He recalled another combat crew training accident in Sioux City during practice runs for P-47s on bombers, when one P-47 got too close and collided with the B-17, killing everyone.

In the event of emergencies when crew members had to bail out, they did the standard "count to ten and pull the rip cord." Their instructors told them to tie their regular pair of shoes to the back of their parachute harnesses because once on the ground they would need them to survive and find their way to safe haven. There was always an airman who asked what to do if his chute malfunctioned. He was told "if it doesn't work, bring it back!"

After Combat Crew training at Sioux City the crew was sent back to Lincoln, Nebraska for staging for overseas. When they were issued their clothing they knew which "theater of ops" they were going to because if it was "Sun Tans" (light clothing) they were going to the South Pacific. Fortunately, in Dick's view, he was issued the OD's (which were wool and gabardines) which meant the European theater.

Around the middle of September, the crew said their farewells. They were designated as Crew FE-350-FA, assigned a brand new B-17G, Number 44-8269, and directed to fly to Grenier Field in Manchester, New Hampshire, where they received fuel, a briefing on the Atlantic crossing, life rafts, survival gear and cargo racks in the bomb bays.

It was at this time that the crew noticed a huge difference in aircraft performance. Throughout the training missions in the States, the B-17s were flown on 80 octane fuel, but now for the trip overseas and throughout the combat tours, 100 octane fuel was used. Dick remembered that when the throttles were forward, it pushed you back in your seat, that's how much difference the higher octane fuel made.

Their first stop was at Goose Bay, Labrador, where they received a "Welcome to Labrador" letter. They found themselves deep in a conifer forest, in a settlement consisting of a small Hudson Bay store, a few modest homes and primitive military structures. It was a fascinating experience, the first time Dick, having grown up in land-locked Kansas, had experienced the scent of a pine forest and the first time he had eaten fresh ocean seafood. They were weathered in at Goose Bay for several days. While there, they were briefed on the approach and landing procedures for the emergency air strip located at the head of a fjord in Greenland where it was made clear that the approach had to be perfect.

From there they made an uneventful trip to Iceland where they spent another two days waiting for weather and were finally cleared for takeoff to the British Isles. For the young airman from Wichita, as with all the young servicemen, this was a totally new, anxiety-ridden experience, entering a theatre of war on a different continent. As Dick recalls, the fears and apprehension began to settle in. "When we left Labrador and headed out over the ocean, I thought to myself, 'What the hell am I doing here?' That's exactly what I thought."

This was another long, uneventful flight. The newly minted crew landed at the air base at Valley, the time of their arrival in Wales happening to coincide with the end of blackouts there. What a great welcome to the UK this turned out to be because the crew got to take part in the celebrations, and what a celebration it was.[71] The blackout had been a prolonged and disruptive source of stress to the Welsh so everyone was elated to see it end and was in a partying mood. This happy circumstance was due to the steady weakening of the Luftwaffe, Allied air supremacy, and the eastward push of the Allied armies, which greatly reduced the capability of Nazi bombing raids. What remained of the Luftwaffe was diverted to the defense of the German heartland and to action on the Eastern Front.

The next day they surrendered their new aircraft and were taken by train to London, then the town of Diss, then by truck (containing six crews) to their assignment with the 100th Bomb Group at Thorpe Abbotts. At the train station in Diss, the newly arrived crews were loaded into an army truck to be taken to Thorpe Abbots. En route, Dick casually asked the GI truck driver, "How are things going at Thorpe Abbotts?" The driver, without hesitating, coldly replied, "You guys are the replacements for the six crews we lost yesterday."

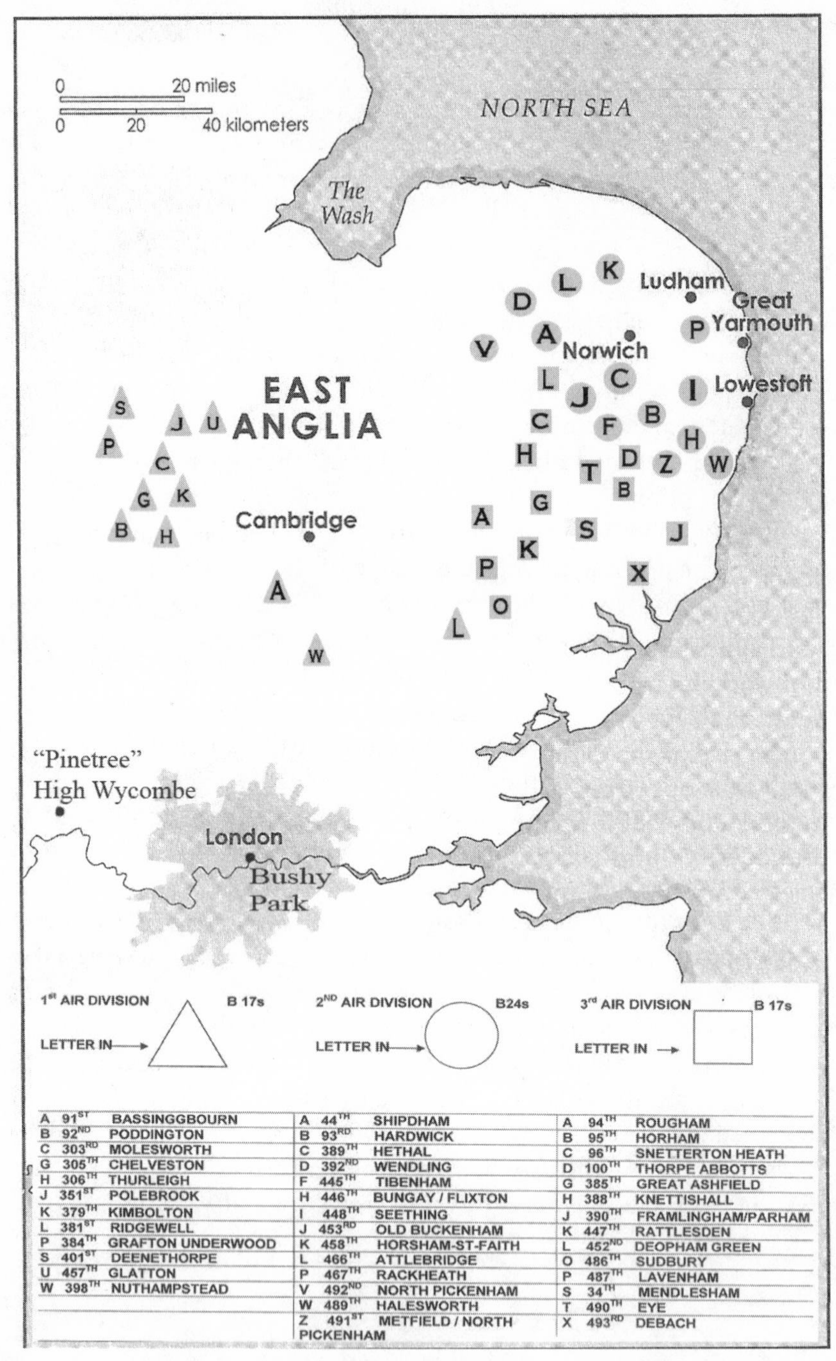

Map of East Anglia with Bomb Groups in each Air Division plotted using their respective symbols. (Courtesy of Sam Hurry, Trustee, 100th Bomb Group Memorial Museum, Thorpe Abbotts)

8

WELCOME TO THORPE ABBOTTS

The Village of Thorpe Abbotts has existed since at least the 11th century, as its name is listed in the great Norman census, The Domesday Book, which was compiled just after the conquest of England by the Duke of Normandy, William the Conqueror. In fact, Thorpe is a word of Viking origin meaning daughter though also a Scandinavian origin meaning outlying farmstead or hamlet. Thorpe Abbotts was a quiet, picturesque village in the rolling English countryside in the county of Norfolk, a distance of only five kilometers from the nearest small town, Diss, and about 100 miles northeast of London. It consists of quaint old country inns, thatched cottages, ancient churches and gardens, and surrounding pastoral farmlands.

The region was best described by writer John Nilsson in his book *Story of the Century*: "Norfolk County caught by nature in the midst of a yawn, lies back from the North Sea, a potpourri of nature, its roads undecided of direction, the myriad villages, the fields looking as though a supernatural painter with a huge paintbrush had splotched them with hues of green; and the farmers, craggy-faced, silent in their small fields, walk by their wagons under the sullen sky."

Only 60 years ago, when Thorpe Abbotts rubbed the sleep from it eyes, it found itself snuggled against a large bomber base, named "The One Hundredth Bombardment Group, H." The H stood for "Heavy." The tranquil solitude of this village was replaced by the deafening roar of bomber engines and the ceaseless activity associated with the hundreds of B-17 heavy bomber aircraft and thousands of airmen of the United States Army Air Force who had made Thorpe Abbotts the base for the 100th Bombardment Group of the mighty Eighth Air Force. It was here that history would be made.

Thorpe Abbotts, home of the 100th Bomb Group, was one of 124 US heavy bomber bases in the UK at the time. The total area of the airfield at Thorpe Abbotts was about 500 acres. This included three runways, with the main runway being 6,300 feet long, one of the longest in the Eighth Air Force. There were also 300 individual buildings, three and a half miles of perimeter track with hardstands, eleven miles of cement road, three and a half miles of sewers, five miles of water mains and fourteen and a half miles of drains. The scale of the construction project was staggering. For this one bomber base, 490,000 square yards of concrete was poured, 4,000,000 bricks were used, and 330,000 cubic yards of soil had to be excavated. Yet this was only one of the 124 American bases built by British contractors in what became the largest construction project in the history of Great Britain. The cost of construction for Thorpe Abbotts alone amounted to one million pounds.[72]

Like all bomb groups, the 100th consisted of four squadrons, with each squadron having nine to twelve B-17s. The squadrons of the 100th were the 349th XR, 350th LN, 351st EP and the 418th LD, the reason for the out of sequence squadron numbers never having been really explained to Dick. It turns out that each bomb group, when initially formed, consisted of only three squadrons. Later, the USAAF added a fourth bomb squadron but the numerical sequence was already broken with the formation of other bomb groups. Therefore, each bomb group ended up with one bomb squadron out of sequence. The two upper case letters following the squadron number were code letters unique to each squadron. Three bomb groups comprised a combat wing., The 100th, 95th and 390th Bomb groups made up the 13th Combat Bombardment Wing with its headquarters at Horham. The 13th Combat Wing, along with two other Wings, the 4th (HQ at Bury St. Edmunds) and the 45th (HQ at Snetterton Heath), belonged to the Third Air Division whose headquarters was at Elvden, Suffolk.

The base at Thorpe Abbotts was like a small city, except that it had been constructed on farm land, some of which was still under production. Like any small city it had a police force, a post office, a fire department, a store (Post Exchange or PX), water and sewer utilities, a church, small hospital and recreational facilities. In support of their bombing missions, there were units responsible for ordnance, armament, communications, transportation, photography,base engineering, and aircraft and engine maintenance. They had a giant filling station that pumped 1,000,000 gallons of gasoline per month! The Red Cross and the Royal Air Force were also represented. It was a very big and complicated business. Buildings were of two types, prefabricated corrugated steel Quonset or Butler huts, or structures assembled from pre-cast concrete panels. There were also pillboxes and anti-invasion defenses, but some structures had to be built above ground due to drainage problems at the airfield. The control tower (a museum today) was a standard USAAF type.[73]

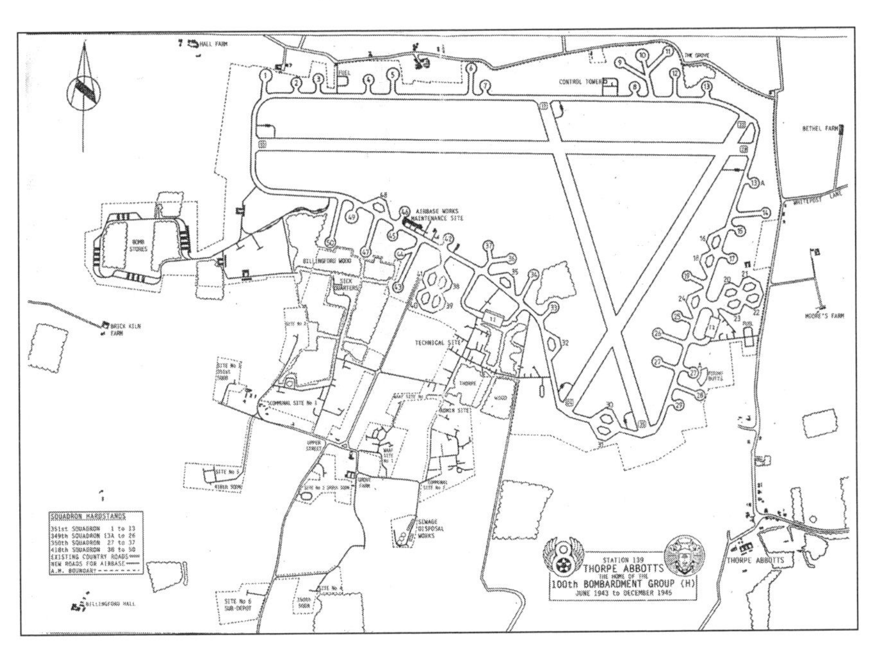

Base layout of Thorpe Abbotts, home of the 100th Bombardment Group. (Courtesy of Sam Hurry, Trustee, 100th Bomb Group Memorial Museum, Thorpe Abbotts)

The permanent staff and flight crews were located in different parts of the base. Officers and enlisted personnel occupied separate quarters with officers assigned to a concrete barrack building. This concrete structure was a former RAF building. Heat was provided a few hours per day by a small stove which burned coke, a form of coal. This stove was in the middle of the room and would burn coal as long as the ration lasted, then when that ran out, furniture or anything else the men could find would be fed into it. Dick recalled, "There was one airman, [Name Deleted], who just for the hell of it would throw in cartridges. It's a wonder nobody was killed by it. One airman used an old oil burner to rig up an ingenious heating system that burned used oil from a tank installed in the ceiling that would drip down a copper tube into the stove where it would burn."

The problem of shaving with a 110 volt razor on a 220 volt circuit was solved by a small variable resistor in a wooden Kraft cheese box. It was homemade, but apparently safe! The barracks building had two privies that were on either side of the front door. There were 12 beds (six on a side) and clean sheets every day. Each bed had a dresser on the side and a place to hang your uniform. This dresser is where Dick kept a fifth of Three Feathers Bourbon (any bourbon was hard to come by in the UK) which he intended to open upon completion of his tour of duty. Colonel Jeffrey, Commanding Officer of the 100th Bomb Group, was quartered next door to their barracks. The latrines were nearby and were heated and supplied with hot water.

Despite base security, it was not unusual to run across prostitutes using the latrines. Given the security, it was also surprising how close to the base perimeter civilians, usually with children, were allowed to go.[74] For a bath, the officers would have to leave the building, clothes and footwear in tow and walk outside to a quonset hut that had the bathing facilities. The hut had a dirt floor, no lights, and illumination only by candle with ten tubs each in an individual room and always water on the floor from previous bathers. There were 2 x 8 planks to keep your feet out of the water. The tubs were old and encrusted with a rusty brown residue from many other bathers. As Dick recalls, "You really didn't care how many guys used it or the last time it was cleaned, you just wanted a bath."

Recreational facilities consisted of a church and two Clubs, one for enlisted personnel and one for officers. Church was, to many, an important part of life on the base.

The Officer's Club at Thorpe Abbotts had the only circular bar in England. Dick remembers guys who would walk out smashed, breathe in some oxygen and then hold a match in front of them and blow flames straight out. Of course, if you were hung over, the best thing for you was oxygen! Drinking was usually avoided if there was a likelihood of flying the next day. But many of the flight officers were dedicated patrons of the Club. It is possible that some of the aircraft accidents were caused by excessive drinking the night before.

THE ACCOUTREMENTS OF AN AIRMAN

An airman's flight clothing was based on temperatures as low as 50 degrees below zero. Most of the crew used the blue, electrically heated suits (nicknamed Bunny suits) and heavy-lined clothing. Some found that it was hard work flying in formation, and that perspiration was a problem. Many wore winter underwear, woolen uniform pants and shirt, maybe a sweater, and woolen flight coveralls; a "bomber jacket; silk gloves, woolen gloves, and lined leather gloves; silk socks, heavy English "fisherman" socks, soft leather 8" Bass "Hunter" boots, and heavy lined flying boots. They wore a regulation flying helmet with built in earphones, added a steel combat helmet on the bomb run, and used a throat microphone for communication.[75]

Other flight gear included a .45-caliber Colt semiautomatic pistol in a shoulder holster, parachute harness (the "chute" was under the seat), an inflatable life vest, and good sun glasses. On the bomb run they would add a steel "flak vest" as well as the steel helmet. They carried a small escape kit which included maps, a compass, a phrase book, signal mirror, money and escape photo.

SUPPORT PERSONNEL

The ground crew consisted of a very dedicated team who were assigned to each squadron of B-17s. Depending upon the squadron size, the team consisted of two officers and up to 100 enlisted men. A line chief was in charge and had three flight chiefs, twelve crew chiefs and 48 mechanics, with a crew chief and four mechanics looking after each B-17. When the number of bombers in a squadron was raised from 12 to 18, six more crew chiefs were added and the number of mechanics assigned to each ship was reduced from four down to two or three.[76] These men considered their individual aircraft to be their special object of tender, loving care, and developed a continuing affectionate relationship with it. They worked in the paved areas in which the planes were parked, which were called hard stands. There was a concrete hard stand for each parked B-17. The ground crews would work, usually in a tent shelter, next to each parked plane before each mission. They had the responsibility of assuring the completion of any servicing or repairs of propellers, oxygen equipment, the bomber's superstructure and armaments.

Ground crew would transport wooden crates containing belts of .50-caliber shells which were loaded next to each gun, and the guns and turrets were thoroughly checked. Armorers placed bombs on long, low trailers which were then pulled by tractor or jeep to the planes, hoisted into the bellies of the B-17s with hand-operated winches, and hung on shackles in the bomb bay.

One can only imagine the emotional and psychological trauma the ground crew experienced when their crew and aircraft did not return from a mission. Each plane to which they were assigned was really their "special baby." At the same time, ground crews often resisted the tendency to become emotionally attached to the crews of those same aircraft. These emotional bonds were often avoided to lessen the trauma of losing an aircrew.[77]

The mechanics worked all night if needed, in freezing cold and rainy weather, testing the controls, inspecting the brakes and landing gear, checking the fuel tanks for leaks and the tires for burns. They left no stone unturned, examining the four engines, listening very carefully for any symptomatic indication of trouble revealed in the pitch or intensity of the sound. All too frequently, engines had to be replaced due to flak damage or just plain war weariness due to excessive usage on missions. Sheet metal workers would measure the damaged aircraft for patches, assuming the bomber was still considered airworthy. The air crews really owed their lives to the thoroughness and dedication of the ground crews in keeping their ships airworthy. It is also acknowledged that the ground crews received very little credit.[78]

It was typically the case that dozens of engines had to be replaced on a given squadron's bombers over the course of a year. This made it unlikely that any given bomber crew would complete its tour flying the same bomber throughout. For example, Dick's crew flew several bombers over their 34 missions, for which he recalled the names of only two, "Old Shillelagh" and "Reluctant Dragon."

Many times, engines which were replaced still contained parts that were fully functional and hence reusable. Mechanics could use these parts to rebuild other engines. Despite the meticulous maintenance, every airman realized that in addition to the nerve shattering tension of going through enemy fire, the danger of unexplained mechanical bugs, clogged fuel lines and malfunctioning controls could each spell doom, as did fog and unexpected storms or crew errors. The probability of survival and seeing their friends and comrades lost weighed heavily on an airman's psyche, and could have a devastatingly stressful effect on morale, impairing judgment and efficiency. According to Dick, this was more of a potential problem in the earliest part of the air war before long-range fighter escorts when two out of three bomber crewmen did not survive.

Very early in the morning of a mission, even before the crew was awakened, the armorers would load the planes with bombs and ammunition while fueling teams would fill the tanks to a level determined by the mission's round trip distance, predicted wind speed and the selected cruising altitude. For a mission deep into Germany, known as a maximum effort, nine tons of fuel were required. Usually, the fuel load made up roughly half of the plane's total load.

After each mission, intelligence officers debriefed the crew as a group. As the crew entered de-briefing, they were given two shots of whiskey to relax them. Usually, this was administered by Red Cross girls. Then they were taken to debriefing rooms for intelligence information. Information was sought about the enemy's response to the mission, the intensity of flak, the Luftwaffe tactics, if new, whether any previously unrecognized Luftwaffe units had participated, what aircraft were seen going down and whether there were any chutes seen.[79]

Dick's crew flew practice missions over England for several weeks. Their first order of business was training in radio procedures, assembly procedures (getting each aircraft into its assigned position in a bomber stream with 1,000 other aircraft was a complex and difficult procedure), combat formation flying, and instrument landing procedures. The training for aerial combat was sometimes as hazardous as the combat itself. The English countryside was strewn with the wreckage of training accidents, both bombers and fighters, sometimes the two together in a jumble.

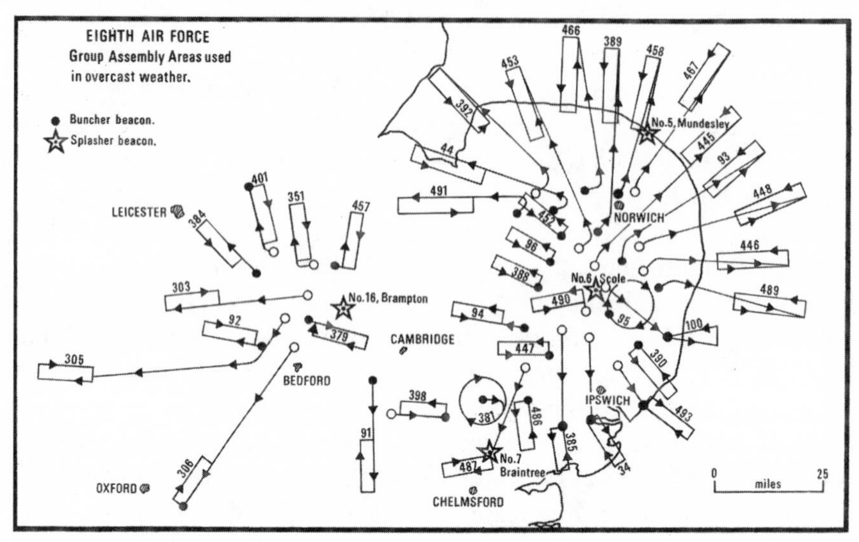

Bomber group assembly areas in overcast. Each bomb group assembled as shown in its assigned air space in the skies of East Anglia. Buncher and Splasher beacons are shown. (From *The Mighty Eighth War Manual* by Roger A. Freeman, courtesy of Orion Publishing Group)

Most of the training accidents were due to bad weather conditions, with fog and icing being the main culprits. The weather and English landscape were a far cry from the crew's training experience in South Dakota, New Mexico or Nebraska. The weather in Western Europe in 1944–45 was frequently the worst possible for formation flying. Instead of good weather during takeoff, assembly, en route to the target, over the target, and on the return to base, the crews had to often overcome fast forming fog and thick cloud cover over England and the Continent, which led to many horrendous accidents. In 1943 alone, there were 20,000 major accidents at bases in the US, with 5,603 airmen killed, while over the course of the war, 15,000 airmen were killed during training accidents in the US and overseas.[80]

During one of the practice missions of Dick's crew, as they were returning to base, their landing was almost perfect and they could hardly feel the wheels touch the ground. In fact the wheels hadn't touched! They were still about 50 feet above the runway, but in landing mode. They realized what had happened and applied full power just as they hit the runway. When they were again airborne they found that the right landing gear had broken, but was still attached to the aircraft. They had three options: try a landing on one wheel; try a belly landing with the good wheel up; or abandon the aircraft and bail out. The crew voted for the one-wheel landing at the emergency airfield with a runway two miles long. It was a smooth landing on the good wheel. They cut the power and had almost stopped when the right wheel folded up into the wing. The aircraft became scrap![81]

Regardless of the benefits and successes of these practice missions, and the occasional screw-ups, there were no instructors, observors or check pilots on board to evaluate a crew's readiness or to meet any kind of performance criteria. The main purpose was to acquaint the crews with extremely variable weather and flying conditions, the topography of East Anglia, and the difficult task of forming up with large numbers of other aircraft.

Dick's pilot, Lieutenant Gene Jensen, recalled, "The Germans were the official enemy, but from my standpoint, weather, formation flying, pilot error and limited air traffic control get equal billing!" In Lt. Jensen's view, their battle with the enemy started with takeoff, the "enemy" being an overloaded aircraft, limited visibility, the hazards of assembly and formation flying, the hazards of return: oxygen, exhausted pilots, instrument conditions and more aircraft than airspace. "We saw many aircraft explode in mid-air, especially the B-24, and we know there were mid-air collisions. We had several near misses! It was a deadly game from the minute the throttles were 'walked' forward for the takeoff until the return to the hardstand. A crash on takeoff, a mid-air collision or a crash on landing were all just as deadly as fire from enemy aircraft or flak."

The critical process of assembling typically 1,000 bombers into battle formation over the crowded skies and generally poor weather conditions of England was extremely perilous. It required precise coordination and control to place each bomber combat wing into its "box" (i.e., allocation of airspace within which to maneuver) at the required position and altitude, at a given time, even under the best weather conditions. To successfully assemble 1,000 bombers through heavy overcast into formation above the thick cloud deck was even more formidable.

To enable assembly and the needed timing for each combat wing of three bomb groups to form up, while minimizing the possibilities of collision, a system of radio beacons called Splashers (powerful, permanent, medium frequency beacons used by all the Allied bombers) and Bunchers (medium frequency, lower powered beacons, usually located on airfields) were used. Each beacon provided checkpoints for use with the radio compass in the cockpit. This gave each pilot a guidance on his position relative to that radio beacon.

By 1944, the procedure had been optimized to the point that all mission assemblies followed this procedure regardless of the weather conditions. The bomb group assembly would begin with each of three groups (forming a combat wing) assuming the same orbit about their assigned Buncher at different altitudes. Each individual bomber, just after takeoff, would follow a briefed bearing for typically five minutes, then make a slow turn toward their combat wing Buncher, making a circular climb at a prescribed rate of 300 to 350 feet per minute at 130 to 150 mph, and continue orbiting the Buncher with a leveling out at a briefed altitude. The squadrons within each bomb group assembled at different prescribed altitudes, as did the three groups of a combat wing relative to their briefed positions in the formation, either lead, high or low. These latter positions were each separated by 1,000 feet of altitude.[82]

Each group leader fired red, green or yellow flares from the cabin roofs of the group leaders' planes to identify the lead squadron to the high and low squadrons of each group. Squadrons would keep circling until they found their groups. It took maybe an hour from takeoff to form three squadrons into a compact group in stagger formation with the low squadron down to the left of the lead squadron and the high squadron up and to the right of it.

Under the worst conditions, when instrument procedures had to be used with Bunchers to break through layered clouds or thick overcast, each bomb group was assigned its own, well-separated assembly areas to try to minimize the deadly risk of collision. It was absolutely critical that the approach to these isolated assembly areas was followed meticulously. Bombers took off at 30-second intervals and climbed for two to four minutes before turning on to their prescribed course. Each bomber reached the group assembly area using the Buncher signal to maintain their position while climbing in the "soup." These allocated assembly areas were typically rectangular with a 15-mile "length" and only a five-mile "width," the latter being the distance just needed to turn the formation through 180 degrees.[83]

During the week preceding Dick's arrival at Thorpe Abbotts, the 100th had lost 12 aircraft and 108 airmen over Ruhland alone. Following procedure, the new pilot, Gene Jensen, flew his first mission with an experienced crew, gaining some initial experience in an attack on Bremen. Dick's and the rest of the crew's first combat mission came on the 15th of October, 1944, to Cologne.

9

LEGEND OF THE "BLOODY HUNDREDTH"

The 100th Bombardment Group had become legendary soon after its activation in 1942. Its reputation preceded, in large part, the arrival of Dick and his crewmates in 1944. Aside from the swagger, drinking and skirt-chasing that all red-blooded bomb groups carried out, by January of 1943 there had been episodes of acting up, heavy drinking, unrestrained ribaldry, violation or disregard of combat rules, and other assorted disciplinary problems in the Group. The newly arriving "virgin" aircrews would tend to imitate the behavior of some of their superiors.[84]

By the time Dick and his crewmates arrived at Thorpe Abbots, the 100th Bomb Group had also taken on a dubious and rather distinctive reputation in battle, and was known as the "The Bloody Hundredth." The source of this nickname remains controversial to this day. Its origin began in the aftermath of the Regensburg raid on August 17, 1943, a mission whose objective was the destruction of the Messerschmitt-109 aircraft-and-assembly shops in the northeastern part of the city. If the mission was successful, some 30 percent of Germany's single-engine fighter aircraft production would be wiped out. Naturally, hundreds of Luftwaffe aircraft rose to defend the factories.

It was recognized that a bomber with wheels down over enemy territory was taken to indicate aerial surrender. A rumor (or was it?) had spread that a damaged B-17 in the 100th BG had strayed from the bomber stream and was surrounded by a swarm of Focke Wulfes and Me-109s that pulled up alongside the stricken B-17 to escort it to a German airfield.

Suddenly the B-17 waist gunners opened up on them with their .50-caliber machine guns, shooting down several German fighters. The enraged Luftwaffe pilots shot the B-17 down. Nothing could have infuriated the Germans more. As the story goes, this incident marked the bombers of the 100th for special attention in a bomber stream and meant that Luftwaffe fighters would look for the square D insignia of the 100th as they charged through the bomber streams.[85,86]

If this incident ever happened, it may have been unintentional. It's possible that the bomber's electrical system was damaged or shorted out, actuating the landing gear assembly without the crew knowing it. Another possibility is that the intercom system was knocked out and the gunners never heard the pilot say that the landing gear was being lowered before they opened fire. The pilot who was thought to be involved in the incident was Robert Knox of the 100th Bomb Group in the aircraft "Pickelpuss," but his surviving crewmembers gave contradictory accounts of the incident. Moreover, surviving German pilots involved in the same incident gave no indication that Knox's landing gear was down nor that the Germans had lost any fighters in the episode.

Ironically, such an incident was documented to have happened to a crippled B-17 with a destroyed intercom so that the crew could not have heard the surrender signal. However, this bomber, piloted by James Regan, belonged to the 390th Bomb Group![87] If there were two incidents on the same mission, know one knows for sure. While every bomb group in the Eighth Air Force suffered tough losses, the 100th always seemed to bear the heaviest beating throughout the war, and it was often the case that if an airman told someone he was in the 100th, the response was "you were lucky to survive."

Other mythical stories of the 100th abound, for example that newly arrived crews at Thorpe Abbotts were told to not even unpack their belongings because they would not be there long. Or the lieutenant who arrived late at Thorpe Abbotts, ate dinner and flew a mission the next day and was shot down! He would be forever known as "The Man Who Came To Dinner."

Certainly, the heavy losses suffered by the 100th on the Regensburg raid (nine bombers lost), along with the attack on Bremen on October 8, 1943 (seven losses), the marshalling yards at Munster on October 10, 1943 (twelve losses) and the "Big B" (Berlin) on March 6, 1944 (fifteen bombers lost) helped solidify the moniker "The Bloody Hundredth" by the time Dick arrived.

The 100th Bomb Group did not end up with the most losses among B-17 bomb groups in the Eighth Air Force by the time the war was over, but as Harry Crosby (a 100th Group navigator) pointed out, "When we lost, we lost BIG!"

10

GROUND WAR SITUATION, POST D-DAY

At the time of Dick's arrival at Thorpe Abbotts in the fall of 1944, the war was hardly winding down, despite optimistic predictions after the collapse of the German front in Normandy, and the ferocity of the fighting on the ground had only intensified as the Allies pushed eastward against tenacious German resistance.

Following the June 6, 1944 D-Day landings of Operation Overlord, the buildup of Allied forces was very rapid, despite the lack of usable ports. The landings had proceeded successfully, due in large measure to the supporting air campaign which had established air superiority over Western Europe. The RAF had destroyed German radar installations along the coast and saturation-bombed five key marshalling yards in the immediate vicinity of the landings, while 1,200 heavy bombers of the Eighth Air Force had carried out a complex and dangerous tactical bombing of the beach defenses, risking friendly-fire damage to ships. All of this created confusion and panic among the German defenders just before the landings, and, from studies of German reaction just prior to and during the invasion, a complete surprise was achieved.[88]

In the following weeks, troops and supplies poured into the beachheads in an unending stream. By 1 July, 1944, nearly a million men, more than a half-million tons of supplies, and nearly 180,000 vehicles had been brought ashore along the beaches of Normandy. During an attempted British breakout around the city of Caen, heavy bombers were used in close tactical support to bludgeon German defenses. Unfortunately, the destruction and friendly fire damage they brought had the effect of blocking rather than assisting the Allied ground forces, and German armored units further blocked an advance in that sector.[89]

On July 25, another massive air bombardment was coordinated with an attack by US ground troops on either side of St. Lo to achieve a substantial breakthrough of German lines. General George S. Patton's US Third Army exploited this breakthrough by advancing toward Brittany. Their objective was to secure the ports in that area, desperately needed for the required supplies and logistical support.[90] The Allied plan was to capture Breton ports and then surge east to seize areas as far east as the Seine River, thus allowing sufficient room for air and supply bases. The overall objective was to advance into Germany on a broad front.

General Dwight D. Eisenhower and the Supreme Headquarters Allied Expeditionary Force (SHAEF) had controlled strategic bombing during and after Operation Overlord, but by September of 1944, control of the Combined Bomber Offensive reverted to the control of the Combined Chiefs of Staff (CCS). Across this broad front in the field under SHAEF in Western Europe, the deployment of Allied forces can be defined by two sectors, one in the north and one to the south. In the south, General Omar Bradley's 12th Army Group, consisting of the 3rd US Army under General Patton, the 9th US Army under General William Simpson, and the 1st US Army under General Courtney H. Hodges comprised the principal American ground forces. In the north, Field Marshal Sir Bernard Montgomery's 21st Army Group, consisting of the 1st British/Canadian Army under General Lieutenant-General Harry Crerar and the 2nd British/ Canadian Army under General Sir Miles Dempsey made up the major ground forces.

Opposing this broad Allied front, the German Army, under the overall command of Field Marshal Gerd von Rundstedt was deployed in the northern sector with Army Group B under Field Marshal Walter Model, consisting of the 5th Panzer Army under General Hasso von Manteuffel (after Oct. 23), the 7th Panzer Army under General Erich Brandenburger, the 1st Parachute Army under Colonel-General Kurt Student, and the 15th Panzer Army under General Gustav-Adolf von Zangen. In the southern sector, Army Group G under Colonel-General Johannes Blaskowitz, consisted of the 1st Panzer Army under General

Otto von Knobelsdorff and the 19th Panzer Army under General Friedrich Wiese.[91]

To the east of the German lines formed by these two Army Groups, the vaunted Siegfreid Line (called as such by the Allies; to the Germans simply the Westwall) would present a formidable obstacle to any Allied advances into Reich territory. The fortified line stretched on a roughly north-south axis from the Swiss border in the south (near Basel), to Strasbourg to Karlsruhe (along the Rhine) to Saarbrucken (along the Saar) to Aachen, then all the way north to Kleve in the Netherlands (near Nijmegen). Thus, this gigantic barrier in the form of a continuous concrete-reinforced defense system extended from Holland all the way to the Swiss border. In 1939 alone, the Westwall had 16,455 constructions, to which was added substantially more structures by 1944 when there were 14,000 pill boxes along the 300-mile-long line.[92]

Although the Germans casualties were very heavy (nearly a million casualties on all fronts during the summer of 1944), the Reich still had millions of troops in service. The Wehrmacht hastily organized nearly 230,000 of these soldiers into "fortress battalions" to defend the Westwall. Although Nazi propagandists touted the invincibility of these defenses to the German people, their construction had slowed following the fall of France in 1940 in favor of the more forward Atlantic coastal defenses. Only with the Allied advances in the West in the summer of 1944 did the Germans quickly begin further work on the line along their own territory.

One effect of a few years of neglect was that grass and shrubbery had grown around the gun emplacements, making them practically invisible from the air, almost so to advancing Allied infantry. Particularly below Luxembourg, the Germans were able to use old French Maginot Line emplacements, turning them around to face attackers from the west. Having learned the importance of stealth in the face of Allied air superiority, the Germans did not reinforce their line with blatant new construction but instead practiced elaborate skill at camouflage, even as as they set up new anti-tank guns, machine-gun nests and infantry trenches all along the border.

By the time the Allies arrived on the ground, the Siegfried Line, if not impenetrable, was extremely strong. The hundreds of pillboxes

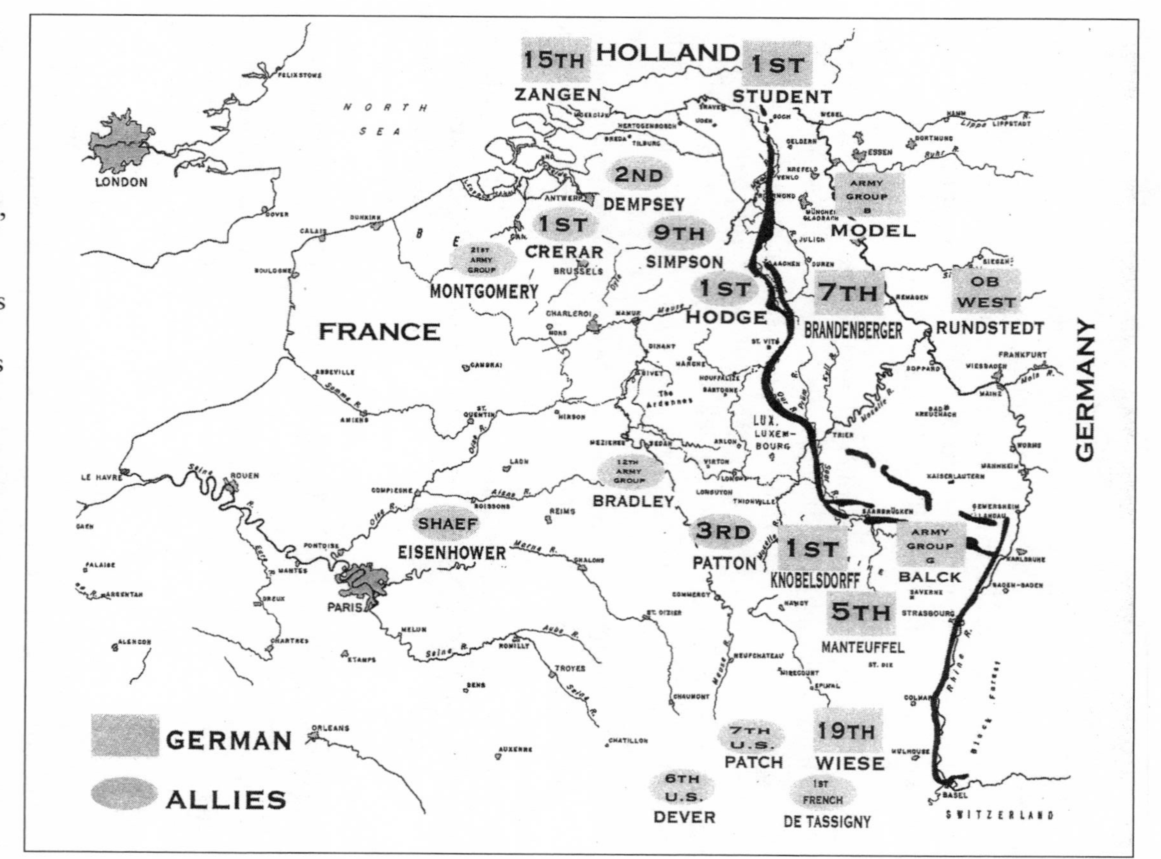

Situation map, ground war in Western Europe, shows the approximate positions of Allied and German rmy groups and individual armies in the early autumn of 1944.

with interlocking fields of fire, were supported by an extensive system of command posts, observation posts, and troop shelters. Furthermore, the Germans had carefully integrated their man-made obstacles, such as "dragon's teeth," with the contours of the terrain.[93] Having abandoned France, German manpower and supplies no longer had to cross a rickety rail or road network under the eyes of Allied airpower to reach the front. Now that they were closer to home, men and ammunition were readily available on the border of the Reich. In early September, Hitler installed one of his ablest commanders, Field Marshal Gerd von Rundstedt, in command of the German armies in the West and charged him with the defense of the Westwall.

The Allied Offensive in the Fall of 1944 was directed toward assaults against this formidable barrier. Hitler planned to stop the Allies at the Siegfried Line long enough for the Wehrmacht to regroup and mount a major counteroffensive. For the Allies, the principal thrust east was to be to the north of the Ardennes Forest in Belgium with General Montgomery's British 21st Army Group. A secondary thrust by General Bradley's newly formed US 12th Army Group, comprising the US First and Third Armies, was to be made south of the Ardennes. The northern route was chosen because it led directly into the Ruhr area where Germany's industrial power was concentrated.

General Eisenhower now altered his original plan, abandoning the idea of stopping at the Seine and instituting instead a determined pursuit of the enemy toward Germany. Because the ports of Cherbourg and Brest were too far west to support the rapidly advancing Allied movements, a new strategy was implemented calling for the capture of Channel ports and especially Antwerp, the finest port in all of Europe. Exploiting the new situation, General Eisenhower reinforced the British by sending the US First Army close alongside the 21st Army Group toward Aachen in a drive toward Antwerp. Only Patton's Third Army continued east on the subsidiary axis south of the Ardennes.

Cherbourg remained the only major port supplying Allied forces in northern France, and advances to the east had been so rapid that the logistical supply system was simply unable to keep up. Thus, the Allied drive eastward began to grind to a halt for lack of supplies, chiefly gasoline for the tanks and armored vehicles. The British took

Le Havre and several Channel ports, and on 4 September 1944 they captured Antwerp, its port fortunately still intact. But Antwerp could not yet be used to relieve the growing logistical crisis because the Germans denied the Allies access to the sea by retaining control of the Schelde Estuary.[94,95]

The newly activated US Ninth Army in Brittany under Lt. General Simpson took Brest late in September, but the port had been completely destroyed, and in any event its location so far from the scene of action precluded its usefulness in solving logistical problems. The failure of the campaign in Brittany to achieve useful results, as well as Montgomery's failure to anticipate the Germans' blocking the approaches to Antwerp, are considered major Allied blunders.

Meanwhile, the invasion of Southern France (Operation DRAGOON) got underway. With the release of shipping and landing craft from OVERLORD, it had finally become possible to carry out this long-planned operation. While the battle of the Argentan-Falaise pocket was still raging, on 15 August 1944, Lt. Gen. Alexander Patch's US Seventh Army invaded the Mediterranean shores of France southwest of Cannes. On 15 September, the US 6th Army Group became operational under command of Lt. Gen. Jacob L. Devers and, with the US Seventh Army and General Jean de Lattre de Tassigny's First French Army, passed from control of Allied Force Headquarters to the control of Supreme Headquarters Allied Expeditionary Force (SHAEF).[96] Henceforth, these forces from the south continued toward Germany on the right of Patton's Third Army.

Opposing the Allied thrust from southern France was the German Nineteenth Panzer Army commanded by General Friedrich Weise, consisting of seven infantry divisions and the 11th Panzer Division. The coastal defenses opposing the invasion had been similar to Normandy but not as extensive or formidable in terms of artillery and numbers of troops.[97]

In Italy, following the landing at Salerno by General Mark Clark's Fifth Army in September 1943, Allied advances had, by 17 June, 1944, driven the Germans to a defensive line (the Trasimene Line) stretching from the eastern to the western coast, roughly seventy-five to eighty miles north of Rome. Once the plain of Foggia had been liberated, the Fifteenth Air Force began operations from the Italian mainland. Hitler reinforced Field Marshal Albrecht Kesselring's Southwest Army Group with eight more divisions, partly by stripping occupation troops from other sectors, including Denmark, Holland and Russia, and transferring two full divisions from the Balkans. He also allowed Kesselring to retain the formidable Hermann Goering Panzer Division which had been scheduled for transfer to France.

Kesselring directed a brilliant delaying action by sacrificing second-rate units, laying mine fields and demolitions and exploiting the stone structures of villages and farms for defensive resistance. The Tenth Army, commanded by General Heinrich Goffried von Vietinghoff, and the Fourteenth Army under General der Panzertruppe Joachim Lemelsen fought a tenacious defensive action while Kesselring was able to shift units as needed along an east-west network of roads to strengthen weakened positions. By December of 1944, the Germans had withdrawn to the Gothic Line, Kesselring's last major line of defense, a newly constructed, heavily fortified defense line strategically located along the mountain chain dividing central Italy from the Po Valley. Here both opposing armies were exhausted and halted major actions for the winter.[98]

On the Western Front, logistical problems had become acute by the autumn of 1944. Although the US First Army under Lt. Gen. Courtney H. Hodges had penetrated the Siegfried Line in several places, the lack of supplies and fuel prevented exploitation of the breakthroughs. Bad weather, terrain that restricted maneuver, and the dense fortifications along the German border combined to create obstacles of major proportions.

Eighth Air Force operations and mission objectives in Western Europe were also influenced in part by events on the Eastern Front and the strategic requirements of the Soviets pushing against the Wehrmacht forces in Poland, East Prussia and the Balkan states. The war in the East diverted millions of German troops, civilians and slave labor to construct anti-tank obstacles, fortifications and defensive structures to oppose the inevitable Soviet onslaught. On the other hand, factories, plants, production facilities and raw materials were lost to the Germans as the Soviet forces advanced, hence affecting the equation used in targeting priorities. For example the Romanian oil center of Ploesti, the target of dozens of Allied bombing raids, was overrun by Soviet troops in August 1944.

Thus, while Allied assaults were raging ahead in Western Europe, the Soviet armies were achieving stunning victories and gradually liberating virtually all of their territory from the gains achieved by the

Situation map, ground war in Eastern Europe, shows the approximate positions of German army groups and individual armies and Soviet fronts in the early autumn of 1944.

Germans during Operation Barbarossa, their invasion in 1941. The Soviet Union's early defeats were due in large part to Stalin's military blunders but, unlike Hitler, Stalin learned his lessons well, allowing his ablest commanders much more autonomy in planning and carrying out combat operations. Hitler took the opposite approach, taking military matters increasingly into his own hands.[99] In the fall of 1944, Soviet armies stood on the Vistula River in Poland.[100]

For sixty-seven days the Polish resistance struggled against the armored might, firepower and aircraft of the brutal German occupation of Warsaw while Stalin ordered the Soviet forces, for political reasons regarding the shape of the new Polish government to come, to remain disengaged across the river simply watching. The bitterness of Poles toward this Soviet indifference to their suffering persists to this day. The resistance finally capitulated on 2 October 1944.

In the Fall of 1944, the German forces on the Eastern Front facing the Red Armies were aligned along a roughly north-south axis stretching from the Baltic Sea and Gulf of Finland in the north to the Balkans, Hungary and Yugoslavia in the south. The northernmost Wehrmacht deployment was Army Group Center commanded by General Hans Reinhardt. In East Prussia, Army Group Vistula was positioned under the direct control of Reichsfuhrer Heinrich Himmler, replaced in December 1945 by Colonel-General Gotthard Heinrici, who later was to direct the brilliant, if ultimately futile, defense of Berlin. Army Group North Ukraine under General Josef Harpe was centered on Silesia, southern Poland and Czechoslovakia, while Army Group South Ukraine, commanded by General Johannes Friessner, was centered in Hungary and Romania. Army Group E under the command of General Maximilian von Weichs, and later Colonel-General Alexander Lohr, was centered in Yugoslavia, and made up the southernmost flank of the German line on the Eastern Front.[101]

Continually pushing westward against the Wehrmacht formations were eleven Soviet "Fronts," each Front having the rough equivalent strength of a US Army Group. A Soviet Front thus consisted of three to ten separate armies with each army comprised of roughly 100,000 troops so that every Soviet Front involved up to one million Red Army soldiers.

From the Baltic Sea to Yugoslavia, the Soviet Fronts in the Fall of 1944 extended from north to south in the following alignment. The northernmost flank consisted of the Leningrad Front commanded by Marshal Leonid Godonov, the Third Baltic Front led by Colonel-General Ivan Maslennikov, the Second Baltic Front under General Andrei Eremenko, the Fourth Baltic Front under the command of Marshal I. K. Bagramyan, the Third Belorussian Front under General I. Chernyakbovsky, the Second Belorussian Front commanded by

Marshal Konstantin Rokossovsky, the First Belorussian Front which at first was also commanded by Marshal Rokossovsky, then given over to the celebrated Marshal Georgi Zhukov in November 1944, who led one of the two-pronged surges toward the capture of Berlin.

To the south of the First Belorussian Front was the First Ukrainian Front under the leadership of Marshal Ivan Koniev. It was Koniev who would lead the relentless drive, in competition with Zhukov, to receive credit for capturing the ultimate prize, Berlin. The southernmost flank of the Soviet lines were held by the Fourth Ukrainian Front under General I. Ye. Petrov, the Second Ukrainian Front led by Marshal Rodion Malinovsky, and the Third Ukrainian Front under Marshal Fydor Tolbukbin.[102]

Lt. Richard Ayesh in Sioux City Iowa, after graduation from combat crew training where he and his crew first met and worked together before flying to England in a new B-17G bomber.

Bombardier cadets swearing an Oath of Secrecy that they will protect the secret Norden bombsight, just before it is being shown to them for the first time.

Bombsight trainer "high-chairs," as part of bombardier training at Midland, Texas and other locations.

Bombardier cadet training inside a B-17 looking toward the rear with bomb racks fully loaded with 100 lb. bombs, each bomb fastened to the shackles mounted on the bomb rack in the bomb bay.

Dick and his first wife, Mary Kay, in Wichita, Kansas just before he left for England.

Dick's bomber crew at Thorpe Abbotts, England. Left to right: Jim Roberts, radio operator/gunner, John Gonda, navigator, Gene Jensen, pilot, Dick Ayesh, bombardier, Jim Millet, co-pilot, Joe Latiolait, waist gunner, Henry Sublet, tail gunner, Floyd Thomasson, engineer/top gunner. Not shown: Robert Byrd, ball turret gunner.

The North American P-51 Mustang, seen here with drop tanks that extended its range to over 600 miles from East Anglia in England, enabling it to escort bombers on the deepest missions over Germany.

The Lockheed P-38 Lightning, seen here (a P-38M) modified as a night fighter guided to a target by its own airborne radar. It was used as a low-level fighter bomber for strafing and bombing as well as for escorting bombers on shorter range bombing missions over Occupied France.

The Republic P-47 Thunderbolt, known as the "Jug." Used for vital bomber escort early in the air war but only for shorter distance bombing missions over France due to its limited range.

A still intact Messerschmitt Bf-109 shot down and on display to the public in the main square at Bolton, Lancashire, England.

Two captured German night fighters: foreground, the Messerschmitt 110C and in the background, the Junkers 88, both equipped with Lichtenstein radar and aerial radar arrays in their nose.

Front view of the world's first operational jet fighter, the Messerschmitt 262 with its four 30mm cannons seen in the fuselage. This front profile presented problems to the bomber crews because it resembled the profile of a P-51 Mustang with drop tanks.

Another view of the Me-262. With a range of 650 miles, a service ceiling of 38,000 ft. and a top speed of 540 mph, its production and deployment were (fortunately for the Allies) delayed by Adolf Hitler's insistence that it be converted to a fighter-bomber.

Lt.General Carl "Tooey" Spaatz, overall commander of the United States Strategic Air Force (USSTAF), whose headquarters was located at Bushy Park, London, code-named WideWing.

Major General James Doolittle, who assumed command of the 8th Air Force in January, 1944 and introduced numerous innovations and changes in tactics which enhanced the effectiveness of strategic bombing. Doolittle's VIII Bomber Command headquarters was at High Wycombe, code-named PINETREE

Formation of 100th Bomb Group B17Gs flying over the Bavarian Alps.

Dick Ayesh (right) being de-briefed by an intelligence officer following a mission.

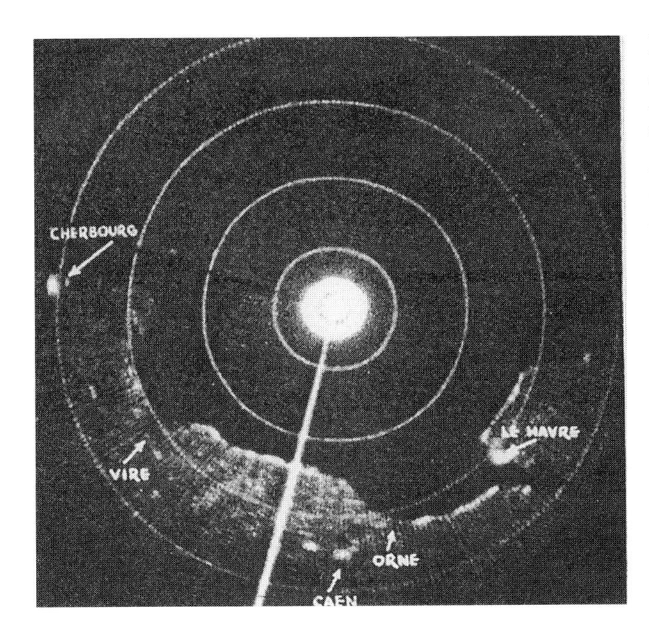

Radar Scope photo of H2X "bombing through overcast." This photo was taken over the D-Day beachheads at Normandy, 30 minutes before the invasion. Note the clear demarcation of the shoreline from the ocean and the bright reflections of Caen and the Cherbourg Peninsula. The small flecks are ships approaching the beaches.

A vertical view of a three-dimensional model of the German synthetic oil plant at Bohlen, prepared by the 325th Photo Wing of the 8th Air Force from aerial photo-reconnaissance. Detailed models like this were constructed for major facilities to enhance bombing accuracy.

Heavy flak concentration (barrage) encountered by a formation of B-17G's in a mission over Bremen, Germany.

Box barrage of flak from radar-directed German 88mm anti-aircraft artillery against a formation of B-17s over Merseberg, Germany. The white cloud is from the explosion of a B-17 which took a direct hit.

Before and after aerial strike photos of Duren, Germany, revealing the effect of saturation bombing which nearly totally destroyed the city. Duren was at a key strategic location between Aachen and Cologne.

The railroad marshalling yards at Fulda, Germany was struck in four different missions by the 8th. Marshalling yards were critical transport targets because here the cars of military supply, equipment and troop trains were coupled or de-coupled, sorted and divided onto separate destination tracks. At these yards, train repairs, maintenance and re-conditioning were also disrupted.

The Scholven Buer synthetic oil plant at Gelsenkirchen, Germany after 27 separate bombing attack by the 8th and the RAF dropped a combined total of 12,400 tons. Multiple strikes were required not only to correct inaccurate drops but also because of the remarkable speed with which the German repair efforts got such plants back into operation. Note the undamaged bullet shaped bomb shelter at mid-left.

The ruins of Cologne, its famous Cathedral still standing, after heavy RAF bombing at night and 8th Air Force bombing during the day.

Strike photo of central Berlin taken by a 100th Bomb Group crewman revealing the Reichstag, Tempelhof airport, and other landmarks.

The Norden bombsight seen mounted in the nose of a B-17G. The bombardier was seated in an armor-backed chair just behind the Norden.

An attack by a Luftwaffe Messerschmitt 410, approaching from behind on a 100th Bomb Group B-17G.

Dick Ayesh and his dad, Samuel, in front of the family home in Wichita just after returning from England.

Dick and his second wife, Mid, just after their wedding in LasVegas.

11

AIR WAR SITUATION, FALL 1944

The air war was the absolutely key lynchpin of the Allied war in Western Europe. Aside from the obvious implicit priority of defending British and US territory, the top priority of the Allies was to fight a decisive, offensive air war against Germany until the utter defeat of the Reich. Following many lessons learned in the North African campaign early in the war, Allied airpower was reorganized in 1942 so that the command of the air force went to airmen rather than ground officers, missions became offensive rather than being defensive, air assets were no longer spread thin among different ground units and were no longer largely tactical in nature.

The Eighth Air Force, with its command center at High Wycombe (VIII Bomber Command), early on adopted a strict policy of high-altitude strategic daylight bombing of military targets and war production facilities in the civilian sector that supported the German war effort. This strategic principle carried more danger for the planes and crews but resulted in more precise destruction, as well as minimizing, as much as possible, civilian casualties and other collateral damage.[103] There was to be no night bombing or intentional area bombing by the USAAF.

Some bomber advocates believed that strategic bombing alone was capable of defeating Germany, while other planners held that strategic bombing could only weaken the German war effort and that a ground invasion would be required for its surrender. The use of the Eighth as a tactical force suffered from the same failures as the RAF had experienced earlier: collateral damage and unacceptable friendly fire casualties, e.g. at the St. Lo Breakout when the 4th Infantry Division was bombed by B-17s with the loss of at least 370 troops. After Normandy the Eighth devoted virtually its entire effort to strategic bombing.

Early on, it was felt that heavy bombers, sufficiently armed and flying in formation to maximize their firepower, could present a defensive barrier sufficient to make it to the target and return without fighter escorts. Moreover, the best chances of hitting the highest priority targets were during daytime. Unfortunately, this daytime go-it-alone strategy without fighter escorts ignored the variable weather conditions over Europe, target obstruction by smoke and decoys, and Luftwaffe opposition and anti-aircraft artillery. Attacks on submarine pens and ball bearing factories, which were frequent targets early in the bomber campaign, proved ineffective.

Starting in January 1943, the Casablanca Conference declared the destruction of German war industry by strategic bombing as a major objective. The highest priority was given to destroying Germany's oil and lubricant production, submarine construction, aircraft, ball bearings, synthetic rubber and military vehicles. In general, the primary war industry targets were located in regions surrounding the following cities: Essen, Dusseldorf, Cologne, Hanover, Hamburg, Berlin, Leipzig, Schweinfurt, Saarbrucken, Merseberg, and Stuttgart. Secondary targets were surrounding Bremen, Munich, Ulm, Regensburg, Kassel, Furth, Erfurt and Dresden.[104]

Prior to D-Day, the Allies had finally achieved air superiority in Western Europe due largely to a change in fighter escort tactics instituted soon after General Jimmy Doolittle arrived in Theater. The arrival of General Doolittle, who replaced Major General Ira Eaker as commander of the Eighth Air Force, marked a major transformative milestone in the execution of the air war. First, on January 4th, 1944, the US heavy bombers and fighter escorts in England flew their last mission as a subordinate part of VIII Bomber Command. The Fifteenth Air Force, established in Italy, and the Eighth Air Force, were organized under a centralized headquarters and designated as the United States Strategic Air Forces (USSTAF), located at Bushy Hall. Then, VIII Bomber Command was officially re-designated Eighth Air Force on February 22, 1944. General Carl Spaatz returned to England to command the USSTAF.[105]

General Spaatz, commander of the USSTAF, and Doolittle, commander of the Eighth Air Force, saw the advantage to be gained over the Luftwaffe by freeing up the deadly P-51 fighter escorts from just performing escort duty protecting the bomber streams and turning them loose on airborne German fighters before they attacked and while they were on the ground as well as the factory facilities that produced them. The opportunity to carry out this large assault on German aircraft had long been planned but the required good weather over an extended period of several days never prevailed until February 20th, 1944. Thus unleashed was a huge, relentless assault on the fighter resources of the Luftwaffe both in the air and on the ground by P-51s and P-47s as well as Heavies, that would forever be known as "Big Week" (see Chapter 12).

While there was still plenty of fight left in the Luftwaffe after D-Day, its ranks had been decimated to the extent that Allied planes ruled the skies prior to and after Operation Overlord, and German fighters were relegated to primarily a defensive posture in the German heartland. Nonetheless, in the final year of the war, the bomber crews still faced a Luftwaffe defending the Fatherland and capable of wreaking havoc on any of their missions. This would continue until the supply of German aviation fuel and lubricants was diminished to a trickle in the late spring of 1945.

By mid-1944, Eighth Air Force had reached a total strength of more than 200,000 people with an estimate that more than 350,000 Americans served in Eighth Air Force during the course of the war. At peak strength, Eighth Air Force had forty heavy bomber groups, fifteen fighter groups, and four specialized support groups. It was capable of dispatching an air armada of more than 2,000 four-engine bombers and more than 1,000 fighters on a single mission to multiple targets.[106]

12

THE NERVE CENTER AT HIGH WYCOMBE

The very heart of planning, intelligence, target selection and operations in the air war over Europe was the headquarters of the Eighth Air Force Bomber Command (aka VIII Bomber Command), code-named "Pinetree." All Eighth Air Force bombing operations were planned here.

The secret installation was located about 30 miles northwest of London at the former Wycombe Abbey Girls School at High Wycombe in Buckinghamshire. The town was known primarily for its furniture building industry. The site was remote, well-screened by trees and lacked significant features when viewed from the air, making it difficult to spot in aerial photography even by the most clever photo interpreter.[107] "Pinetree" was conveniently and intentionally only four miles from RAF Bomber Command's headquarters, code-named "Southdown" in the Chiltern Hills. This close proximity greatly facilitated the close cooperation between the USAAF and the RAF which continued throughout the war. British radar and communications systems were integrated with USAAF operations centers, and weather and intelligence information was shared.[108] Weather and photoreconnaissance flights, preceding and following missions, were carried out mostly by RAF high-altitude Spitfires for the USAAF. Each morning, the USAAF commander would attend the 9:00 AM briefings of Sir Arthur Harris at RAF HQ where mission and target decisions were made for the next night's RAF bombing objective.[109]

The classrooms within Wycombe Girls School building itself were converted to offices which served as the administrative offices of the

Eighth Air Force under both Major General Ira Eaker (1942–44) and Lieutenant General James Doolittle (1944–45). The entire "Pinetree" complex was sited on over 200 acres in the southeastern quarter of High Wycombe. Clusters of buildings were constructed on the grounds, as was a tent city, all of which was needed to accommodate the roughly 12,000 male and female military personnel.

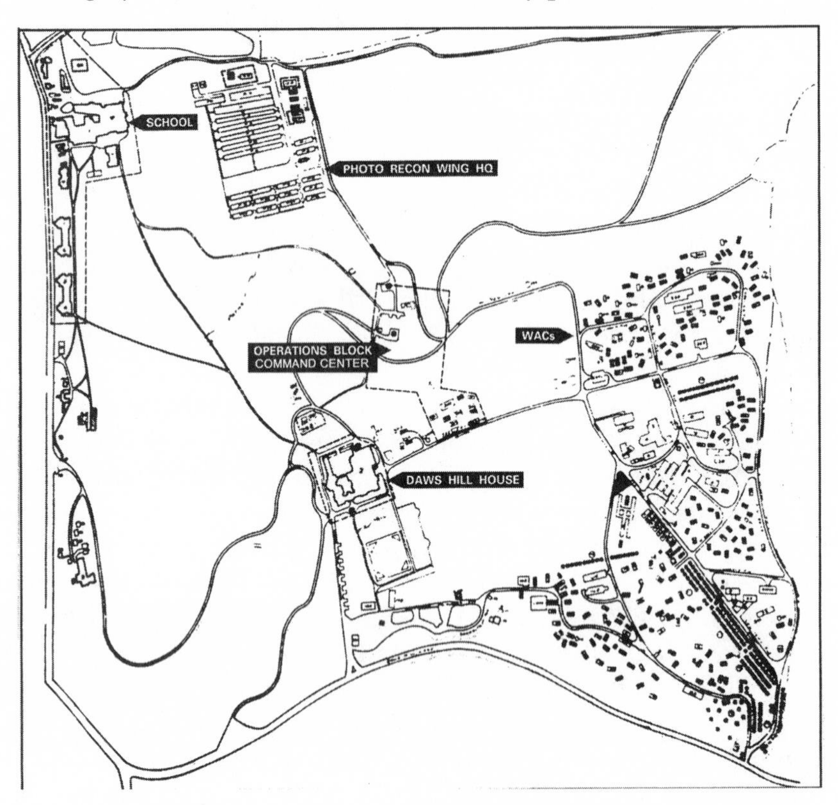

Layout of Eighth Air Force Bomber Command HQ, High Wycombe, codenamed Pinetree. (Courtesy of *After the Battle* magazine)

But by far the most remarkable structure in the entire complex was the "Pinetree" command center for VIII Bomber Command. It was situated entirely underground and encompassed three floors extending over 23,000 square feet. The command center was covered by 10 feet of concrete, above which was 25 feet of soil, while the exterior walls of the huge subterranean structure were in excess of six feet thick! The perimeter of these outer walls was actually recessed from the surrounding strata by a void three to four feet in width in order to absorb the shock of an explosion, while all internal walls were five feet thick. The entire structure was protected by gas-tight doors along with an air filtration system and air conditioning which maintained the temperature inside at 67 degrees Fahrenheit. Emergency power supplies, water and provisions were available to enable the complex to continue functioning on its own in case of isolation due to wartime or natural calamities.[110]

Every mission of the Eighth was preceded by an operational staff conference in the underground war room at High Wycombe. The commander (General James Doolittle during Dick's tenure in the 100th) would hold a daily briefing attended by the command's entire staff of intelligence officers, meteorological officers and navigation officers, and would directly order attacks on specific targets to occur the next day.

The staff weather officer would begin with a report on the selected target areas and secondary targets and the expected weather at all of the bases during takeoff and return. A large map on the wall exhibited red lights for bases that were closed due to weather and green lights for ones that were open. Damage assessments were reviewed from graphic representations and recon photos from missions that had already occurred, on the highest priority list of strategic targets. Estimates were made by specialists on how much more bombing effort would be required to destroy remnants of earlier targets. Aiming points for the bombardiers, ingress and egress routes to and from the target, assembly points and rendezvous instructions would be specified. Specialists on fighter escort requirements for a mission would estimate how many aircraft were needed for escort and how many were needed for strafing. The intelligence on locations of enemy antiaircraft batteries and Luftwaffe bases would be reviewed and plotted to assess the anticipated enemy resistance. Intelligence officers would apprise the staff of any new German developments, their offensive and defensive capabilities and the success achieved in previous raids.

This preparation included the latest information on the status of the ground war, particularly on how far the Allied troops had advanced. They would also cull useful information from debriefings of bomber crews and that of captured enemy pilots and captured aircrews, as well as gun camera film from fighters and target photos. Operations statisticians were occasionally called upon to provide summaries of past missions and trends, while supply, maintenance and communications experts would point out any problems that might affect future operations.[111]

A briefing officer would describe the mission in general terms, e.g. how many bombers and fighters were available to be sent and what type of target(s) they were attacking.

The bomber controller would state the takeoff times, the time over target and the bomber routes. The fighter controller would present the planned operations for the fighters. All of this would include any questions General Doolittle might have to make sure nothing was overlooked and to issue any necessary command decisions. Following the selection of targets for the next day by the commander, senior staff officers would draw up the details of the bombing operation which would then be sent from High Wycombe by teleprinter to the relevant Air Division headquarters.

These division headquarters were the only recipient of direct communications from Pinetree. Each Air Division (1st, 2nd and 3rd) would communicate information to the Combat Wings and from there the operational information was communicated to the Bombardment Groups. Prior to this, a provisional "heads-up" communication was made to the Bombardment Groups identifying the targets and bomb loads for the next day so that the preparation of the crews and aircraft for action could be started. Then the crews were briefed early in the morning of that day's mission. This procedure was repeated every day until the end of the war.[112]

The types of intelligence and its acquisition, as well as the target selection criteria employed by the American and British air commands, was obviously of paramount importance to the successful execution of the air war. Yet, this topic has received little attention in the mainstream literature on the Second World War in general and the air war specifically. In order for strategic bombing to be effective, it could not operate blind. Intelligence from aerial photo-reconnaissance and ground intelligence were absolutely critical to target selection, disposition of enemy defenses, locations of camouflaged war factories, decoy factories and post-mission bomb damage assessments in occupied Europe.[113] This was carried out primarily by photo-reconnaissance missions of the RAF and USSTAF.

The techniques of photo-reconnaissance evolved significantly during the war from crude but clever beginnings. Allied efforts were advanced tremendously through the ideas and pioneering aerial espionage of the Australian aviator, Sidney Cotton, who, under cover as a salesman of aeronautical products, actually carried out airborne espionage across Germany before the war even began! His concept of aerial espionage rested upon the use of small, very fast camera-equipped aircraft able to evade Luftwaffe planes, present a small cross-section and be stripped of guns and radio in order to make room for extra fuel, and be able to fly at high altitude. His concept led to the abandonment of slow, lumbering bombers, at least by the RAF.

To achieve the ideal recon aircraft, the RAF made modifications to the Spitfire (and eventually the twin-engine Mosquito) which was stripped of its guns, radio and any other dispensable accessories to lighten its weight. This would enable it to rapidly achieve ceiling, extend its range and carry a battery of cameras. Initially, two fixed F/24 cameras with five-inch lenses pointed downward were mounted. Still another problem had to be overcome. At the very high altitudes needed for the planes to operate most safely, the extremely low temperatures cracked film inside the cameras, and the lenses frosted over with condensation. Sydney Cotton solved this problem by improvising ducts that sent warm air from the Spitfire's engine blowing across the cameras. This crude heating system was eventually replaced by electrically-heated camera covers.[114]

These specially fitted Spitfires were very reluctantly assigned due to the shortage of fighters needed to protect the homefront. Even then, in order to avoid destruction, the photo-recon Spitfires had to fly at 35,000 feet and were painted a dark green to prevent detection, or at least minimize it. Silhouetted against the sky, they were very hard to detect. The early cameras were designed to be used at only 10,000 feet where the plane was vulnerable. Unfortunately, the telephoto camera technology was such that at 35,000 feet it yielded a scale of only 1:72,000 so that 1 inch on the photo was only 1 mile on the ground. Eventually, eight-inch lenses were employed which gave a scale of

1:45,000 at 30,000 feet. This was followed by 20-inch lenses and culminated in f/52 cameras with 36-inch lenses giving a photo scale of 1:13,000 feet at 40,000 feet! This could yield the type of traffic on a railroad siding, the layout of a radar installation, or the state of construction of a new U-Boat.[115]

American photoreconnaissance efforts began with the P-38 Lightning, which was usually equipped with three wide-angle cameras for general coverage and two long-lens cameras to zero in on target areas. Much of the progress on the American side was due to George W. Goddard, the US Chief of Photo Research, who was primarily responsible for the introduction of high-powered lenses.

Although to a large extent, US photo-recon efforts relied mostly on British techniques and aircraft like the Spitfire and Mosquito, by mid-1943 the US reconnaissance capability had grown substantially. The P-38 became a key component and American reconnaissance missions, which also included modified B-17 bombers.

The designation F-9 (F for "Foto") was assigned to photographic reconnaissance conversions of existing bombers. Sixteen B-17Fs were converted to long range photographic reconnaissance configurations by having their bombing equipment removed and replaced with photographic equipment. Some cameras were installed in the nose and in the aft fuselage as well. Some defensive armament was, however, retained.

The designation F-9A was assigned to an unspecified number of B-17Fs that were converted to a photographic configuration in a manner similar to that of the F-9 but differing in some camera details. Tri-camera units (see below) were an effective way to increase many-fold the area covered by photographic exposures.

All of these planes were re-designated F-9B after further camera changes. For photo-reconnaissance at night, they used a "flashlight bomb," a 50-pound cylinder of magnesium whose explosion illuminated a ground area and triggered a photoelectric camera shutter. The light of the explosion caused electrons to be released by the photoelectric effect, giving rise to an electric current which activated the shutter.

The designation F-9B was assigned to 25 photographic Fortresses obtained by adapting some existing F-9As and by converting other B-

17Fs. The designation F-9C was assigned to ten B-17Gs converted for photographic reconnaissance in a manner similar to the F-9, F-9A, and F-9B conversions of the B-17F. In the F-9C, a chin turret of the B-17G had been replaced by a housing for tri-metrogen cameras, the best cameras for wide coverage. These tri-camera units consisted of three synchronized cameras in the nose of a light or heavy aircraft. The cameras had a six-inch focal length metrogen lenses, one taking 9x9-inch vertical shots of the area directly below the plane and the other two cameras taking 9x9 oblique shots to the right and left. By the end of the war, a total of 71 B-17s were converted for photorecon use.[116,117]

In order to make full use of the high-altitude espionage, the photos had to be analyzed by the most highly-trained, expert photo interpreters. These specialists included both men and women in the service who were particularly skilled at gleaning intelligence from intricate photo interpretation. Some of these individuals would translate the photos into three-dimensional models of the target area by using the precise dimensions of objects in the target area determined by the use of stereoscopic images (pairs of photos examined through a stereoscope). The modelers would then build the target area that included each natural and man-made feature more than a few feet high in the target area. Artists painted the landscape in the colors of the foliage appropriate to the season. Using these models, bomber crews could walk around the models, getting a sense in depth of what the target would look like from any direction or altitude.[118]

Due to the absence of adequate intelligence at the outset of the air war in Europe, the nature of "strategic bombing" had to undergo a number of evolutionary changes with time. The original pre-war notion of precision daylight bombing against industrial production targets required a far better understanding of German industry than had existed, and was considered untenable by many until the arrival of adequate long-range escort aircraft in December 1943. Precision efforts continued through the late winter(weather permitting) but was soon diverted to support Operation Overlord. The bomb tonnage dropped against Germany declined during this period. Following the initiation of Overlord, the USAAF in Europe came under General Eisenhower's control and was used in support of the armies—at first tactical during the Normandy breakout and then in highly concen-

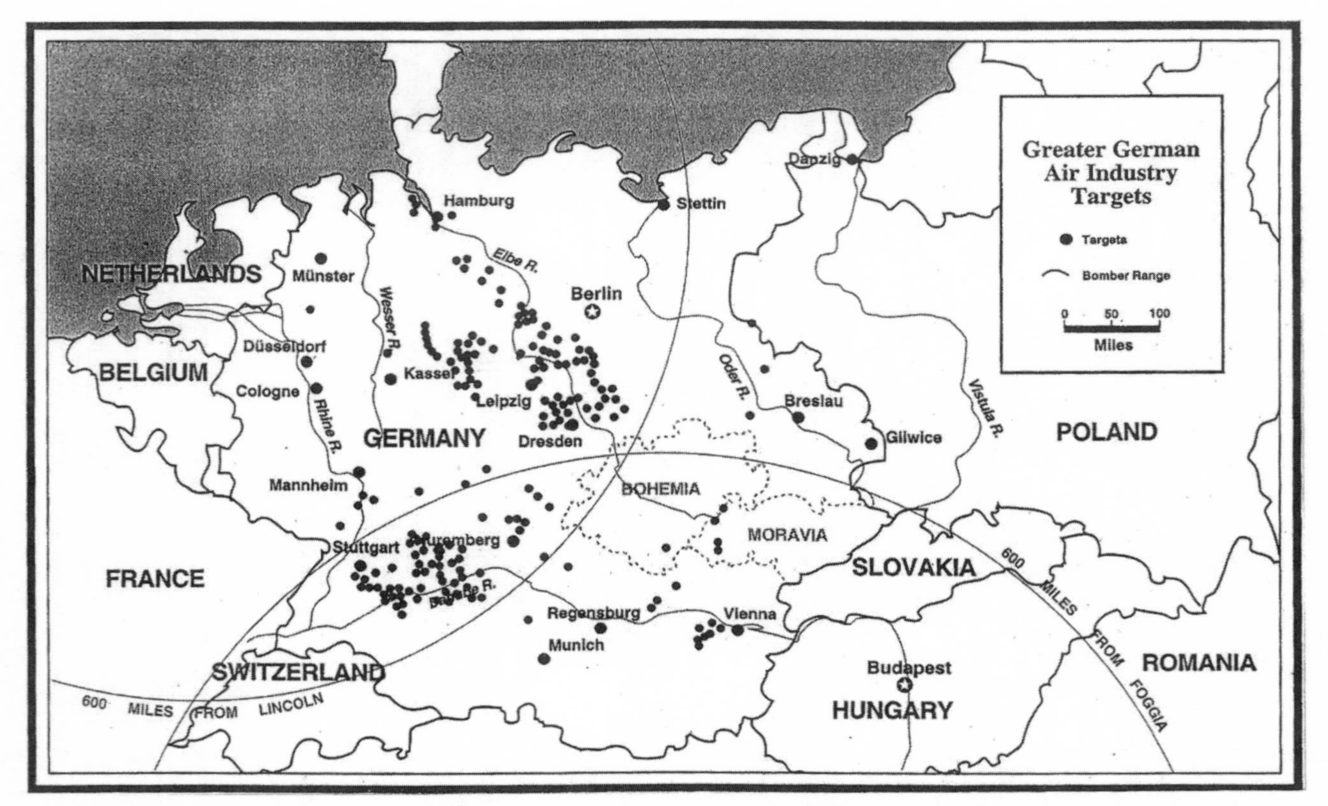

German air industry targets. (From *Carl Spaatz and the Air War in Europe* by Richard G. Davis)

trated attacks against the German synthetic oil and rail transportation networks to enable the Rhine crossings.[119]

Among the most influential intelligence groups engaged in target selection for the Eighth Air Force in Europe was the Enemy Objectives Unit (EOU), which was a subdivision of the Economic Warfare Division of the American Embassy in London. This little-known group was extremely powerful in formulating and advocating US strategic bombing decisions. The EOU was crucial because, although the USAAF had committed itself to daylight, precision bombing over Europe, the intelligence (aside from British intelligence), underlying doctrine and target selection criteria had not yet been formulated. Nor had any one strategy unfolded yet to determine what it would take to carry out massive bombing while being attacked by Luftwaffe fighter aircraft.[120]

Amazingly, the members of the EOU were not primarily military, or even trained in military science. They were mainly trained as economists, a clear indication that a crucial objective of US bombing was to weaken the German war economy as a means to victory. Thus, the EOU developed and applied criteria for target selection based upon the impact on Germany of one target system versus another with points within a given target system if the bombing accuracy was available. For example, a large complex of factories within which one targeted subset would have more impact on Germany's war effort would be favored for selection over another industrial complex.

There were analyses of particular German industrial plants or installations designed to establish the most vulnerable point of attack. These studies would involve visits by EOU personnel to the nearest equivalent installations in Britain as proxies, utilizing as much intelligence as London could provide, not only about the plant itself but also on its projected impact in its economic sector and how that sector would affect the war effort.

Thus, the EOU was guided by the principle of how the destruction of the minimum number of targets would have the greatest, fastest and most long-lasting direct military effect on the battlefield. This assessment would take into account the ways in which it was predicted the Germans would respond to the effects of the attack.[121]

As D-Day approached, EOU became part of Operation Octopus

to assist the Twenty-First and Twelfth Army Groups, the Allied Expeditionary Air Force, G-2, SHAEF, and the British Air Ministry. While still primarily tied to the Eighth and Fifteenth Air Forces, the EOU probably had its greatest operational impact through its influence on bureaucratic battles between the Americans and their proponents on the one hand and the British and their proponents on the other. These internecine conflicts involved clashes of personality, vested interests and unforeseen events, as well as doctrine. EOU played a role in three major bureaucratic battles, which, in a literal sense, determined the shape of the air war in Europe. These three major crises were documented as: (1) daylight strategic bombing by American forces versus area (city) bombing as carried out by the RAF; (2) priority of attacks on marshalling yards versus attacks on oil targets; and (3) the optimum tactical targets in support of the D-day invasion.[122]

The first crisis was precipitated when the Eighth Air Force had taken the bold initiative of attacking German aircraft production, then concentrated in central Germany, before the protection of long-range P-51 fighter escorts were available for the bombers. With slave labor and manpower drafted from other sectors, German single-engine fighter production expanded dramatically, according to photo-reconnaissance, which revealed that German fighter production had increased from 381 in January 1944 to 1,050 fighter aircraft in July 1944. The hard-won Allied air supremacy achieved before D-Day was clearly endangered if the German expansion plan was permitted to continue unabated.

The American attacks forced the Germans to disperse their production, and December production was reduced to only 560 planes. However, a heavy price was paid in terms of the loss of US life and aircraft. An outcry of criticism arose in Washington as well as in London about the heavy losses. British supporters of area bombing seized the opportunity to argue that a crisis in German morale could be brought about if the US bombers would abandon daylight bombing and join the RAF in night attacks. However, the American military was not about to abandon its fundamental commitment to daylight precision bombing, especially when the needed long-range fighter escorts were about to enter the European theater. EOU played a central role in the defense of American doctrine. As recalled by Walter Rostow, "The issue was settled, as it often is in public policy, by an event, not an argument."

That event was Big Week! USAAF meteorologists had predicted that the week of February 20 to 25 would be ideal for such a widespread attack. In the week beginning February 20, 1944, the whole US bomber force, conforming to a long-laid plan, was dispatched to attack German aircraft production from one end of Europe to the other. It was estimated that about 100 US bombers and crews would be lost. Remarkably, the number lost was only 22. On February 20th, a force of over 800 "heavies" was assembled with the 1st and 2nd Bomb Divisions sent to the Messerschmitt Bf-109 plant complex at Leipzig and the 3rd Division sent to Posen in eastern Poland. When the 1st Division crossed into Germany, the Luftwaffe seemed to put up every single and twin-engined plane in their air arsenal including the usual Me-109 and FW-190s but also Ju-87s, He-111s, Do-17s and FW-189s.[123] This unlikely defeat of the Luftwaffe by the American long-range fighters (and Heavies) marked the emergence of the USAAF as a powerful, mature, fighting force.

The second major crisis arose over the relative merits of bombing marshalling yards versus bombing oil targets. The main downside of bombing marshalling yards in Occupied Europe was the anticipated large-scale loss of civilian life, since marshalling yards were usually located in cities. Both involved intense debate in which, at the bureaucratic level, General Spaatz was opposed by Eisenhower's deputy, Air Chief Marshal Arthur Tedder and part of the RAF, and at the intellectual level, EOU was squared off against Tedder's one-man brain trust, a civilian named Solly Zuckerman. Zuckerman was an expert on the sexual and social life of apes who, in the service of his country, applied his fertile intellect to the physical effects of bombing and became a bombing strategist with a very strong character. As Rostow noted, "There are Americans, and some British, who to the end of their days, regarded the last year of the struggle in Europe as a war against Solly Zuckerman rather than Adolf Hitler."[124]

A plan to bomb German oil production was drawn up, approved by Spaatz as early as March 5, and sent forward to Eisenhower and Tedder. The judgment underlying the plan was that a radical reduction in oil supplies was the optimum way to reduce by strategic bombing the fighting capability of the German ground and air forces.

However, Solly Zuckerman, basing his judgment on his experiences and lessons learned in the air war in the Mediterranean, persuaded Tedder to support focusing attacks on western European railway marshalling yards. Oil targets, according to this picture, were to be deferred until after D-Day. General Eisenhower decided in favor of Tedder and railway marshalling yards were chosen despite the projected loss of French civilian lives, primarily on the grounds that it would provide some immediate help in the D-Day landings and their aftermath, whereas the military effects of the oil attacks might be less immediate. However, on April 5, the Fifteenth Air Force successfully attacked Ploesti ostensibly to destroy marshalling yards in the immediate vicinity of the refineries. That is, Ploesti happened to be on the standard marshalling yards target list! This insubordinate attack had, in effect, been successful and significant immediate effects on the German oil supply could be detected by Allied intelligence.[125]

Therefore, on May 12, Eighth Air Force Heavies attacked a substantial group of oil targets in central Germany, including the most important facility, at Leuna (Merseberg). ULTRA intelligence promptly and unambiguously provided evidence of German panic as they elevated the defense of their oil production to that of overriding priority, even above fighter plane production. Though German aircraft production began to rise in dispersed factories later in 1944, there was insufficient aircraft fuel to train the pilots and fly the planes. From a peak of 180,000 metric tons production in March 1944—before the fortuitous attack on Ploesti oil— aircraft fuel production was down to an incredible 10,000 tons by September 1944.[126]

The third major bureaucratic battle raged over the optimum tactical targets in support of D-Day. Tedder and Zuckerman again argued that railway marshalling yards would suffice; but Rostow and the EOU argued for isolating the Normandy battlefield by taking out three rings of bridges, above all the Seine-Loire Rivers complex. The influence of the American air force and, ultimately, General Omar Bradley's and General Montgomery's ground force headquarters, were lined up in support of the bridge concept.[127]

It is important to point out that many British experts backed the American precision bombing effort not only as good allies, but because the intelligence requirements were more exacting and challenging than for the British area bombing of cities or railway marshalling yards, where all that was really required were good surface maps.

The P-51 long-range fighter, which helped win virtual total air supremacy over Germany, proved essential to validating the American commitment to precision bombing. That validation and the air supremacy it provided was essential to the Normandy landings, the consolidation of the bridgehead, and the attacks on oil. It not only virtually grounded the German Luftwaffe, but also radically reduced the mobility of German ground forces on the Western and Eastern fronts in the last year of the war. General Adolf Galland, chief of the German fighter force and a fighter ace himself, summed up an extended analysis as follows: "The raids of the allied air fleets on the German petrol supply installations was the most important of the combined factors which brought about the collapse of Germany."

Air Chief Marshal Sir Arthur Harris (aka Bomber Harris), commander of the RAF Bomber Command, was a redoubtable opponent of the oil offensive and referred to its advocates (including EOU) as "the oily boys." Against his will, the RAF was forced into the oil offensive and played an effective role. Harris' final word is a bit grudging, but on the whole, a gracious capitulation: "I still do not think it was reasonable at that time, to expect that the (oil] campaign would succeed; what the Allied strategists did was to bet on an outsider, and it happened to win the race."

More importantly, able military leaders learned that they needed intellectuals—not only physical and social scientists, but bright, innovative civilians. It was proven that non-military people could work well in a military setting. This forged marriage under the desperate pressure of wartime led to institutionalized links between the intellectual sector and national security that exists to this day in the form of the CIA, RAND and other national defense-related intelligence organizations.[128]

13

THE AIR WAR ON SYNTHETIC OIL

The historic old city of Merseberg, situated in East Prussia on the River Saale, is one of the oldest towns in Germany. It was the favorite residence of German monarchs, including King Henry I (Henry the Fowler) and Emperor Otto I. Like most cities in Europe, its long history is culturally rich and punctuated with momentous events. Among its most beautiful buildings are its cathedral, founded in 1015 and rebuilt in the 13th and 16th centuries, and the Episcopal Palace built in the 15th century. Merseberg also served as a key German outpost for subduing the Slavs and Poles and was an Episcopal See from 968 until its suppression in 1561 during the Protestant Reformation, when the bishopric passed to Saxony. From 1657 to 1738 the city was the seat of the Dukes of Saxe-Merseburg. In 1815 at the Congress of Vienna, following the final defeat of Napoleon at Waterloo, Merseberg became part of Prussia.

The city had suffered calamities in the Peasants' War and during the Thirty Years' War. But at the beginning of the 20th century Merseberg underwent a transformation that would ultimately make it the most heavily fortified city in all of Germany. This transformation would doom much of this beautiful city to destruction with the deaths of 65 percent of its population in an inferno of explosions and flames. For it was here, between 1909 and 1913, that the pioneering work by Carl Bosch and Friedrich Bergius (who shared the Nobel Prize in Chemistry for it) set forth the scientific principles of the catalytic high-pressure ammonia synthesis, making Merseberg a center of the petrochemical industry.

It eventually became a fortress city, protected by 1,000 flak guns and Luftwaffe fighters, because here was located Germany's largest, most important, synthetic oil facility, the giant Leuna works. At its wartime peak, Leuna employed 36,000 workers. The story of Merseberg in the first half of the 20th century is therefore intimately associated with the story of the air war against synthetic oil in World War II.

Starting with World War I, the overriding importance of oil was fully appreciated by nations engaged in mechanized warfare. As Marshall Foch stated, "In war a drop of gasoline is worth a drop of blood," while Lord Curzon reflected that the "the Allies [in World War I] floated to victory on a sea of oil." In World War II, the need for oil was on a vastly larger scale and, to the German war machine, was more than an absolute necessity.[129]

Oil fields were discovered in Germany during an intensified drilling program in 1930–1934 but she lacked sufficient "native" oil within her national boundaries to fulfill the enormous needs of her military forces. Moreover, even with the importation of oil from central Europe (Ploesti in Romania and oil fields in Hungary), there was an insufficient supply to enable Germany to conduct a future successful war effort.[130] This petroleum shortfall forced Germany to produce synthetic oil.

There were two primary processes used in German synthetic petroleum production: the Fischer-Tropsch process and the Bergius hydrogenation process. Fischer-Tropsch, developed by Franz Fischer and Hans Tropsch at the Kaiser Wilhelm Institute for Coal Research in 1925, synthesized liquid hydrocarbons from a "synthesis" gas composed of carbon monoxide gas and hydrogen using metal catalysts. The "synthesis" gas was created through a reaction of coke or coal with steam and oxygen, at temperatures over 1,652 degrees Fahrenheit. The process produced liquid fuels such as diesel fuel and gasoline out of solid combustible black coal.[131]

The second process, known as the Bergius method, was developed twelve years earlier than Fischer-Tropsch by Friedrich Bergius in Hanover. It involved the direct liquefaction of coal, called hydrogenation, into synthetic crude oil, which could then be processed in refineries to make gasoline. The Bergius method worked best with brown coal and geologically young black coal. The Bergius hydrogenation method also yielded more petroleum per ton of coal than the Fischer-Tropsch process.[132]

In 1934, anticipating future needs, the Germans began to expand their lubricating oil processing facilities to obtain maximum production from native crudes. Lubricating oils, though principally derived from petroleum, require either special kinds of petroleum or special processing, or both, for their manufacture. The factors affecting the German lubricating oil situation are thus somewhat different from those governing fuels. They required refinery plants in large numbers. Just before the war, Germany's capacity for refining was three million tons a year. The refineries were centered in the Hamburg and Hanover areas with a secondary concentration of refineries on the Rhine and Ruhr rivers at Emmerich, Dortmund, Dusseldorf and Regensburg.

The decision was made to try to fill motor fuel requirements from synthetic oil (Fischer-Tropsch and Bergius) in the hope of satisfying lubricating oil needs from native petroleum. By substituting raw unrefined oils for some lubricants, by stressing the regeneration of used oil, and by generally guiding consumption and production, Germany was able to satisfy lubricating requirements with a minimum of processing expansion. During the war, stocks of lubricating oil were fairly well maintained, except for brief crises brought about by pinpoint Allied strategic bombing.[133]

Amazingly, the German petroleum industry received assistance from a rather unlikely source. Through a partnership between the German petrochemical giant I.G. Farben and the Standard Oil Company of New Jersey, Germany embarked on a massive program to produce synthetic fuels from its plentiful domestic coal supplies, a process called hydrogenation. This initiative included a number of I.G. Farben processes like carbonization, hydrogenation, Bergius, Fischer-Tropsch and Winkler, aided by the American partnership. Indeed, this German-American pre-war partnership fueled enormous controversy because it was seen by many as being overtly supportive of the Nazi regime.[134]

In 1942, Germany was producing about 800,000 tons of natural crude, only a small fraction of its needs. The lack of sufficient native crude oil forced prewar Germany to import a large portion of what

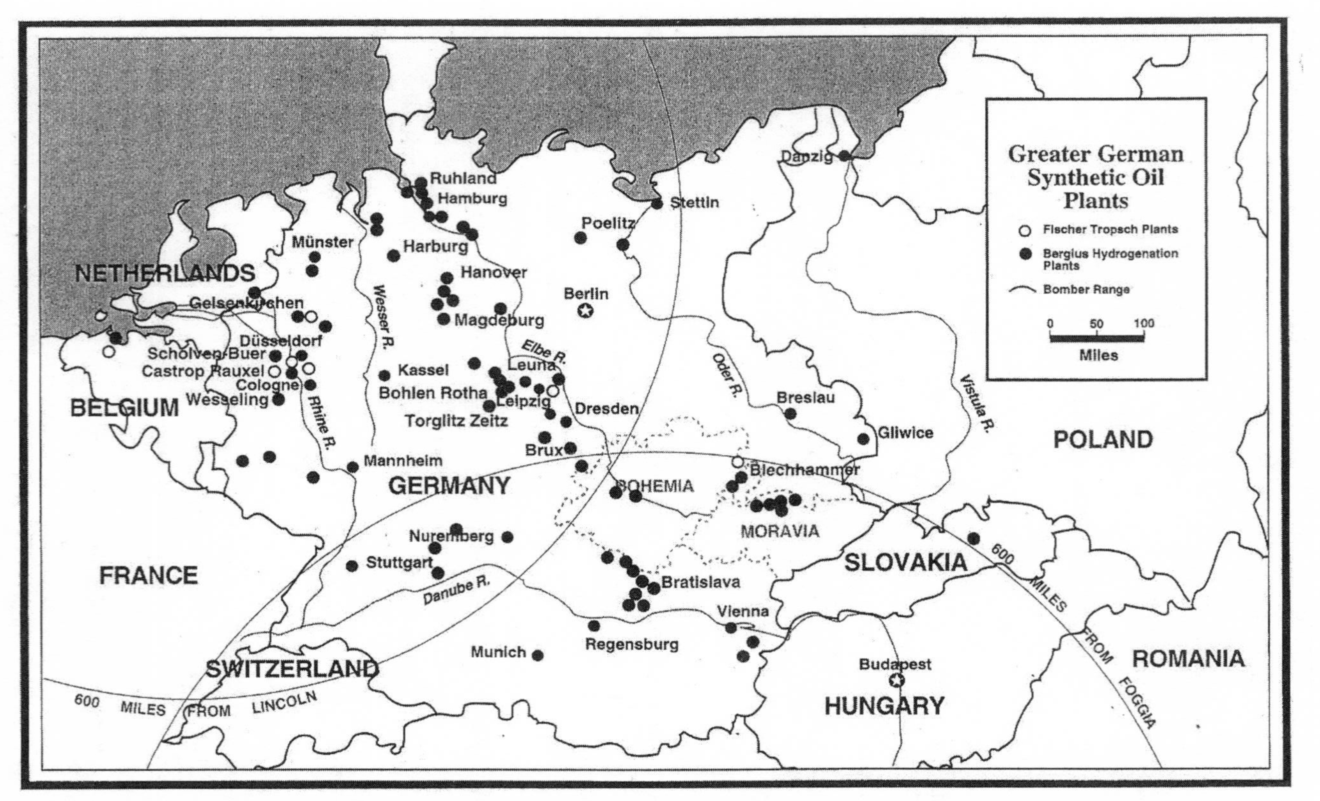

German synthetic oil plants. (From *Carl Spaatz and the Air War in Europe* by Richard G. Davis)

she consumed. The crudes or semi-finished materials imported were chosen to fit the eventual products manufactured. In general, lubricating oil was manufactured from wax-free crudes, which only required light refining. Ploesti in Romania and oil fields in Hungary provided more than 25 percent of refined crude oil such as liquid fuels. Nevertheless, domestic production of liquid fuels and other refined oil products was small but important to the German war effort.[135]

Petroleum needs were essentially being met until the Allies began to concentrate their air attacks on fuel targets. In August 1943, intense attacks were carried out against the heavily defended oil refineries at Ploesti. The attacks began with a bold and very costly low-altitude attack in August 1943. In this first raid, nearly one-third of the 180 participating bombers were lost, with most of the rest damaged. Ploesti was eventually flattened by bombing, but only after 24 raids with the tragic loss of 305 bombers and 3,000 men. In fact, oil shipments from Ploesti continued and briefly increased until April 1944 when air raids resumed. The sustained attacks during 1944, together with the mining of the Danube River reduced Romanian oil shipments to a trickle. Finally advancing Russian troops took over what was left of Ploesti in August 1944.

With the loss of its chief source of imported oil, the maintenance of a steady flow of oil was only possible via synthetic oil facilities. Thus, synthetic oil plants were given very high priority by the Reich and were very heavily defended because now the German war effort depended upon them exclusively..

Synthetic oil was principally produced by the Bergius Hydrogenation process at Leuna, Politz, Scholven, Gelsenkirchen, Troglitz, Magdeburg, Wesseling, Bohlen-Rotha, Lutzendorf, Welheim, and Blechhammer (Siliesia). Of these, the Leuna works was the most important. Unfortunately for the Allies, faulty intelligence had actually delayed the air attacks on synthetic oil plants and their chemical industry by-products.

During the last two years of the war, the role of strategic bombing became even more critical to shortening the conflict. By February 1944, large-scale bomber raids into Germany resumed with a 1,000-bomber raid at the end of the month and attacks on Berlin in March 1944. By September 1944, German petroleum production was reduced to 25 percent capacity. Thus began a series of crippling blows to the Nazi war machine. By 1944, the Ruhr Valley (Happy Valley to the airmen) was largely devastated.

The large-scale bomber raids were carried out against high priority targets like marshalling yards (where troops and supplies were concentrated for transportation by train to the various frontlines), the armaments industry, tank factories and aircraft assembly plants Indeed, these attacks could slow down the war effort by disabling transportation, destroying factories for tanks, aircraft, munitions and flak. These facilities, all crucial to Hitler's homeland defense, were heavily protected and camouflaged. In parallel, British area (city) bombing would disrupt communications and create confusion. However, the very highest priority targets for the Americans were the synthetic oil refineries and chemical plants. Their destruction had the greatest potential of actually shortening the war, thereby saving countless lives, both civilian and military.

Since the Germans recognized that the loss of synthetic oil would be a death-dealing blow to the Reich, each synthetic oil refinery was highly protected by hundreds of anti-aircraft batteries, including the ubiquitous and deadly 88mm guns, and Luftwaffe aerodromes in close proximity. There were 57 synthetic oil facilities in Germany in October 1944, each defended by hundreds of 88mm and 20mm and 30mm batteries, each battery consisting of four to six guns. Moreover, each refinery had to be hit more than once to hope to knock it out.

The Allied target prioritization in the fall of 1944 clearly reflects the importance of oil and industrial targets. For Dick and his crew mates, their specific targets in 1944 manifested this prioritization. Their targets were primarily marshalling yards, tank factories, the Leuna Synthetic Oil Refinery, I.G. Farben Chemical Plants (a few kilometers from Auschwitz-Birkenau), airfields, plane factories, troop concentrations and Tegli munitions and flak factories.

As the bombing of the synthetic oil plants finally picked up, production dropped steadily, and by July of 1944 every major plant had been hit. Before the sustained bombing effort on this key industry, the synthetic plants were putting out an average of 316,000 tons of oil per month and 175,000 tons of aviation gas. By June, 1944, this fell to 107,000 and 30,000 tons, respectively. By September 1944, German production was reduced to an all-time low with just 17,000 tons of oil and 5,000 tons of aviation fuel being produced per month. But the main problem for the Luftwaffe was the lack of trained pilots well before aviation fuel supplies became critically low. Nearly 1,000 Luftwaffe pilots were lost in the first four months of 1944 which included Big Week. Many of these men had considerable experience and could not be quickly replaced.[136]

The Germans took extreme measures to repair and reconstruct the oil plants. An oil czar was appointed, Edmund Geilenberg, who was given almost unlimited resources in men and materials to repair the plants and quickly restore production. Geilenberg used as many as 350,000 men for the repair, rebuilding and dispersal of the bombed plants and for new underground construction. The synthetic oil plants were huge, complex facilities which could not easily be broken down and dispersed. Efforts toward dispersal and underground construction were not completed by war's end. Geilenberg was, however, able to bring bombed synthetic oil plants back into at least partial production in a remarkably short period of time.[137]

The classic example of this intense air war on synthetic oil targets is the Leuna works at Merseberg. Leuna was the largest and most important of the Reich's synthetic plants and protected by a highly effective smoke screen and the heaviest flak concentration in Europe. Bomber crews viewed a mission to Leuna as the most dangerous and difficult assignment of the air war. The oil refineries in the Leipzig area like Leuna were protected by no fewer than 1,000 flak batteries of different caliber with Leuna being the most heavily defended. At its wartime peak, Leuna employed 36,000 workers and was more heavily defended than Berlin itself.

Leuna was hit on May 12,1944 and put out of production. However, post-war investigation of plant records and interrogation of Leuna's officials established that a force of several thousand men had it back in partial operation in about 10 days.[138] It was the second day in a row that the Eighth Air Force visited Merseberg. Merseberg was an eight-hour trip for bomber and fighter crews lucky enough to make it back to England. Over 500 of the 1,000-plus flak guns in the Leipzig area ringed the Hale-Leuna refineries. With Merseberg being the third highest priority Allied target in Hitler's Reich, the lethal flak and

Luftwaffe fighter protection surrounding it would bring down high numbers of American bombers and fighters.

Leuna was again hit on May 28 but resumed partial production on June 3 and reached 75 percent of capacity in early July. It was hit again on July 7 and again shut down, but production started two days later and reached 53 percent of capacity on July 19. An attack on July 20 shut the plant down again, but only for three days; by July 27 production was back to 35 percent of capacity. Attacks on July 28 and 29 closed the plant. The 100th Bomb Group, to which Dick's crew belonged, lost eight B-17s on the 29 July mission, where intense, accurate flak plus Luftwaffe fighters attacking at Staffel (squadron) strength or greater added up to disaster for the bomber formations entering the area. The swift German fighters took no mercy on wounded B-17s, pouncing on any lame-duck stragglers to finish them off. The 100th Bomb Group's loss accounted for slightly more than half of the 15 American bombers that fell at the hands of the Germans on that Merseberg mission.

Despite the heavy losses suffered by the Allied forces, the Eighth Air Force continued to hammer away at Merseberg and other refinery targets. Further attacks on August 24, September 11, September 13, September 28 and October 7 kept it closed down. However, Leuna got started again on October 14 and although production was interrupted by a small raid on November 2, it reached 28 percent of capacity by November 20!

Although there were six more heavy attacks in November and December (largely ineffective because of adverse weather), production was brought up to 15 percent of capacity in January 1945 and was maintained at that level until nearly the end of the war. From the first attack to the end, production at Leuna averaged nine percent of capacity. All together, there were 22 attacks on Leuna, 20 by the Eighth Air Force and 2 by the RAF. Due to the urgency of keeping this plant out of production, many of these missions were dispatched in difficult bombing weather. Consequently, the degree of bombing accuracy on Leuna was not high as compared with other targets. To win the battle with Leuna a total of 6,552 bomber sorties were flown against the plant, 18,328 tons of bombs were dropped, and an entire year was required.[139] A saying attributed to German workers engaged in rebuilding the damaged synthetic oil works was "Today we have finished rebuilding the plants and tomorrow the bombers will come again." German consumption of oil exceeded production from May 1944 onward. Accumulated stocks were rapidly used up, and in six months were practically exhausted.

The loss of oil production was sharply felt by the Wehrmacht and Luftwaffe. In August the final run-in-time for aircraft engines was cut from two hours to a half hour. For lack of fuel, pilot training, previously cut down, was further curtailed. Through the summer, the movement of German panzer divisions in the field was hampered increasingly by the fall in fuel production, as well as by losses in combat and mounting transportation difficulties. By December the fuel shortage had reached catastrophic proportions.[140]

When the Germans launched their Ardennes counteroffensive (the Battle of the Bulge) on December 16, 1944, their reserves of fuel were insufficient to support the operation. They planned to rely on capturing Allied stocks. Failing in this, many panzer units were lost when they ran out of gasoline. In February and March of 1945 the Germans massed 1,200 tanks on the Baranov bridgehead at the Vistula River to check the Russians. They were immobilized for lack of gasoline and overrun. Thus, on both the Eastern and Western Fronts, the tangible evidence is overwhelming that the bomber war on petroleum was a towering blow to military operations by the Reich.

14

GERMAN DEFENSES AGAINST BOMBERS

In an air war, the defenders are not only military personnel but also civilians whose resolve and courage under air attack and their willingness to continue working under perilous conditions and high risk in war production were absolutely crucial to their nation's survival. Thus, homeland security and response to air attack, including the organization and response of shelters, food, public transportation, power supplies and hospitals, were indispensable defensive measures as critical as military defenses.

The military defense of the Third Reich against bombers was diverse, sophisticated, flexible and deadly. They employed Staffeln of day and night fighters, searchlights, radar, flak, barrage balloons, camouflage, and fighter command and control.

The Reich produced an incredible number of Flugabwehr-Kanone or "flak" guns, most notably the 88mm guns, not only for front line defense and anti-tank use (when loaded with armor-piercing shells) but also as part of coordinated, radar-directed flak and searchlight systems to provide an umbrella of protection for their major industrial cities and the critical synthetic oil facilities.

Heavy flak typically consisted of the highly effective and ubiquitous 88mm cannon set up in anti-aircraft mode, and 105mm guns. As early as 1942, over 15,000 88mm cannons formed the bulwark of flak defenses for Germany, arrayed in flak belts stretching across Holland and Germany, in some places nine miles thick. The 88mm anti-aircraft artillery was effective up to an altitude of roughly 26,000 feet and the 105mm guns even higher. German 88s could fire 22-lb. shells at a rate of 15 to 20 rounds per minute. It took only seven seconds for an 88mm shell to reach 18,000 ft. This excellent gun proved very effective, especially when aimed with the use of radar. The shells exploded at a preset altitude according to their timed fuses, sending metal shrapnel flying in all directions.[141] The German 88s had the obvious advantage that they all used the same standard shells and required only a single production line, facilitating production, re-supply and rapid replacement.

Barrage balloons used by the Germans were teardrop-shaped balloons anchored close to the ground with steel cables to deter low-level attackers. In 1944–45, the Germans experimented with guided surface-to-air missile systems, or SAMs, far ahead of the Allies but were unable to deploy them before the war ended. They tried to conceal targets using smoke pots and camouflage as well as decoy structures built to replicate the appearance of factories and even petroleum facilities from the air.

The lightest German flak artillery typically consisted of heavy 12.7mm machine guns and 20mm towed cannons easily set up for anti-aircraft uses. The 20mm flak guns were served by four men and were typically towed behind a vehicle. Some were set up in flak wagons, a light tank body with four 20mm cannons mounted on it. They fired 20mm exploding shells up to 6,500 feet at a rate of 280 shells/minute. These guns were used primarily against low altitude enemy aircraft. Although their range was too short to be used for protection against bomber attacks on major cities, they did provide protection for important military installations, railroads, bridges, highways, important road junctions and the smaller cities and towns. These lighter guns could take a heavy toll on any low flying Allied aircraft.[142]

The German medium flak guns were typically 37mm towed by trucks or half-tracks and manned by as many as eight men. These munitions had a much longer range than the 20mm guns and were more deadly. They used tracers and shells with percussion fuses which exploded only upon direct impact. They were employed to protect higher value targets and were often combined with light flak guns in the field, or with heavy flak guns in cities. They fired a 37mm contact-exploding shell to almost 15,000 feet at a rate of 250 shells/min. The rising flak barrage they delivered into the bomber stream was visible as globes of yellow or red to the air crews.[143]

A German flak battery consisted of a central electric power unit, in a command post in charge of four to eight 88mm guns linked together by telephonic data transmission from a fire controller to the guns. From 1944 until the end of the war, two to five of these heavy flak batteries were combined to form Grossbatterien, which could have up to forty 88mm flak guns, firing rectangular patterns of shells called box barrages. Each battery was controlled by a single predictor which estimated where the aircraft would be by the time the shell reached it and thus improve aim. Therefore, as many as two dozen guns could be brought to bear on a single bomber at a time.

The searchlights were sited in threes with a sound locator which located the position of an aircraft by fixing on the sound of its engines. The range of the sound locators was about 6,000 yards but, in view of the time taken for the sound to reach the instrument, the calculated position of the target could be up to a mile behind its actual position, which had to be compensated for in the aiming. During daylight the predictor crews followed the aircraft by telescope or field glasses but at night the sound locators directed the searchlights (which had a range of 14,000 yards in clear weather) but cloudy sky conditions reduced the effectiveness of the unit. The firepower also increased as larger caliber guns were introduced including 105mm cannon.[144]

In 1944 flak accounted for 3,501 American planes destroyed, 600 less than planes lost to enemy fighters in the same time period. Constant demand for front line troops for the German army meant that many of the flak crews included elderly men, schoolboys, and even POWs. German secondary school students fifteen and sixteen years old were called up as "flak helpers" both for setting up and for even manning medium and heavy flak batteries. Even heavier flak guns gradually appeared, including a 128mm behemoth. The 128mm consisted of two barrels three feet apart on a single mounting.[145] German flak accounted for 50 of the 72 RAF bombers lost over Berlin on the night of March 24, 1944. An incredible 56 bombers were destroyed or crippled by flak during a B-17 raid on Merseberg in November of 1944.

By January of 1944, there were 20,625 flak guns (7,941 heavies guns and 12,684 light/medium guns) with 6,880 searchlights defending Germany.[146] Stationed on other fronts were another 9,569 anti-aircraft guns and 960 searchlights.

Since the 88s were extremely valuable assets against tanks as well as aircraft, the number of 88mm guns diverted to air defense was always questioned. By some estimates 3,343 shells costing a total of 267,440 Reichsmarks ($107,000) were required to bring down one Allied bomber. By the end of 1944 it was taking about 33,500 rounds for each aircraft downed, compared to the 4,057 rounds required in 1942.[147] On the Eastern Front, these 88mm guns were desperately needed against Russian tanks. Their availability in the East could have nearly doubled German anti-tank strength.

This shortfall of guns (and the manpower to operate them) in the East and its concomitant consequences can therefore be attributed to the pressure of the massive Allied bombing campaign. Ammunition usage soared from a monthly average of 500,000 shells in 1941/42 to 3,175,400 shells in December 1944, due in large part to the defense against bombers. At peak strength, over two million soldiers and civilians were tied down to ground anti-aircraft defenses. Indeed, 30 percent of all gun and 20 percent of heavy ammunition production went for air-defense in 1944.[148] This bears testimony to the immeasurable impact of the heavy strategic bombing campaign of 1944–45 by the USAAF and RAF in assisting the Soviet armies on the Eastern front and in achieving final victory.

For continuously pointed flak fire, flak bursts occur at regular intervals along the direction of the bomber. However, this was effective only if the bombers flew on a steady course between the initial point and the bomb release point long enough for German fire controllers to plot a probable route at the flak batteries. Bombers could use evasive tactics against continuous fire by losing altitude from the initial point in a series of irregular drops at irregular intervals as well as weaving horizontally, then gaining altitude just before the bomb release point.[149] Often bombers would make a feint before reaching the initial point as though on a path to another target, then resume their path toward the real target once reaching the initial point. For predicted concentrations of flak fire, flak barrages would be directed at set points once the probable (predicted) course was plotted by the controller. Predicted concentrations of bursts could be higher than continuous fire.

Flak was the nightmare of bomber crews because it wasn't predictable, you couldn't see it coming, and if you swerved to avoid the bursts in front, you could just as easily fly into the next set of shells. They exploded in daylight with puffs of black smoke with little red interiors, and made muffled "krumppp" sounds when heard from inside the planes due to the high levels of noise in the bombers. At night they flashed quickly yellow or red and disappeared.

Even if flak artillery did not score a direct hit on a bomber, the effect of the high velocity metal shrapnel could be devastating if the burst was close enough to an Allied plane. Flak could knock out an aircraft within about 30 yards of the shell burst, but the shrapnel from the explosion was still capable of inflicting serious damage up to 200 yards from the burst center. The shrapnel ripped into the thin metal skins of the planes, damaging and disabling equipment and killing or horribly wounding to the airmen.

When a flak burst hit close, the shards of shrapnel banged through the aircraft and pinged off more solid surfaces. With a direct hit from an 88mm or larger shell the aircraft would stagger, sometimes stall, and fill with smoke and screaming wounded airmen. Sometimes a wing would fold up and the bomber would go straight down in flames. Other times the entire aircraft would simply vanish in a dirty ball of fire, smoke and bits of plane and human flesh. Many other times the aircraft and men would fly on, riddled with holes but still fighting. Frequently, these crippled aircraft would have to try to land somewhere without lights, damaged undercarriages, missing engines and wounded or dead crew members. Often they bombed their targets only to die afterward in a crash landing on the continent or in England.[150]

Due to the redeployment of anti-aircraft guns as the Eastern and Western Fronts continually shifted inward, the flak experienced by American bomber crews actually became more concentrated. The gun emplacements were heavily fortified and part of the ground defense system. Anti-aircraft armor was put around the guns.

When guns were diverted to the Russian Front for example, this led to a weakening of the Reich's defenses. Eventually, the demand for guns in other theaters of operation weakened air defenses. Major German cities and industrial centers, like the Ruhr Valley were surrounded by more than two hundred 88mm flak batteries.[151] Each flak battery consisted of six to eight 88mm guns, many radar-controlled or mounted on railroad cars which were able to follow the bomber stream and keep it under attack. Trains were built carrying flak guns which ran between Cologne and Frankfurt. Radar-guided 88mm guns fired "predicted" flak which could shoot down individual bombers at high altitudes.

Gradually, the Reich's flak defenses thickened and became harder to break through without great losses. It was the intent of the Germans to make the flak defense so overwhelmingly costly that the Allies would call off the attacks. The main aim of flak was to try to break up the interlocking-fire defensive bomber formations of high low and lead groups to cause damaged aircraft to fall out of formation and give the fighters an in to the group. In this way the bombers could be picked off one by one. By 1944, the loss of territory in occupied Europe actually led to intensification of the flak defenses by redeploying 88mm artillery into increasingly smaller regions as Reich forces retreated. Despite this development, as Dick recalled, "flak was never as bad as going in without the fighter escorts."

The other dreaded major threat to Allied bombers was German fighter aircraft. Of all the aircraft types deployed by the Luftwaffe for air defense, three fighters were the most effective and deadly to penetrating Allied bombers. These were the Bf-109 (Messerschmitt-109), the Focke-Wulf-190 and the Messerschmitt-262, the world's first operational jet combat aircraft.

These three aircraft are discussed exclusively here because they also comprised the vast majority of the Luftwaffe's defensive aircraft against bombers and were the most competitive against the Allied fighter escorts. For example, many types such as the twin-engined Messerschmitt Bf-110 were vulnerable and relatively ineffective against the bombers and their escorts or were not as frequently seen attacking the bomber streams. However, the Me Bf-110 was an all metal monoplane which carried a wide angle airborne radar set enabling it to become a successful night fighter. Likewise the Junkers-88 was the most versatile German bomber. It was twin-engined, all metal and best deployed as a night fighter or torpedo plane.[152]

Perhaps the plane most identified with Luftwaffe bomber defense was the Messerschmitt Bf-109. It was flown by most of the top German aces in both the Eastern and Western fronts. Roughly 30,000 Me-109s were built. The basic design philosophy by Willy Messerschmitt was to place the most powerful engine into the smallest airframe. This proved to be a very successful formula that could be continually modified for improved performance. The weaknesses of the Me-109 were primarily its cramped cockpit, poor rearward visibility, and narrow track undercarriage that made ground handling difficult. Furthermore, its control forces became progressively heavier as speed increased. Thus, its maneuverability was very good at low and medium speed, but deteriorated greatly at high speed. And its relatively short range was a liability on both the Western and Eastern fronts, severely restricting its tactical usage.[153,154]

By 1940, the latest version, the Me-109D, had received the long-awaited Daimler-Benz 600 engine, and its top speed was up to about 320 mph. The Messerschmitt model that bore the brunt of the subsequent Battle of Britain was the 109E. It first came into service in 1939, and by 1940 was the first-line Luftwaffe fighter. The "E" model was powered by the Daimler-Benz DB 601A, a supercharged, 12-cylinder inverted Vee engine with fuel injection. It developed 1,100 hp at 2,400 rpm. This gave a top speed of 354 mph and a best climb rate of 2,990 ft/min. The 109E compared very closely in performance to the British Spitfire I and II, the premier British fighters of the Battle of Britain. Again, its main drawback as a bomber escort was its limited range, which led in large measure to the British triumph in the Battle of Britain.[155,156]

Purely as a fighter, the 109E was among the best in aerial combat. By the early part of 1941, German squadrons were receiving the Me-109F, powered by the up-rated DB 601N, which incorporated a power boost system for brief emergency use. This engine was nominally rated for 1,200 hp. Its more streamlined nose, retractable tail wheel, rounded wing tips (rather than the traditional "clipped" tips of the earlier models), cantilever horizontal stabilizer, and 900 rpm, 20mm cannon made it, for a time, the best fighter in the air.[157] Maneuverability was enhanced, and top speed was up to 382 mph at 17,000 feet with a best rate of climb of 3,640 ft/min. The next version, the "G," or Gustav, first appeared at the end of 1942. This was to became the most numerous ME-109 model of all, produced in many variations. Performance was again up with the maximum speed in excess of 400 mph at altitude. Power was provided by a bored-out DB 601 called the DB 605, and this engine, which had some early reliability problems, was rated at 1,475 hp at takeoff. The Gustav was used on all fronts for the rest of the war.[158]

In summary, the basic Me-109 had a wingspan of 32 ft. 6 in., length 28 ft. 9in., height of 8 ft. 1 in., and a Daimler-Benz 601, 12 cylinder. Vee, 1,100 horse power engine. It had a maximum speed of 354 mph at 16,400 ft., a best climb rate of 2,990 ft/minute at 13,150 feet, a service ceiling of 30,100 ft. and a combat range of 412 miles at 16,400 ft. Its empty weight was 4,431-lb. and its loaded weight was 5,600-lb. The Me-109 carried armaments consisting of two 7.9mm fuselage guns, and two 20mm wing cannon (one on each wing).[159]

The Focke-Wulf 190 (hereafter FW-190) was powered by a Bavarian Motor Works (BMW) 14-cylinder twin-row air-cooled radial engine. This engine delivered 1,760 horsepower and, coupled with the aircraft's excellent handling qualities, gave the early FW-190A models a clear superiority, for example, over the RAF's Spitfire Mark V in terms of speed, climb, dive, and roll rate.

The FW-190's wingspan was 34 ft. 5 in., length 29 ft. 1 in., height, 12 ft. and was powered by a BMW 801D 14 cylinder radial, 1,760 horsepower engine with 3,000 rpm at 18,000 ft. The FW-190 had a maximum speed of 395 mph at 17,000 ft. and 390 mph at 20,000 ft. Its best climb rate was 3,280 ft./min. at 17,500 ft. with a service ceiling of 37,000 ft. and a range of 820 miles. The FW-190's maximum weight 9,200-lb (8,580 normal) and its armaments were two 7.9mm machine guns, and four 20mm cannons.

There was also superb armor protection for its pilot. The typical armament, was two 7.9mm machine guns in the engine cowling, two Mauser 20mm cannon in the wing roots, each of which could fire 700 rounds per minute, plus two slower firing (450 rounds per minute) Oerlikon 20mm cannon farther out in the wings.[160,161]

There was also an extended range version with racks under the wings and fuselage for drop tanks or munitions. The 1943 version of the plane was the FW-190A-5. The primary variants of the A-5 included air superiority, bomber destroyer, and ground attack versions. This version put out up to 2,050 horsepower. An A-6 version got a new wing structure and replaced the slower firing outer wing 20mm cannons with faster firing Mauser cannons.

The FW 190A-8 version of 1944 incorporated other improvements, including increased fuel capacity for longer range, and an improved power boost system to improve high altitude performance. It could achieve a speed of 405 mph at 17,000 feet. Its best climb was down to 2,756 ft./min. at 16,100 ft. But by 1944, the Luftwaffe needed a new power plant to keep the FW-190 competitive with the latest Allied fighters. The FW-190D was the result. The FW-190 model D was a much modified fighter which used the standard Focke-Wulf wings and tail plane with an extended rear fuselage and a longer and heavier Junkers Jumo 213 engine. This raised the top speed up to 436 mph, best climb rate up to 3,642 ft./min.), and eventually 458.5 mph (at 38,080 ft) in the D-12 model. These "long nose" models were more difficult to handle but kept the Focke-Wulf competitive in performance with the best Allied fighters until the end of the war.[162]

The Me-262 "Schwalbe" ("Swallow") was the world's first operational turbojet aircraft. First flown as a pure jet on July 18, 1942, it proved much faster than conventional aircraft. Development problems, Allied bombings, and flawed Luftwaffe leadership contributed to delays in mass production. In one of the war's biggest blunders, Adolf Hitler, in 1943, approved mass production, but only if the aircraft was used primarily as a fighter-bomber. On July 25, 1944, an Me-262 became the first jet airplane used in combat when it attacked a British photo-reconnaissance Mosquito flying over Munich. As a pure attack fighter, the Me-262 was devastating against Allied bomber formations. The bombers, however, destroyed hundreds of Me-262s on the ground. More than 1,400 Me-262s were produced, but fewer than 300 actually saw combat. Most remained on the ground awaiting conversion to bombers, or were unable to fly because of lack of fuel, spare parts or trained pilots.[163]

The Me-262 had a wingspan of 41 ft., length of 34 ft. 9 in., a height of 11 ft. 4 in. and a weight of 15,600 lbs. It was powered by two Junkers Jumo 004s, each having 1,980 lbs. of thrust. It could attain a maximum speed of 540 mph, a cruising speed of 460 mph, a range of 650 miles and a service ceiling of 38,000 ft. The Me-262's armaments consisted of four 30mm MK-108 cannons, plus the ability to carry 1,000 lbs. of bombs.

15

ON THE EVE OF COMBAT

The eve of a first combat mission had to be an absolutely terrifying time for a young airman. The intense preparations preceding each mission helped keep the anxiety at bay but the sinking feeling and lonesome foreboding at takeoff afflicted many. All of the training they had received was about to be tested under the most stressful conditions.

There really was no typical mission. Each one varied with the number of hours flown, the highly variable weather patterns, encounters with enemy fighters, anti-aircraft artillery, mechanical problems and fatigue. For Dick Ayesh, the many events and unexpected experiences were recorded in his combat diary which he faithfully kept mission by mission each time he returned to Thorpe Abbotts.

No crew members knew the night before a mission where the next day's bombing run would occur. However, since the maximum fuel load for the B-17 of 2,780 gallons was just sufficient for the most dangerous missions deep into Germany, the airmen could guess where they were going before being briefed by finding out how much fuel had been loaded overnight. That is why when a sergeant would awaken Dick and his crew members (usually around 3 or 4 in the morning) by shining a flashlight in their faces, the first question they asked him was "What's the fuel load?" As Dick recalls, "That usually told how hard the mission would be, since the more fuel, the deeper into enemy territory and the longer the mission. Of course when we were scheduled to fly a combat mission, we got 'fresh' eggs. If we had a stand down, no flying, then it was powdered eggs!"

Once up, the crew had maybe 60-90 minutes to go out in the cold, shave, eat their fried eggs and go to the briefing. A close shave was critical because your oxygen mask had to fit tightly to your skin to avoid leaks. At the briefing, roll call took place, followed by the announcement of the target destination. As W. Griswold Smith of the 100th observed, "If it was an oil facility or the Big B [Berlin], you could usually hear a murmur or a shiver roll back through the briefing room." Dick recalled that "when the curtain was pulled back and we saw that the mission was to Berlin or an oil facility like Merseberg, there was just silence—no joviality or talking, just very quiet."

Dick's job was to make all the effort of the ground personnel and the flight crews worth the cost. What would be the use of going through all this if the bomb load was not on target? Once over the target the rest of the crew was helpless—the pilots were not flying the plane, the gunners were not defending it, and the navigator had no navigation to consider until after bombs away. Simply put, the B-17s were sitting ducks during the bomb run.

At last, when cleared for takeoff, the precarious and tedious assembly of the bomb groups started. Each squadron of six bombers usually had to puncture through overcast, emerging above the cloud deck and continuing the long climb inexorably upward at roughly 300 feet per minute to base altitude. An unparalleled description of the always complex and nerve-wracking assembly was provided by Beirne Lay.[164] "Now the sky over England was heavy with the weight of thousands of tons of bombs, men and fuel being lifted 4 miles straight upon a giant aerial hoist to the western terminus of a 20,000 foot aerial highway that led east."

Each group leader fired red, green or yellow flares from the cabin roofs of the group leaders' planes to identify the lead squadron to the high and low squadrons of each group. Squadrons would keep circling until they found their groups. It took maybe an hour from takeoff to form three squadrons into a compact group stagger formation with the low squadron down to the left of the lead squadron and the high squadron up and to the right of the lead. Lay described the view from his ship in the last element of the high squadron of the entire procession: "The air division looked like huge anvil-shaped swarms of locusts . . . deployed to uncover every gun and also permit maneuverability." Many B-17s trailed the climbing stream as spares in the event any ships aborted due to mechanical failure during the hard climb. Once assembly was complete, these backup B-17s returned to base.

Once the assembly of all the squadrons into group formation was complete, the stream of maybe 1,000 bombers headed across the English Channel. Once over the water, gunners checked their weaponry. Already they were searching the skies for enemy fighters, and the B-17s would shudder as gunners fired short bursts to test their guns. The pungent smell of burnt cordite filled the cabins and the planes trembled to the recoil of the nose and ball turret guns. Dick recalled a concern that the shell casings, kicked out at fairly high velocity from the machine-gun fire, could themselves damage a friendly aircraft. And already the RDF screens of the Germans were recording the approaching bombers and the sector controllers of the Luftwaffe's fighter belt in Western Europe were alerting their Staffeln of FW-190s and Me-109s. Soon all hell would break loose as the stream would run the gauntlet of fighter attacks and flak bursts and the tight formations would inevitably begin to loosen. Any wounded stragglers from the bomber stream would become easy prey for predatory German fighters.

In Dick's words, "Anyone who has really been in combat will tell you—most of what went on was very uncoordinated. Everybody was scared to hell. Nobody wants to get killed. If you talk to anybody who has really been in combat, there are no heroes. You just do your thing and pray that you don't get hurt or get killed or shot or anything like that. By the grace of God you got through. Anyone who was in combat knows that. Early in the war, only one out of three airmen survived. Then later, with fighter escorts, two out of three survived. That made me feel better. I'll take those odds any day, instead of one out of three. During a mission I was as small a target as I could be. One airman, a pilot, just came in after eight missions and said he could not fly combat anymore. It took a lot of guts to do that but it happened. Everyone is made differently. There was no loosey goosey stuff going on like you saw in 'Catch 22' and several other movies about the air war. It was all business."

For Dick personally, the prospect of being severely wounded or an amputee was worse to him than death. He put his personal feelings at the time into words: "If I'm wounded I'd just as soon go down. I did not want to be part of a person. I really meant that. I prayed a lot and always carried a picture of the Virgin Mary with me. The chaplain would send a letter to each guy's church telling them that you went to church before each mission. So when I returned home, my priest, Father George Cohlmia at St.George in Wichita, was very pleased and proud. He always beamed when he saw me."

The spectacle of an air battle during the approach to target was something so surreal that it can only be described by those who were in them. There is probably no more evocative and chilling description than that of Bierne Lay[165] relating what he witnessed on the costly Regensburg raid. As he described, "In the bomber stream, all manner of jetsam flew backward in the slipstream: emergency hatches, exit doors, prematurely opened parachutes, bodies, assorted fragments of B-17s and German fighter fragments, all manner of smoke, sheets of orange flame. Even airmen making delayed jumps would hurtle through the formation, clasping their knees to their heads to minimize their cross-sections and revolving like divers doing triple somersaults, barely missing propellers and fuselages of ships. Fighters were exploding, B-17s dropping out of the stream in every state of distress and disintegration, American (white) parachutes and German (yellow) parachutes floating down while 20,000 feet below on the green-carpeted ground, the funeral pyres of smoke from downed fighters and bombers, the white dots of maybe 60 parachutes at one time seen floating downward became routine."

The spectacle was so fantastically surreal, Lay's brain was numbed to the actuality of death and destruction all around his ship so that he stated had it not been for the knots and squeezing in his stomach and nausea keeping him aware of reality, he might easily have been watching an animated cartoon in a movie theater.

Few would guess or even believe that the Air Force lost more planes from anti-aircraft fire than from the much more dramatic fighter attacks. In fact, flak destroyed 3,501 American planes in 1944 alone. This was 600 more than met their doom by fighter plane opposition during that same year. What made a B-17 even more of a sitting duck, it was usually flying with a head wind to slow the plane down and thus make the bombing more accurate.

As Dick recounts, "The flak you see has already exploded. Its the flak you don't see that scares the hell out of you. The ones you don't see shudder the whole damn airplane and you hear metal crunching against metal. On one mission we had 80 hits on our ship. If you got hit in the gas tank and it leaked onto the turbosupercharger, and you were lucky enough to notice it, then you'd bail out right quick. The plane would explode in seconds. When hydraulic fluid was burning, the inhalation of its fumes made you sick. When we encountered enemy fighters, the fight did not last very long. But it was like passing through a swarm of deadly bees, things happened so fast."

Of 350,000 airmen stationed in England with the Eighth, 26,000 were killed, which was the highest percentage of mortality of all the service branches in World War II. For example, the percentage killed in the Air Corps was three times higher than the US Army and twice as high as the percentage of fatalities suffered by the Marine Corps during the entire war in the Pacific. Being an airman aboard an Allied bomber was arguably the most dangerous job in the entire war, probably ranking in peril with submariners and service in the Luftwaffe.[166]

The emotional roller coaster that airmen experienced was excruciating and relentless throughout their tours and was nothing short of pure hell. They had to endure the nerve shattering stress of not knowing from day to day whether you would be alive the next, the lack of a place to hide 25,000 feet above the ground, the most frigid conditions imaginable, flying under weather conditions that would have grounded any civilian aircraft, the life or death dependence on your supply of oxygen, the terrifying bomb run itself when the plane was a slow moving target for intense flak barrages, German fighter attacks; the shock of seeing your friends butchered and killed on board with no medics available, the trauma of the long flight back to base often in a crippled ship with horrendously wounded and dead crew members on board with you. It is little wonder that wartime correspondent Andy Rooney frequently remarked that it was in many respects "tougher to be an airman in the Eighth Air Force during the war than an infantryman."

The probability of survival and seeing their friends and comrades lost had to weigh heavily on an airman's psyche and, in some cases, have a devastatingly stressful effect on morale, quite possibly impairing judgment and efficiency. This and the combat stress became unbearable for many and led to emotional and mental breakdowns. As reported by historian Donald Miller in Masters of the Air,[167] fully 4,000 to 5,000 out of 225,000 airmen in the Eighth in combat were treated as emotional casualties and a further 2,100 airmen were grounded due to neuro-psychiatric disorders. Others were grounded because of 'lack of moral fiber,' in other words, they just could not take it." As Dick stated, "Everyone is made differently and it took a lot of guts to admit it."

Dick's moment of reckoning, his first combat mission, was to bomb marshalling yards in Cologne. So begins his diary with its first entry on October 15, 1944.

16

MISSION-BY-MISSION (I): From Fall 1944 to the German Counter-Offensive

Along with commentary, Lt. Dick Ayesh's combat diary is reprinted here verbatim, save for some revises of spellings, abbreviations and punctuation for clarity.

* * *

#1—Sunday, October 15, 1944

Mission—Cologne Marshalling Yds.
Load—16-250# G.P. & 4 M-17 Incen.
Bomb Alt.—25,000ft

This was my first mission so everything was very new to me. We bombed by instruments due to solid undercast. Flak was moderate to intense and accurate. 11 out of 13 ships received battle damage. We got a hit in #4 prop. We were #2 of Hi element of the Lead Sq. Mission was 7 1/2 hours long.

* * *

Commentary

Each squadron consisted of 12 planes and flew in formation according to the following positions, lead, high and low. This was a protective formation to maximize firepower on attacking aircraft.

Dick's B-17 had a bomb load of sixteen 250# general purpose bombs (GP) and four M-17 incendiary bombs. The bombs were released at an altitude of 25,000 feet. His first three missions were against railroad marshalling yards in Cologne and Munster where German troops and supplies were being transported by rail to support the German divisions operating against the American and British breakout into the Ardennes following D-Day. Cologne was very close to the center of Army Group B under Field Marshall Model with vital north-south rail connections to supply the 1st, 7th and 15th Panzer Armies and a short distance from the Siegfried Line. By mid-October 1944, the First Army under General Courtney Hodges had overrun part of the Siegfried Line in the vicinity of Aachen so this mission was also in support of the assault on the West Wall in that sector.[168]

When bombing was done by instruments due to solid undercast, this meant that airborne radar known as H2S (British) or H2X (US), also known as "the Mickey," was used to try to identify the location of the target.

* * *

#2—October 17, 1944

Mission—Cologne Marshalling Yds.
Load—34-100# G.P. and 2-M-17 In.
Bomb Alt.—27,000ft.

Our position was #2 in the low element of the high sq. All groups were bombing at the same time which indicated a wide target area. We encountered heavy accurate flak and were bounced around quite a bit by accurate flak bursts. Observed one B-17 blow up. We received a hole in the left flap which was of a minor nature. Saw no enemy fighters and bombing was done by instru. as we found a complete 10/10 undercast at the target. After landing, learned one Navigator in the 350 sq. was killed. Was an 8 1/2 hr. mission.

* * *

Commentary

A flak burst, usually 88mm shells, could lift a B-17 100 feet if it was nearby. When an airman saw a flak burst, it was already too late. The sound of shrapnel striking the plane was sharp. It took an 88mm shell about seven seconds to reach 20,000 ft. Over Berlin, B-17s flew through as many as 20 miles of flak batteries, as many as 520 guns. This was a terrifying experience and always dreaded by the crews.

On the bomb run from the IP to the target drop, the bombardier had taken control of the plane and had to keep it steady and smooth, somehow remaining cool and oblivious to all of the death and destruction happening around him. Evasive action could take place only after bombs were released, but on the straight and level bomb run the waist gunners would throw out handful after handful of "Chaff," sometimes called "Window." These were strips of aluminum foil that would confuse the German radar aiming devices. Once you entered into the range of the AA guns, hope was placed on jamming the enemy radar by foiling their aim and altitude. The crew had their flak vests and steel helmets on. They were notified when it was safe to remove them after leaving enemy territory. The helmet was a modified GI steel helmet and the vest was a series of overlapping metal plates sewed into a cloth jacket which covered their torsos, front and back. The helmet covered down over their ears and the back of their necks. There is no doubt as to the added protection all this gave them, but equally as important was the psychological value of doing what you could to protect yourself from danger.

Another device used by the Eighth Air Force was an electronic jamming unit which went by the name of "Carpet." It sent out radio signals on the same frequency as the German AA radar, thereby confusing their aim. Each combat wing had some planes of each group with a Carpet transmitter. The Germans also used ground optical range finders to detect the bombers' altitude and direction. There was no way to foil this method of aiming their guns. The flak impacts have been described as sounding like gravel hitting a tin roof. Vicious chunks of metal would rip through the planes. When the 88mm shell reached a predetermined altitude, it exploded. The shrapnel spread out like an inverted cone.

* * *

#3—Sunday, October 22, 1944

Mission—Munster Marshalling Yds.
Load—14-250# G.P. plus 4-M-17 Incendiaries.
Bomb Alt.—25,000ft

We were flying #6 in the lead Sq. Flew in over the Zeider Zee, made a wide circle and bombed Munster on the way out. Encountered no Flak but did see a few rockets. I had 2-250# GP and an Incendiary hang up and went back to kick them out and passed out for lack of oxygen just as I was about to step into the Bomb Bays. The engineer gave me oxygen and I began to feel better. We brought the bomb back. Rack malfunction. We took off this morning in a heavy fog at 1015 and landed at 1630. Bombing was by H2X.

* * *

Commentary

The Zeider Zee was a well-known navigation point in Holland on the flight path back to East Anglia. The rockets Dick reported were air-to-air rockets mounted under the wings of a Luftwaffe fighter. H2X, otherwise know as "Mickey" to Eighth airmen, as an airborne radar package. Originally developed by the British as H2S, it was an early type of ground image radar which aided navigators and bombardiers to locate targets. It was sometimes called bombing by PFF, Mickey or H2X. The lead B-17 would have a radar dome instead of a ball turret for the "Mickey Operator" to guide the other B-17s to the bomb release point. GEE, an earlier radar aid, was successfully jammed by the Germans, had limited range and never achieved a position close enough to get within 1/10 mile of the target. H2X used its beams to indicate ground features, giving airmen a rough indication of the territory below with readings that distinguished water, open fields and built up areas. Eventually, the H2X radar emissions could be tracked by German ground radar making the flak much more accurate.

* * *

#4—October 26, 1944

Mission—Tank Factory at Hanover
Load—20-250# G.P.
Bomb Alt.—27,5000ft

We flew #3 in lead of Hi Sq. We took off in a heavy fog and mist. 2 Forts collided over Buncher 28. We had a solid undercast all the way in and out. Heavy Flak at the target but it used carpet and I'm sure it helped immensely. We were alerted for "bandits in the area" but I didn't see any E/A. Upon return, we had to make an instrument descent over the Buncher and came in at 400ft. Field was lit up with lights and flares. Route in over the Zeider Zee and out. Take off 0930 and landed at 1730.

* * *

Commentary

E/A in Dick's diary denotes enemy aircraft. A "Buncher" was a radio homing beacon for certain groups on the coast and "Splasher Six" was the Splasher beacon closest to Thorpe Abbots. The "Buncher" beacon was used so the groups could assemble prior to departing for the mission. Buncher 28 was a navigation marker on the English coast. CAVU means "ceiling and visibility is unlimited."

* * *

#5—November 2, 1944

Mission—Merseburg (Leuna Syn. Oil Refinery.)
Load—20-250# G.P.
Bomb Alt.—28,000ft

Our position was #2 in the lead sq. Target area was 5 to 10/10 coverage so bombing was done by PFF. The flak was very, very intense and accurate. We got 12 hits—flap, wing, nose, and bomb bay. (Radio operator) Jim Roberts was hit by a piece of flak which lodged in the zipper of his jacket just in front of his throat. His flak suit absorbed most of the momentum of the piece. I saw one Fort blow up and after the bomb run there were quite a few stragglers. We saw no enemy fighters altho we were briefed for 500 of them in the area. Route in over the Zeider Zee—bombed on a heading of 90 deg. then did 180 turn and came home. Take off at 0730 landed at 1630. November 3, Our mission to Hamburg was scrubbed. I learned yesterday that 1st Div. was attacked by 400 E/A. We lost 41 bombers. Also saw ship 991 which received a very near hit on right tail and fin. The tail was riddled and looked like a sieve. The tail gunner was mangled so badly that they took him out piece by piece. I could see pieces of his head still lodged in the shattered plexi-glass. Blood was dripping out of the comp. A blanket was covering his remains but you could still see pieces of his flesh. They had to wash him out with a hose. It was the most horrible sight I've ever seen or ever hope to see.

* * *

Commentary

Bombing by PFF meant, to the Eighth Air Force daylight bombing, that bombing was done by H2X and was used when there was solid overcast, as in this case, and the target could not be seen by the bombardier.

An attack by 400 Luftwaffe aircraft is an indication of how heavily defended were Merseberg and other synthetic oil facilities. The number of German planes defending also belies estimates that the Luftwaffe was nearly totally crippled by the autumn of 1944. By the time of this next mission, the Western Front had receded to the area of Metz in the north and Lyon in the south but the Allies had not yet entered the territory of the Reich on the ground. Unbeknownst to Allied intelligence, Hitler and staff were in the final planning stages on the Bulge counteroffensive. In the next mission, the primary target was cancelled and instead a raid on the giant I.G. Farben chemical plant at Ludwigshaven was carried out.

This was the chief Allied goal of ending the war by destroying the enemy's fuel supply and synthetic oil facilities. Merseberg, site of the world's largest synthetic oil refinery, and one of the most heavily guarded. Indeed, it was the most fortified stronghold in all of Germany, making a bomber attack extremely perilous. As Dick recorded that the flak was "very, very intense and accurate" and that though they encountered no enemy aircraft, intelligence warned of 500 Luftwaffe fighters in the area of Merseberg. It was protected by highly effective smoke screens and the heaviest flak concentration in Europe. A plywood replica of Leuna was built 4 miles south of the main refinery to deceive bombardiers. Thousands of workers restored Leuna back into production to some level. Just after the war, the US Strategic Bomb Survey studied plant records and interrogated officials. Leuna had been bombed 13 times between May 12, 1944 and mid-October near the time of Dick's mission. A total of twenty two attacks were carried out on Leuna during the war, twenty bombing attacks by the USAAF and two by the RAF.

* * *

#6—Sunday, November 5, 1944

Mission—Ludwigshaven (I.G. Farbin chemical plant-mfgrs. of poison gas and plastics.
Load—6-1000# G.P.
Bomb Alt.—27,000ft

Our primary target was to bomb the French forts around Metz which were holding Gen. Patton's First Army [*sic*] from adv. We were to bomb 2 miles ahead of our own troops but the area was too cloudy for accurate bombing so we went after the Chem. plant at Ludwigshaven. We were in 100 "A" which was leading the Div. and #3 in the low element. Weather was undercast till we reached the IP, then visual to target. The jerries let us get close then they opened up on us. Flak was very accurate and intense. We collected 43 hits and feathered #3 engine. We came across the channel at 400 ft. Very rough with terrific wind. We crossed England at 300ft. Most of the ships landed at Framlingham. Had prop wash on take off and cross wind on landing. Our flaps were shot out and we had collected hits in every section of the ship. Take off 0700 and landed at 1500. We saw no enemy fighters.

* * *

Commentary

Feathering an engine meant turning the blades of its propellor through a device in the cockpit so that it would not create drag if it was either turning too slowly or too fast (a runaway).

The IP or initial point was where the formation turned toward the target to begin the bomb run. During this time, the bombardier actually flew the plane with the Norden bombsight.

In the next mission, the primary target was cancelled and instead a raid on the giant I.G. Farben chemical plant at Ludwigshaven was carried out. I.G. Farben, (Interssen Gemeinschaft Farben) was the giant chemical and petroleum complex. The importance of I.G. Farben's support for the National Socialist movement was pointed out in a book about the cartel, in which it is stated: "Without I.G.'s immense production facilities, its far reaching research, varied technical experience and overall concentration of economic power, Germany would not have been in a position to start its aggressive war in September, 1939." The importance of I.G. Farben to the plans of the German Nazi Party can be illustrated by a product that an I.G. Farben-dominated company manufactured. It was called Zyklon B, the lethal gas utilized by the Nazi exterminators at Auschwitz, Bitterfeld, Walfen, Hoechst, Agfa, Ludwigshafen, and Buchenwald. (I.G. Farben, being a chemical company even before it was merged with other chemical companies to form the cartel). The company was also the producer of the chlorine gas used during World War I.

But the real importance of I.G. Farben to the war efforts of Adolf Hitler came in the utilization of the process known as hydrogenation, the production of gasoline from coal, created by the I.G. Farben chemical cartel. Germany had no native gasoline production capabilities, and this was one of the main reasons it lost World War I. It was a German scientist who discovered the process of converting coal. Germany was the possessor of large quantities of coal turned into gasoline in 1909, but the technology was not completely developed during the war. In August, 1927, Standard Oil agreed to embark on a cooperative program of research and development of the hydrogenation process to refine the oil necessary for Germany to prepare for World War II. This was of extreme importance to the Nazi war effort, because, by the end of the war, Germany was producing about seventy-five percent of its fuel synthetically.

* * *

A CLOSE CALL AFTER A NIGHT OF DRINKING

Lt. Gene Jensen reported:

"A mission had been canceled after our crew became airborne, and, because of weather we were diverted to a Royal Air Force base in the west of England. On the assumption that the weather would not clear, we arranged for use of a British Army lorry and drove to a nearby village, the site of a Women's Land Army Base. We got back to the RAF base during the small hours of the morning. A few hours later, we got the bad news. The weather had cleared at Thorpe Abbots, and they would be taking off as soon as possible! With the exception of the tail gunner and the pilot (who had a mild hangover), we were in no condition to drive a big aircraft.

I designated the tail gunner as copilot. As we began the takeoff, I realized that we were not getting takeoff power! It took only a few seconds to locate the problem. We'd forgotten to set the turbochargers to takeoff power. The acting copilot (the tail gunner) knew nothing about the aircraft so I let go of the throttle and reached over to adjust the four turbo controls to full setting. That was when I found that he had also forgotten to set the throttle drag! The two righthand engines dropped to idle, and the two left hand engines went to full takeoff power. At about 80 mph the plane made a 45 degree turn to the right and headed across the grass toward the parking area for the RAF bombers. This was a very awkward situation. I couldn't stop, change course, or take off! Then I noticed he hadn't set the flaps for takeoff. When I reset the flaps the aircraft felt like it wanted to fly. I waited until the last moment and retracted the wheels. They cleared the RAF bombers and the row of big trees along their parking area."[169]

* * *

#7—Monday November 6, 1944

Mission—Nuemunster
Load—24-250# G.P.
Bomb Alt.—25,000ft

Our target was up by Kiel and Denmark. We were to bomb an airfield and factory prod. parts and assembling FW 190's. It was to be a visual run but we found 5/10 cloud cover in the area. Flak was light to moderate and below us. After turn off target enemy fighters were reported behind us but I never did see any. Route in was over North Sea and out the same way. We were #5 in the Hi Sq. Take off at 0630 and landed at 1500. It was a beautiful morning and I watched the sun come up, shining thru the clouds.

* * *

Commentary

Kiel was the location of a major U-boat base and busy port on Germany's north coast which was hit many times by Eighth Air Force and RAF bombers.

* * *

#8—Thursday, Nov. 16, '44

Mission—5 Miles Northeast of Aachen.
Load—30-260# Fragmentation Bom.
Bomb Alt.—21,500ft.

We were to bomb Nazi troops in the area which lies between Aachen and Duren, 2 mi. ahead of our own troops (Gen. Patton's First [*sic*] Army). We saw flak enroute to the rally point but it wasn't close. One ship released early and dropped on our side of the lines. Don't know if they hit anyone. Tgt. area was 5/10 coverage. PFF release. We let down over France. This was the first time I had seen much of France and the whole countryside was pock-marked by bomb craters and art. fire. Saw Calais and the white cliffs of Dover. Upon return our part of England was socked in so we circled around for an hour looking for a hole. Finally our gas supply was so low that we had to come in. Made instru. descent. Ceiling was 200ft and visibility was 260 yards. Nearly collided with another Fort when we broke out of the clouds. Ceil. 200ft and vis. 500yds. On the ground. Took off 0700 and landed 1600. One ship crashed on takeoff this morning. Jet jobs over England this morn. We flew the slot in the Hi Sq.

* * *

Commentary

In this case of tactical bombing near Aachen, Dick's diary entry mistakenly identified the 1st Army as being under General Patton. First Army was under General Courtney Hodges where his 5th, 7th and 19th Divisions were assaulting the Siegfried line right at Aachen and punctured the Siegfried line forming a bulge (the Aachen Salient) that extended to Duren and the Roer River. This mission included anti-personnel explosives, 260# fragmentation bombs to inflict maximum damage among troop concentrations.

This diary entry not only refers to the relatively few cases of tactical bombing by Eighth Air Force heavy bombers but also documents that such tactical bombing often led to friendly fire casualties. This happened a number of times during the war by both the USAAF and the RAF. One of the worst such cases was the accidental bombing of US troops by some of the 2,700 bombers which were bombing the German defenses around St. Lo in Normandy to open the way for Operation Cobra, "the St.Lo Breakout," on July 24th, 1944. This tragic error resulted in over 100 US troops killed, including Lt. General Lesley McNair, the highest ranking American officer to die in the war, and hundreds of wounded.

* * *

#9—Wednesday Nov 29, '44

Mission—Hamm Marshalling Yards.
Load—16-250# G.P. and 2 M-17 Incendiary clusters.
Bomb Alt.—24,000ft

We were flying slot in the low sq. Undercast all the way so bombed by H2X. Saw no flak. The reason for flying the slot is because we are to be checked out for lead.

* * *

Commentary

Being checked out for lead was the process of selecting the lead crew including the lead bombardier. When the lead bombardier dropped his bomb load, the other bombardiers would release in synchronism with the lead's release. The lead bombardier was therefore the most skilled person at his job. The lead aircraft at the head of the stream had the lead bombardier. The disadvantage of being lead was that your tour was longer (by several months) and, understandably, you were the prime target during attacks on the bomber stream. The advantage was that you flew only every fifth mission. Hamm was located on the Lippe River about 70 miles west of the Siegfried Line's northernmost sector and to the northeast of Dortmund. The marshalling yards contained troops and supplies in support of General Student's 1st Parachute Army and to strengthen the Siegfried Line. These yards were frequent targets of the Eighth Air Force and RAF throughout the war.

* * *

#10— Thursday Nov. 30, 1944

Mission—Merseburg(Leuna Syn. Oil)
Load—20-250#G.P.
Bomb Alt.—28,000ft

We were flying Deputy lead (lead of 2nd element) of the Lead Sq. Mission was delayed 1 hour because of weather. 10/10 all way to IP then it broke CAVU. 1st Div. going to Leipzig. We missed IP by 20 miles so we had to go over Zeitz to get to the target. There was supposed to be the greatest concentration of flak in the world in this area. There was!! It looked as tho a huge black cloud hung over the target. We were under fire for 20 min. The target itself was obscured by smoke screens and smoke of the groups who had bombed before us. Anderson, who lived in our brk., was flying on our left wing and got a hit between #1 and 2 and went down. (I saw 3 P-51's go down.) Ball turret gunner reported he saw a fire in his wing and later it broke off. He saw 3 chutes. I saw a ship covered with flames shoot up ahead then dive down. It was a ball of fire. It was from the group on our left. The 95th group under us just before bombs away. We got hit in #3 oil line and had to feather it. #4 was hit from the top and spilled oil so we feathered it. Flak sheared the connecting rod from B.B. [bomb bay] motor to door screw and it was impossible to close doors. We dropped down to 20,000 ft and still losing altitude due to the drag caused by the doors being open. Also our turbo's were shot out and we lost a lot of the power of the remaining 2 engines. We started #4 again and by this time we had lost the formation.

(Continued from Nov. 30)

I went back and managed to get the doors closed by turning the screw with my hands and a screwdriver. By this time we were down to 15,000ft and able to maintain altitude. We jettisoned all excess weight i.e., flak suits, guns, ammunition. A lone P-51 flew with us for a few minutes then left. Our electrical system was shot out and the plane was filled with smoke from the burning hydraulic oil. We were 2 1/2 hours away from friendly territory, solid undercast made navigation a good guess because our G-box and fluxgate compass were out. On way out we flew over Coblenz and they nearly shot us down. When we thought we were over friendly territory we let down thru the clouds and broke over the wooded area by Luxemburg. We were lost and trying to get to Brussels or Paris. We weren't particular, however, so we landed at the first airfeild near Cambrai, France. All this time we had been at 1,500 ft because of the low cloud ceiling. 2 other Forts also had landed there. One had no prop and another feathered and the other had a feathered prop. We stayed over night at this field. The guys were very nice to us. The next morning we walked into Cambrai. We ate at a Red Cross Club and drank at an officers club which formerly belonged to the Luftwaffe. That nite we were to leave for Denain to get a ride home. I stored the [Norden] sight in a vault. All our crew got together and went to a small pub where we drank bier and wine. These French people are really funny. Next day we got a ride back by the A.S.C. in a stripped down B-17.

(Continued from Nov. 30)

This field had a good number of C-47's. It was the closest base to the front lines. Here the freight is brought by air and loaded on trucks for the front lines (Red Ball Highway). The field had been hit hard by the Allies and was heavily mined by the Germans when they left. We had an escort of 1100 fighters. We lost 56 bombers this day

* * *

Commentary

Dick walked into what had the day before been a barracks for German airmen. He saw a large of portrait Adolf Hitler adorning a wall, and took charge of a bunk bed for a much needed sleep. On the bunk bed was the name of the German airman, Hermann Schmidt, who had slept in it the night before the airfield was captured.

At the small French pub where Dick and his crewmates were seated at the bar having beer and wine, he casually asked the French barmaid behind the bar how she got along with the Germans. He was sort of expecting her to say something like "those filthy swine, we're glad they're gone." Instead, she just shrugged her shoulders and said "business is business."

For his courage and skill in manually closing the flak-damaged bomb bay doors by straddling the open bay with only a screwdriver and pliers as the crippled plane was rapidly losing altitude and power during this mission, Dick was awarded the Distinguished Flying Cross.

* * *

LT. GENE JENSEN'S ACCOUNT OF MISSION #10

> As they went over the target they took several direct hits on the aircraft. In rapid succession they lost one engine and had an electrical fire in the cockpit which cut off most of the power system. They dropped the bombs, and then found that they could not get the bomb bay doors closed, a piece of flak (shell fragment) had severed the drive shaft for the door closure drive. Then they started to lose power on another engine. The flight engineer had controlled the cockpit fire, and Dick Ayesh, the bombardier, had finally gotten the bomb bay doors closed. In the process they had lost 12,000 feet, and were alone in the sky, easy prey for Nazi fighters. They also realized they had been flying on an unknown heading for some time. It was not the time or place to be lost! The navigator worked out a heading which he thought would take them in the general direction of England. They were essentially flying on two engines, and could maintain an airspeed just above landing speed. Fortunately, there was a total cloud cover, and they did not encounter German aircraft. They did have the company of a P-51 for a short time, but he could not fly as slow as they were

going and had to leave. Eventually, they spotted a hole in the clouds which allowed them to drop through the cloud layer. They were greeted by a welcome sight, a long line of trucks with the white star of the US Army on their roofs. They followed the trucks at an altitude of a few hundred feet, and soon saw an airfield directly ahead. They landed and rolled to a stop, no brakes. They had landed at a fighter field captured the previous day, and German tanks were still burning at the periphery of the field. There was a constant stream of C-47 cargo planes bringing in supplies. During the night the base was strafed and our B-17 destroyed! In a day or so we hitched a ride home on one of the cargo aircraft. We were a very lucky crew!

* * *

#11—Tuesday December 5, 1944

Mission—Berlin
Load—20-250# G.P.
Bomb Alt.—27,000ft

We were to bomb the Tegli Munitions and flak factory in the northwestern part of town. Night take off and assembly. Weather was 10/10 over the continent. Flak was moderate inaccurate. After bombs away fighters hit us and we got to witness a dogfight as our boys chased them off. Gonda, the navigator passed out from lack of oxygen. Ed and I worked on him for hours before he fully recovered. He had been out for 8 minutes. We were flying #2 in hi of the lead. Temperature was -45 degrees Centigrade.

* * *

#12—Tuesday Dec. 12, 1944

Mission—Darmstadt Marshalling Yd.

Load—10-500# G.P. and 2 M-17 Inc.
Bomb Alt.—27,000ft

This tgt. was 20 miles south of Frankfurt. The target area had 5/10 cloud cover but we got a visual run. A bad B missed the target. Flak was meagre. Other groups hit the target. We were #2 in Hi of High Sq. On return to England we found solid undercast and had to peel off and make an instru. descent. We broke out over a convoy and immediately a patrolling P-47 challenged us. We fired a few flares and that seemed to satisfy him and he left. We were coming in at 300' which blew the cowling off, so we feathered it and landed at the 95th(Horam). They interrogated us and after c-ration dinner we got a truck back here.

* * *

Commentary

The many potential hazards that B-17 crews faced upon returning to base in the crowded skies of East Anglia is made painfully clear by this account of Dick's pilot, Lt. Gene Jensen. "They had a defined course to follow when they returned to the base under instrument flying conditions. (Normally) at about 14, 000 feet over the English channel they would start a slow descent until they reached an elevation of about 1.000 feet when they would make a turn toward the Base to pick up the instrument landing system and which would guide them to the runway.

But there was a problem. There would be a thousand aircraft returning at about the same time, crews would be very tired, and in some cases aircraft would have damaged or (have) injured crew members (aboard). Midair collisions happened and near misses were common, giving some lack of confidence in the prescribed instrument landing procedure. Their aircraft had a radio altimeter that could read in 50-foot intervals. The pilot could set the altimeter to flash RED at 50 feet, and then make a cautious descent over the channel. Usually they would break out of the clouds at about 100 feet, (an elevation about equal to the wing span of the aircraft) and fly visual to the base.

On this flight when they broke out of the clouds they were headed directly for a British destroyer and below the level of their masts. Needless to say they retreated into the clouds."

Dick recalled another near miss when, as their B-17 was descending, a squadron of big black Lancaster bombers flew right through their formation, again illustrating how crowded and potentially hazardous the skies were over England.

Yes, fighters and flak were bad, but there were other things that took a dreadful toll of Allied planes. As many as one out of six aircraft lost were from non-enemy causes. Pilot and navigation error, take off and landing, weather, equipment failure, collision between planes in the crowded air space over England, excited gunners hitting friendly planes with machine gun fire in the heat of battle, planes being hit by bombs dropped from higher up in the formation, and just plain horseplay cost many lives.

A B-17 would stall below 100 mph. The pitch and frequency of a prop would tell if the engine was a runaway. The speed of an aircraft engine is determined both by the throttle and pitch of the propeller. The flatter the pitch, the less the load and the faster it will run. When an engine runs away, it is out of control and unless quickly corrected, it will disintegrate and may cause the plane to crash. The tell tale sign was a high pitch sound.

* * *

#13—Monday December 18, '44

Mission—Mainz Marshalling Yards
Load—18-250# G.P. and 2 M-17 Inc.
Bomb Alt.—28,000 ft

We were flying #2 in lead squadron. Clouds were up to 30,000 ft over the continent and we were in the soup all the way. We separated from the division because our H2X equipment went out. (We were unable to find the target.) We made a run on Coblenz but the "mickey" was still out so we brought the bombs home.

* * *

Commentary

The "Mickey" was the H2X airborne radar box. This mission on marshalling yards in Mainz, with its incendiary bombs, was intended to target Nazi troop concentrations and rolling stock in support of Hitler's Ardennes offensive.

* * *

PERILOUS LANDING ON AN ICY RUNWAY WITH A FULL BOMB LOAD

The return to base by Gene Jensen's crew after Mission #13 was aborted turned out to be a very close call. The mission was aborted but they were told to land with their full bomb load! They were also warned that the runway was covered with ice and snow and therefore very slippery. They flew for an hour to reduce their fuel load and hopefully land safely. Unfortunately, they had to land faster than is normally the case without the bomb load. Very quickly, they discovered they were in grave danger. The brakes were useless due to the ice cover, and in order to remain on the runway the engines had to be used, therefore preventing a deceleration.

By the time they reached the end of the runway their ground speed was still 100 mph. It was too late to try to take off again with the heavy bomb load on board. Co-pilot Jim Millet and pilot Gene Jensen pulled the main power switch which stopped the engines. As expected, in a few seconds the plane left the runway at an angle and came to an abrupt stop in the mud with the tail wheel still on the runway. But to make matters far worse, an earlier bomber had crashed into the base bomb dump and when their plane veered off the runway, the bombs were still going off. They were diving for cover each time one would explode![170]

17

LONDON ENCOUNTERS, ROMANTIC AND OTHERWISE

Few would argue that the well-known British description of American forces in the United Kingdom as "over-paid, over-sexed and over here" was probably well-founded. The young GIs were there as saviors and protectors of the Realm and were looked up to generally by the British populace. Inevitably, the stress and loneliness that wartime conditions brought both to the native population and the young GIs led to more and more romances, broken marriages, lovers' quarrels and jealous lovers that inevitably took their toll on the good will of the British public. Therefore, the initially very positive view of Americans quickly began to erode.

Indeed, as described by the American historian Donald Miller, in *Masters of the Air*, the impressions the British public had of Americans was characterized as boastful, materialistic, immature, loud, bombastic, bragging, self-righteous, arrogant, with a lack of courtesy and common decency.[171]

Dick's recollections, after 50-plus years blend and blur but several early encounters are etched in his memory. In his own words, "My recollections of England and the British are mostly very positive. One of the first things I saw on arriving was a two-wheeled cart pulled by a donkey with an elderly couple driving it. And I saw thatched roofs for the first time and remember their smell, musty and hay-like, the scent of something old and decaying.

"It just seemed backward in some ways compared to the States. A lot of the GIs looked down on the English but not me. I loved them but I couldn't understand them! It was not only the different accents I heard but also the different ways they said things, like instead of a car being in the garage or repair shop, it was in the 'works' or the trunk of a car was the 'boot.' I found them to be very courteous. My very first interaction in London was with a taxi driver in one of those little black taxis with a funny air horn. I told him to take me from Charing Cross Station to the Marble Arch, a 3 to 4 minute ride. When I asked him what I owed, he said 10 Schillings and 2 pence. He overcharged me!" There were many reported instances of unscrupulous behavior toward GIs by some British including taking advantage of them through pick pocketing and thievery.

Dick also recalled little rosy-cheeked English kids running up to me and asking cheerily "Any gum, chum? Any spam today, Sam?"

Although the threat from Luftwaffe bombing attacks on England was lessened greatly when Allied air supremacy was established in Western Europe by the time of Dick's tour (see however Dick's diary entry of 4 March, 1945), the threat posed by V-1 Buzz Bombs and V-2 rocket attacks was at its peak and the fears of the British public were greatly heightened. Adding to the hysteria was the real possibility of even more "miracle weapons" unleashed by Hitler.

As if all of the other stresses and sacrifices of war experienced by the British public were not enough, the year 1944-45 saw the terror of German missiles raining down on England beginning with the V-1 flying bomb or buzz bomb. The V-1 ("Vergeltungswaffe 1" or Vengeance Weapon 1) was really the world's first cruise missile. It had a total weight was 4,806-lbs and could carry a 1,874-lb warhead over a distance of 222 miles. Launched from ski-like rails, its thrust gave the missile a speed of 290 to 400 mph. The trajectory was controlled by an automatic gyroscope compass. Between the first V-1 strike against London on June 13th 1944 and the last V-1 attacks on March 29th 1945, a total of 9,251 V-1 were launched against England with 2,419 V-1s striking London. Because of its relatively slow speed, the V-1 could either be shot down by anti-aircraft fire, shot down by RAF fighters or bumped off course by the fighters, causing it to lose gyroscopic control and crash. Nearly 4000 V-1s were either shot down by ground fire, RAF fighters or knocked off course while about 300 were snagged in the cables of barrage balloons.[172]

The V-1's range was pre-set inside the bomb before it was

launched. A tiny propeller in its nose was attached to a counter. Through this link, every 30 rotations of the propeller would count down one number on the counter. When the pre-set counter reached zero, the buzz bomb was considered to be at its target. The engine would cut off as the air hose from the servo mechanism to the rear elevator was automatically cut. This activated a spring mechanism that would force down the elevators, and the V-1 would begin a steep dive. The well-known, terrifying silence when the buzzing sound of the motor stopped was interrupted by a massive explosion.

At the time of the V-1 attacks, Tom Oakley, now a retiree in Brockdish, East Anglia, was a young civil defense gunner in London who described the times vividly. On one occasion, he recalled "I was on duty one night (manning anti -a/c rocket guns) in our local park when I witnessed a string of V-1's following each other like a convoy of London buses. On another occasion (of a V-1 attack), I took a flying leap into a slit trench waiting for the bang" !!!

The V-2 ("Vergeltungswaffe Zwei") was another name for the German long distance rocket A-4 ("Aggregat 4"), a liquid fuel rocket 46 feet long. The V-2 was the immediate ancestor of all launch vehicles and space rockets which followed. Unlike the slow, vulnerable V-1, the V-2 was unstoppable due to its highly supersonic speed (3,378 mph) descending from a peak altitude of 58 miles (97 km) high up in the stratosphere to impact on the ground at a speed of ~ 1,780 mph. The only way to destroy the V-2 was to take out its launch pads. Between the first V-2 strike on London on September 8, 1944 and the last on March 27, 1945, a total 1,358 V-2s struck the city and its surrounding suburbs.[173]

The first V-2s were guided by a radio direction beam for about a minute after launch but the vast majority had no radio guidance. The maximum operating range was 199 miles which was later extended to 236 miles. The V-2 packed a high explosive warhead of 2,150-lb. Even without a warhead, the impact of the rocket itself caused a crater approx. 42 feet deep and 118 feet in diameter.

The V-2 was all the more terrifying since due to its supersonic descent, it was both silent and invisible until impact when the immense blast crater was formed. The destructive power would have been even greater if, instead of penetrating into the ground, the V-2 exploded above the ground through the use of proximity fuses.

The pressure from the British public to eliminate the German rocket threats led to controversy between British leaders and Carl Spaatz over the diversion of USSTAF resources from strategic bombing missions to the newly launched operation CROSSBOW which was a concentrated effort to destroy the launch sites. This ongoing battle pitted Air Chief Tedder and other British commanders and Spaatz who considered his highest priority to destroy transport and oil targets. General Eisenhower finally gave his support to General Spaatz's position that Operation POINTBLANK should have priority over CROSSBOW and that RAF assets should be used in CROSSBOW.[174]

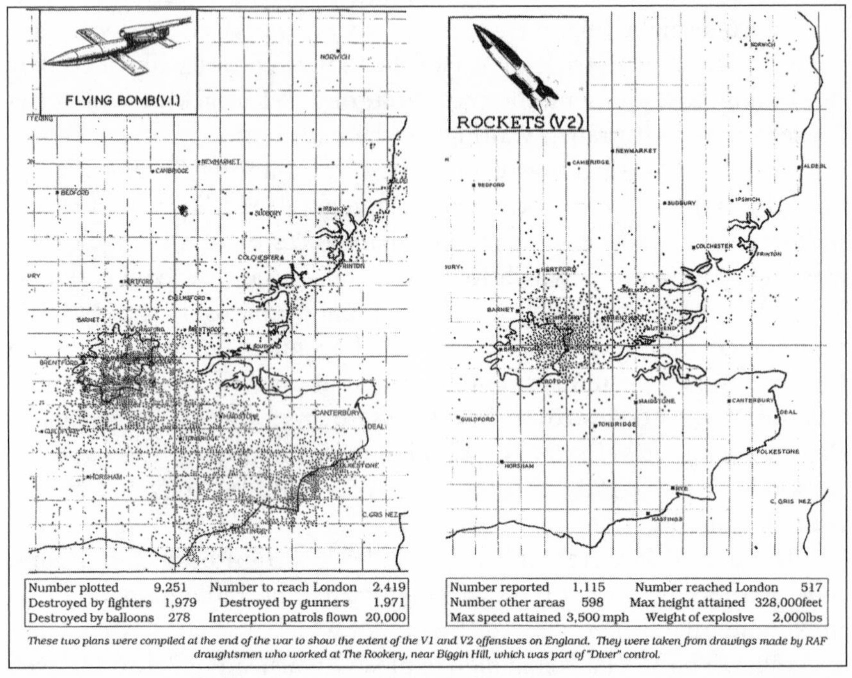

Diagram showing locations of V-1 and V-2 strikes in the United Kingdom. (From *Doodle Bugs and Rockets* by Robert Ogley, 1987, courtesy of Froglet Publishing)

"During one of my passes spent in London," Dick recalled, "I saw the immediate aftermath of a V-2 rocket attack. Unlike the V-1 Buzz

Bombs, you had little warning of a V-2 strike. I saw the damage just after one hit near Selfridges Department Store, which knocked out all of the windows and I remembered the ground shook. I heard two thunderous sounds, one from the impact and the other from the air it displaced, rushing back together after being displaced by its supersonic descent. I went to see the crater which was three stories deep."

Dick recalled, "The English women were beautiful, and lucky for me, they really latched onto officers because they had money. A British Major did not make as much money as a GI sergeant so the British girls tended to want to go with GI officers because they had all the money and could take them shopping."

The ease with which USAAC personnel could meet and have liaisons with British women was the stuff of legend and has been portrayed in several movies like Yank, The Americanization of Emily, Hanover Street, Homefront, etc. There was love and sex everywhere in a country in which most everyone was stressed and lonely, soldiers and civilians alike. Let's face it, the British were stressed too with stringent rationing, German bombing, uncertainty, loved ones away, and fear and apprehension of what the future might hold. British women were lonely for their boyfriends, lovers and husbands, while the Americans, even married ones, indulged in romance, however fleeting and impermanent. Sex was available nearly everywhere, whether the opportunity was free or not. Prostitution was rampant and love encounters occurred even on trains. As Dick recalls, "A lot of things were going on between the cars, especially in the tunnels." Hell, they're all young kids. It was a fun time. Many encounters took place in famous spots like Hyde Park and of course in Piccadilly Circus. You could stand in Piccadilly Circus and just hear people walking but not see anything during the blackout. During blackouts, hookers (known affectionately to many as Piccadilly Commandos) would walk up to you, shine a flashlight under your chin and ask you to make love. If you turned them down, the usual reply would be "So Yank, you think you're better than we are!"

Most everyone knew that the "going rate" varied according to when during a month an encounter took place. Around the first of a given month, the rate was ten pounds because the GIs were paid then. By the middle of the month, the rate was down to five pounds because the servicemen had already spent much of their money, while by the end of the month they were usually broke and the rate was whatever the girls could get.

In 1943, there was an epidemic of venereal disease with a 25 percent higher rate of contraction for GIs in England than at home. Half of these cases were contracted in Piccadilly.[175] Dick saw prophylactic stations on nearly every corner and a curious difference in attitude toward bodily functions, including public toilets with only a divider separating men and women and a common trough carrying the sewage. He soon realized that their attitude toward sex and bodily functions was sure different from in the States. But then their culture is centuries older than ours.

"Of course, the official Army line was for us to avoid such encounters," recalled Dick. "I always recalled a big Irish priest in our class at Air Cadet training in Santa Ana, California who once told us, 'Look at me! I've never had a woman and I could whip anyone of you in this squadron!'"

The Eighth Air Force command recognized that the extreme stress of daily combat missions made it necessary for airmen to have rest and relaxation away from the bomber base. While airmen were allowed to visit local villages if no mission was scheduled, they would also receive a three-day pass once a month. During the middle portion of their 25- or 35-mission tours, they were sent to specific places. They did visit the local villages, but most everyone went into London, a short ride by train, on each of their regular passes. "There was not only an abundance of women and good times but also private clubs and choice places for food and relaxation, like the Reindeer Club and Hotel run by the Red Cross, and Grosvenor House which was strictly for officers. You could get good American food there. The Picadilly Hotel was terrific but it was so crowded, sometimes you could not get in. At Selfridges department store, every other week, they had 'ice' (ice cream) which was not available everyday. Lunch at Selfridges featured beans on toast which I really came to like."

Dick recalled one small restaurant on Fleet Street that featured "steak smothered in onions" that turned out to be horsemeat. At the Mayfair Hotel, a good dinner consisted of chunks of mutton, a small boiled potato and small cooked carrots. In his words, "One of my favorite places for entertainment was the old Windmill Theater which was open all night and I believe still is. They had beautiful girls, great live productions (mostly girly shows) and theatrical acts." This legendary destination for servicemen was featured recently in the movie "Mrs. Henderson Presents," starring Judi Dench and Bob Hoskins.

"The ultimate R&R for an Eighth officer was a "Flak House" and mine was Eynsham Hall, a beautiful English Country Manor near Oxford with its huge fireplaces (you could stand up inside of them) like in Robin Hood movies, silk wallpaper, Fleur de Lis emblems all over, and the feel of a typical castle but without turrets, with nearly every interior structure made of oak. The food was good, we had private rooms and we did not have to get up early in the morning. We'd be awakened by girls each morning serving us orange juice. I remember one of them remarking as I got out of bed, 'My you sure have a lot of hair on your legs!' We were served all meals in a beautiful dining room. Usually there were 50-75 officers there at one time."

Although he would deny it, Dick's frequent liaisons were in no small part due to his good looks and a certain presence that women found alluring, as well as his officer status. "There was a young lady named Valerie W. who I saw as often as I could, four or five times total. I met her when I boarded a train to London, taking a seat in a compartment where a young, blue-eyed well-dressed woman was seated. I approached her, we conversed and she wrote her name and phone number on a piece of paper and told me to call her the next time I was in London. I took her shopping a time or two and on our third date I met her Mom and had dinner with them. Her Mom had used their canned cherry ration to make some cherry tarts for dinner. Valerie's knowledge of aviation was pretty minimal. She had heard our group had lost many bombers on a recent mission and told me how scared she was when she thought she saw my plane returning 'with one of the fans not turning!' I know its going to sound incredible but we actually never did anything."

He continued, "But usually, the encounters with women were shorter. You got to remember that many of their people were gone too and they were lonesome. I remembered riding on a bus in a seat behind a British woman. I noticed she had a little splattered mud on the back of her stockings and so told her about it. She turned to me and said, 'You Yanks sure work fast.'" What happened at her flat, four bus stops later is better left to the reader's imagination.

"I remember once I stopped in a pub for a quick beer. An older, well-dressed woman at a nearby table said, 'Yank come over here. Let me buy you a drink.' She just wanted to talk to me. I guess she was just lonely. Another young woman who lived in Diss in one of the old thatched roof houses did my laundry and made a scarf with my initials, RRA, on it, out of a parachute."

"I think my most amazing encounter in London happened on my first three-day pass. I stayed at the Reindeer Club which was run by Red Cross girls. I was going about town clubbing and happened to notice a stairway leading to a club below the street level. I went downstairs, pushed aside the blackout curtain and heard someone yell 'Dickie boy!' How do you figure out of a city of eight million people, I would run into a childhood buddy, Lt. George Cohlmia, a navigator who sold newspapers with me, gambled with me and used to lag pennies against the wall of the Lassen Hotel in Wichita. I met George the next afternoon at the Piccadilly Hotel which had a glass encased restaurant within the lobby.

"George and I were having a drink (tea and crumpets) when a sergeant with a long winter coat entered the hotel and said there's a woman asking for you outside. He was looking at me. I told him he must mean my friend George because I had just arrived in London and didn't know anyone. He went back outside, then returned and said, 'Lieutenant, no, it's you she wants.' I had her come in. She was a shapely brunette with long hair, blue eyes, about 5'5 or 5'6 and said her name was Bunny.

" She said she had not eaten and was hungry. During the course of this encounter, she told me that in exchange for paying her rent every month, she would do anything I want, anytime I want. Her rent was 7 pounds per month. So I saw her at her 2nd story flat as often as I could, maybe 4 to 5 times. Her flat was heated by a small gas stove that you would have to feed with a 'thru-pence' (three pence) in order for it to work. So the first thing I would do when I came over was feed it."

18

MISSION-BY-MISSION (II): From the Battle of the Bulge to Berlin and Dresden

In December 1944 Adolf Hitler directed an ambitious counteroffensive with the object of regaining the initiative in the West and compelling the Allies to settle for a negotiated peace. Hitler's generals were opposed to the plan, on the grounds that Germany then lacked the resources to sustain a major offensive, but the Fuhrer's will prevailed. The counteroffensive was launched on 16 December by some 30 German divisions against the American front in the Ardennes region. This had been considered a quiet sector used to acclimate new divisions or rest ones that had been battered by previous fighting along the Westwall. Hitler's intention was to break through the front and then drive through Liege to Antwerp in order to cut off and annihilate the British 21st Army Group and the US First and Ninth Armies north of the Ardennes.

Aided by stormy weather which grounded Allied planes and restricted observation, as well as a degree of Allied overconfidence and overreliance on ULTRA, the Germans achieved surprise. They at first made rapid gains, but firm resistance by various isolated American units bought time for the US First and Ninth Armies to shift against the northern flank of the penetration, for the British to send reserves to secure the line of the Meuse River, and for Patton's Third Army to hit the salient from the south. Denied vital roads and hampered by lack of gasoline, the German attack resulted only in a large bulge in the Allied front which barely touched (and then only on one day by reconnaissance units) the Meuse, their first objective.

For the first week of their attack the Germans did have the advantage of dense cloud cover that grounded the Allied air forces. It was not until Christmas Eve that the skies cleared and aircraft engines roared to life on scores of Allied bomber and fighter bases. For Dick, it would be his fourteenth mission.

* * *

#14—Sunday, December 24, '44

Mission—Biblis Airfield
Load—36-100# G.P.
Bomb Alt.—24,000ft

For the past 6 days we have been grounded because bad weather. Meanwhile the Germans have started a push thru the Ardennes Forest into Luxembourg and Belgium. They are threatening Liege. Without air support, we cannot stop them. Today, every aircraft that can get in the air is flying. Our route in took us directly over the German salient where we encountered heavy accurate flak. "Bandits" were reported in the area. It is very clear, visibility is excellent. I saw a B-17 in the group ahead of us get a direct hit and saw him tumble down out of formation. He was breaking up and I could see his wing and tail come off. I didn't see any chutes. I saw another one fall out of formation and spin down. I followed him down and saw him explode right next to a small town. A single chute came floating down beside the wreckage. Another Fort got a hit and disintegrated. A B-26 came by smoking badly and a few seconds later he burst into flames as he tried to crash land. Immediately after E/A were reported in the area, I saw 4 balls of fire in one place and 3 in another which were flaming fighters. I hope they were Jerry fighters. We found our airfield and trained the bombs right across it. Our objective was to hit these fields the Nazi were using to base their fighter support for their push. Flak was everywhere. We could see many groups obliterate small towns and fighter bombers blasting road and rail junctions. When we arrived back at the base it was dark and everywhere we could see ships circling with their lights on. I learned later that there had been a string of bombers 400 miles long going out to hit the Germans. The 100th group had 62 planes out today. We flew #2 of low element of low square. When we landed the fog was thick and a few planes ran off the runway. This caused a congestion which was dangerous for the boys landing.

* * *

Commentary

Often when the fog was so thick that it obscured the runway, the crews would take B-17s and line them up on one side of the runway with engines going to disperse the fog and clear the runway.

Dick recalled the mood at Thorpe Abbotts when word of the German counter-offensive arrived. "They took all of our ground people—cooks, mail clerks and all other non-essential personnel at the Base were taken. Only armorers and crew support were left. This looked bad. This could really prolong the war. Everyone had a sense that things were going to get bad, especially if the Germans got into Antwerp. We all had the same reaction. It was like protecting your star player on a basketball team. You protect him. Everything that could be sent was sent. We wanted to go over and help the guys there in any way we could. That's the way we felt. When the weather lifted, we saw the devastation of the counter-offensive."

* * *

#15—Christmas Day, Dec. 25, '44

Mission—Kaiserslautern M/Y
Load—10-500# G.P. and 2-M-17 Inc.
Bomb Alt.—24,000 ft.

We were leading the Division and #2 in the low of the low sq.

We went around the front line flak. The weather was CAVU. Germany was covered with snow and we could see the results of the bombing the day before. Many little towns were wiped out. In many places, we could see where battles had been fought leaving prints in the snow. Flak at the target was accurate and intense. We hit the target beautifully. It was noon when we hit this town, probably just as they sat down for their Christmas dinner. When we returned to the base fog was covering the runway half so we had to wait for it to move on. Finally we could just barely make out the runway, so we all came in. We found a delicious Christmas dinner waiting for us and later in the evening we had drinks in the barracks. When we took off this morning England was covered with frost and ice and was very peaceful looking—truly a Christmas setting.

* * *

Commentary

The intervention of Allied air power in the Battle of the Bulge was devastating to the Germans. Due to the limited road network in the Ardennes, entire German convoys were caught while stalled in huge traffic jams without cover. Because of the freezing cold, enemy infantry tended to congregate in towns, which were more easily identifiable from the air than field positions.

Part of this great air effort involved a large supply drop at the town of Bastogne, where the 101st Airborne and other American units had been surrounded by elements of several German divisions. Between the resupply of US forces and the devastation of the road network, leaving forward German units starved of fuel and ammunition, the air attacks were pivotal to the outcome of the battle.

At this Christmas, Dick received a most touching letter from his first wife, Mary Kay, which truly expresses in a universal way the feelings shared by loved ones of American troops everywhere, including those troops who, at this Christmas, were in a desperate struggle in the Battle of the Bulge. Mary Kay's letter to Dick is repeated here.

WRITTEN FOR CHRISTMAS—1944

To my husband—somewhere on foreign soil:

This is a Christmas letter to you dear. I hope you will read it Christmas day, so you may feel that I am close to you on this first Christmas that we have been apart.

It's written to thank you for all the other Christmas days that I have had as your wife.

To remind you of our last Christmas in a lonely little town in Arizona, a beautiful Christmas eve when the stars were so clear and bright you could imagine the wonder the Shepherds must have felt when they first saw the Star in the East. And then to take you back still farther to the Christmas before when we were together for the last time in our own place. And still further yet to the one before when we spent the day at your folks house. Count them and add this one, you'll find they make four, think of them now when we are far apart. Physically that is, for in our hearts and minds we are perhaps even closer than we were in those other happier years.

And now will you go with me into the future of next Christmas when we shall be together again; and all the horrid dark days that have passed in the meantime will have faded away like an ugly memory, and the world will be beautiful again. You will know that every little house and each elegant castle the world over owes it's right to Christmas to you and the thousands of others like you who have given up so much to make it so. To make it a decent place for us and all the others like us to raise our children in, and share with them the joys of many a heart warming Christmas to come. You will know you have brought Christmas to boys and girls the world over who have never known one yet, children who were born in a bomb shelter, and have lived in hunger and want and fear ever since. You can know that we shall have peace "In our time". Our time being all the years of fullest living which are before us.

If you will think these thoughts with me, then you can be proud of where you are this Christmas day, no matter where you may be.

There are those who will try to tell you that you have been forced to go to war for political reasons; that you have been sent to another country to fight a war that is not yours; that when some capitalist has made enough, it will be over. But never believe them. You are fighting this war for all humanity; for all who believe in the decency of human relationships; for every man who had a home, a family and a wife he loved and had to tell them goodbye. You are not fighting to make some politician greater, you are fighting for goodness and kindness, without which we are all better off dead.

I wish you could know the joy and pride there is for me in being able to say that my husband is helping to bring hope to the world. So Chin up darling, my very greatest hopes and prayers go with you and all who fly with you. Truly God himself must look with great favor upon you and your kind.

"Mary" Christmas

* * *

#16—Tuesday Dec. 28, 1944

Mission—Coblenz M/Y
Load—20-250# G.P.
Bomb Alt.—26,000ft

The primary target was a road junction in the small village of Luneback but the target was covered by a 10/10 layer of clouds, therefore we bombed Coblenz. Due to solid undercast we bombed by H2X. The flak was low and moderate. Our route in took us right over our supposed drive into Bastogne to relieve the forces holding out there.

* * *

#17—Friday, Dec. 29, 1944

Mission—Frankfurt M/Y
Load—20-250# G.P.
Bomb Alt.—25,000ft

Plan A was the Leuna syn oil plant at Merseburg but it was scrubbed enroute, so we proceeded to Frankfurt. Weather was a broken undercast until we reached the Frankfurt area then it was CAVU. We drove past Frankfurt then turned around and made the bomb run. We could pick out the target the first time we passed the town. The flak was heavy and very accurate. All three squadrons hit the MPI perfectly. It was a superb job of precision pin point bombing. Just after bombs away, Furrer got a hit in #1 engine and started a fire. Most of his crew bailed out but he brought his ship back after the fire had gone out. This was his navigator's last mission. He is now a POW. We lead the 8th air force over the target.

* * *

#18—Saturday, Dec. 30, '44

Mission—Kassel M/Y
Load—12-500# G.P.
Bomb Alt.—24,000ft

It was 10/10 undercast all the way. The flak was heavy but inaccurate. Sunday Dec. 31, '44 On this day the 349th had a stand down and the group went to Hamburg. They met terrific flak and fighters hit them for 15 minutes after they had dropped their bombs. 6 Forts were lost to flak (including our own war weary) and the rest were lost to fighters. We had 15 ships out of the whole group which were able to fly the next day. Gomer, a fellow graduate from Deming went down and is a prisoner of war. I heard Charlie Donoua also a POW.

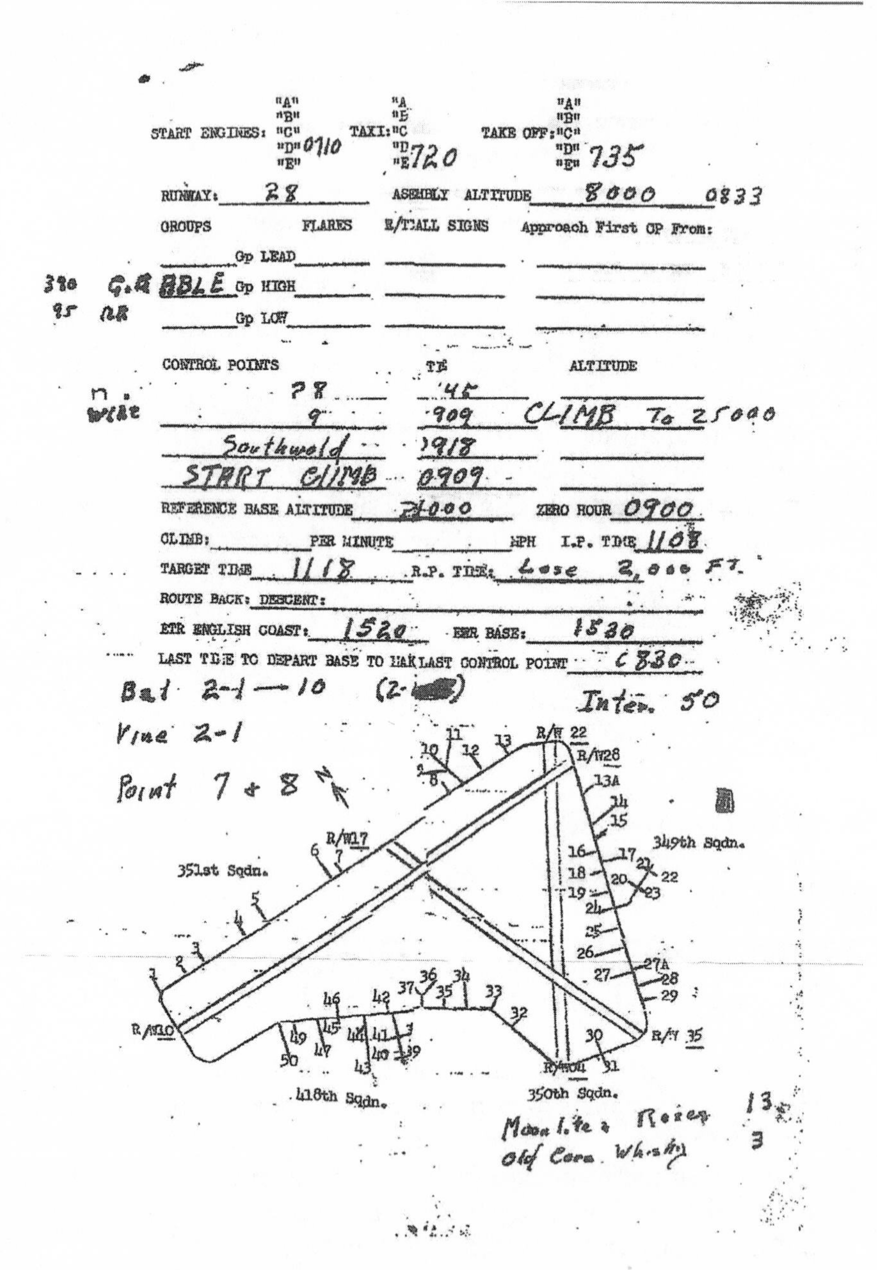

START ENGINES: "A" "B" "C" "D" 0710 "E"   TAXI: "A "B "C "D "E 720   TAKE OFF: "A" "B" "C" "D" "E" 735

RUNWAY: 28   ASEMBLY ALTITUDE 8000 0833

GROUPS   FLARES   E/TAIL SIGNS   Approach First CP From:

Gp LEAD

390 G.R. BBLE Gp HIGH

95 RR Gp LOW

CONTROL POINTS   TE   ALTITUDE

78   '45

9   909   CLIMB To 25000

Southwold   1918

START CLIMB   0909

REFERENCE BASE ALTITUDE 21000   ZERO HOUR 0900

CLIMB: PER MINUTE MPH   I.P. TIME 1108

TARGET TIME 1118   R.P. TIME: Lose 2,000 FT.

ROUTE BACK: DESCENT:

ETR ENGLISH COAST: 1520   ETR BASE: 1530

LAST TIME TO DEPART BASE TO MAK LAST CONTROL POINT C830

Bal 2-1 — 10 (2-)   Inter. 50

Vine 2-1

Point 7 & 8 N

Moon lite & Roses 13
Old Corn Whisky 3

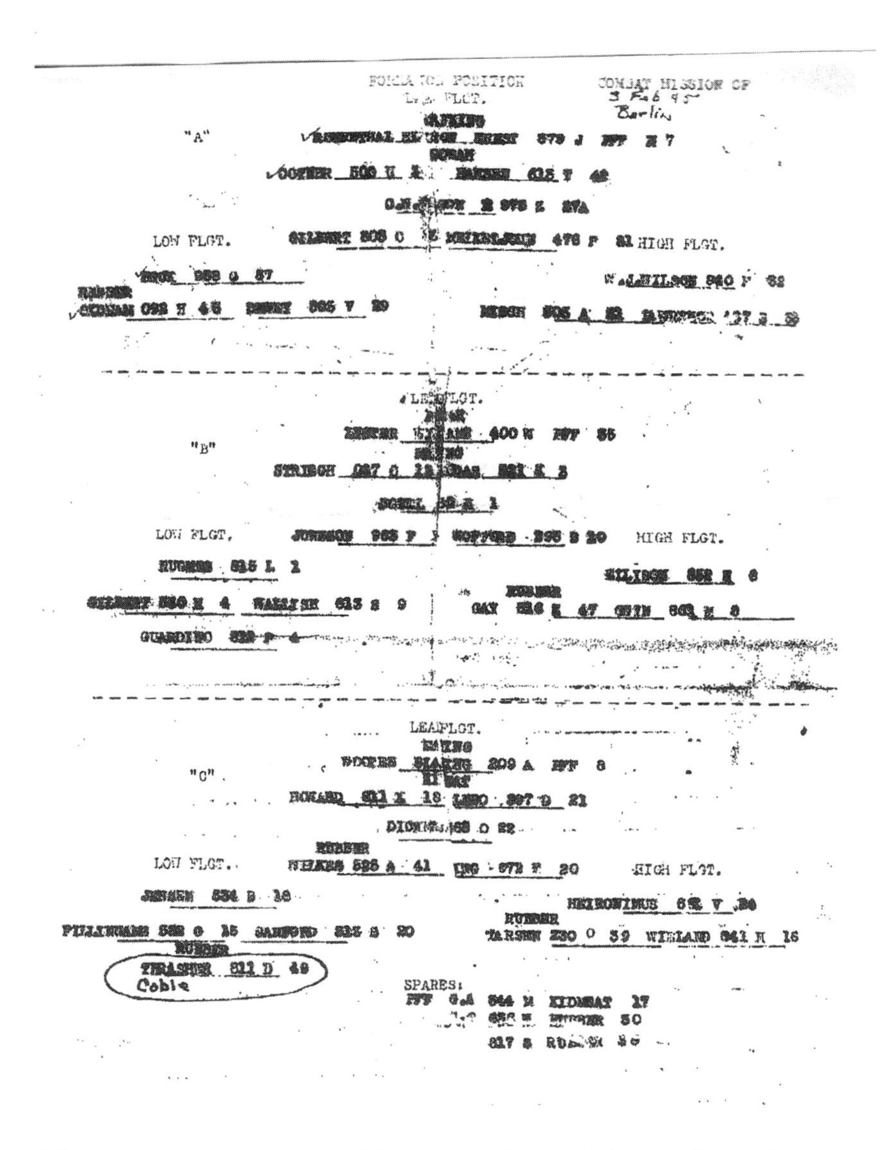

COMBAT MISSION OF
3 Feb 45
Berlin

"A"

LOW FLGT. GILBERT 808 C [illegible] 478 F 81 HIGH FLGT.

DENNY 865 V 10

"B"

LEAD FLGT.

STRIBOH 087 C 18 [illegible]

LOW FLGT. JOHNSON 983 F [illegible] 20 HIGH FLGT.

HUGHES 815 L 2

WILSON 852 [illegible] 6

WALLISH 613 [illegible] 9

GAY [illegible] 47

GUARDINO [illegible]

"C"

LEAD FLGT.

WOOPES [illegible] 209 A [illegible] 8

HOWARD 831 X 18 [illegible] 307 D 21

LOW FLGT. WEAKES 528 A 41 [illegible] 20 HIGH FLGT.

JENSEN 534 B 18

HEIRONIMUS [illegible] V [illegible]

SANFORD [illegible] 20

WIELAND 841 [illegible] 16

THRASHER 811 D 49
Coble

SPARES:
[illegible] 844 M KIDMEAT 17
[illegible] 50
817 S [illegible]

This page and facing: Actual formation sheets of the 100th Bomb Group for the Berlin mission of February 3, 1945. (Courtesy of Jack O'Leary, 100th Bomb Group Memorial Foundation)

* * *

#19—Wednesday, Jan. 3, 1945

Mission—Fulda M/Y
Load—14-300# G.P. and 2 M-17 Incendiaries
Bomb Alt.—21,000ft

The mission was uneventful in that we had a solid undercast and the fighter support was good. Bombed by instruments. We flew #3 in the low element of the low Sq. Route in was down thru the southern part of Germany, then up to target paralleling the front lines. Took off at 0700 and landed at 1600.

* * *

Commentary

By now the German advance in the Ardennes had been halted, and the Luftwaffe had furthermore lost hundreds of its remaining fighter aircraft in a surprise attack on Allied tactical airfields, called Operation Bodenplatte, on New Year's Day.

* * *

#20—Saturday, Jan. 13, 1945

Mission—Mainz-Railroad Bridge
Load—5-1000# G.P.
Bomb Alt.—26,000ft.

We were leading the low element of the High Squadron. Route in was south towards Switzerland then west to target. I believe we missed the bridge. Visual to target then patchy into the target area. The flak was moderate inaccurate. The temperature at flight altitude was -53 degrees Cent. We took off at 0800 and landed at 1500. We came in on the deck at 300 ft.

* * *

#21—Sunday, Jan. 14, 1945

Mission—Derben(undergroud oil storage depot).
Load—6-1000# G.P. RDX
Bomb Alt.—26,000ft

We were leading the low element of the lead squadron. Our route in was over the North Sea—thru the corrider by Cruxhaven—fly to the outskirts of Berlin as an IP—then turn and bomb on a 270 degree heading. Route was by Hanover and Osnabruck. The 13th Combat Wing was leading the division with 95th Group in the lead; 100th Group was second; 390th group was last. Just 3 groups were to bomb this target. We met our escorts (16 P-51s) just after we passed Heligoland. All of Northern Germany was visual. We could see smoke screens around all the big cities around there. Also saw some barrage balloons. As we passed over the Kiel Canal a barge shot flak at us. Observed many German boats scurrying from the harbors in the sea. As we turned and headed for our IP at Berlin we could see many contrails ahead and we knew the Jerry fighters were waiting for us. Our 6 fighters formed in front of us. The E/A came in from 12 o'clock high out of the sun--diving in about 10 abreast. There were about 75 of them. Our escort broke up the company front attack causing the E/A to scatter and make only single attacks on the 95th. After the initial pass at the 95th the E/A passed around us and hit the 390th which was lagging about 5 miles behind. The Jerries shot down the whole low squadron. A lone FW 190 made a pass at us but he pulled up in front of us showing his armored belly. A P-51 shot him down as he stalled there. A terrific dogfight was ensuing and Forts and fighters were going down all over. We hit the target causing huge billowy black smoke to rise to about 10,000 ft. We made the RP at Stendal and headed for home. No flak at the target. As we passed near Osnabruck, I noticed 2 enemy fighters taking off from a field.

I think our escort got them later. Take off at 0730 and landed at 1530.

* * *

#22—February 3, 1945

Mission—Berlin(a building in the center of town.)
Load—10-500# G.P. RDX
Bomb Alt.—26,000ft

Flying lead of the low element in the Low Sq. and leading the 3rd Division. The 1st Div. was to precede us over the tgt. We had been briefed for this target the past 3 mornings but they were scrubbed. The original ship we had this morning cut out on the mags so we changed ships and met the formation just as they departed the English coast. Bandits in the area around Dummer Lake. Flak at the target was accurate and very intense. The target area was visual. About 3 minutes from the bomb release line, 2 ships blew up by a direct burst. All I saw of one was four flaming gas tanks and heavy black smoke. The other went into a spin. It was flaming and later a wing came off. Saw another one get hit and go down on fire. One of our ships in the sq. on our left got hit and was on fire. It pulled up 500ft above the formation then peeled off and headed directly for us. We dived to try to get away from it and it went past us, upside down, just missing us a few feet. Maj. Rosenthal's ship (he was leading the group) began to smoke but he stayed until bombs away then pulled over to our right and 5 guys bailed out. Then it went into a spin. We lost ships out of the group. We bombed in group formation and laid our bombs in the vicinity of Templehof. The city was flaming from the 1st div. attack.

If we got into trouble we were supposed to go to Russian lines. We had a 315 mile per hour ground speed and the lines were just 35 miles away. Learned later that Maj.Rosenthal and 4 others were safe with the Russians and they are coming back here. Take off at 0800 and landed at 1545

* * *

Commentary

This mission to Berlin was a smaller scale version of what was originally intended as a massive Berlin city bombing known as Operation Thunderclap. Intended to totally disrupt communications and inflict 100,000 casualties, it was a concept pushed by Portal and the RAF Bomber Command but rejected by General Spaatz and the Americans because of the massive civilian casualties it would have caused. As it turned out, this raid inflicted roughly 5,000 civilian casualties, far less than the tens of thousands of civilians who would have been killed had the original conception of Operation Thunderclap been implemented.

* * *

#23—February 9, 1945

Mission—Bolin Syn. Oil (visual) Weimer (H2X)
Load—10-500# G.P. RDX
Bomb Alt.—27,000ft
Unable to bomb the primary because of clouds so we bombed an armament factory at Weimar. No flak at the target but plenty in the area. We hit the target. On the way in a lone ME 262 jet plane flew alongside then crossed over us and disappeared in the clouds with P-51's after him. It had a green top and grey bottom with a red nose. Took off at 0800 and landed at 1600.

* * *

#24—Valentine's Day, Feb. 14, 1945

Mission—Chemnitz M/Y
Load—10-500# G.P. RDX
Bomb Alt.—23,000 ft

We were striking in direct support of the Russian armies in

> their drive to Central Germany. Route weather was patchy low clouds and clear with a layer of Cirrus at 20,000 ft. Bandits were reported in the area around Leipzig. On the bomb run the contrails were very dense and persistent making formation flying a problem. Another squadron of planes had evidently turned too early because they came right through our formation. It is a wonder we did not lose a lot of planes. We bombed PFF. Route was over Z.Z. to Leipzig to tgt then out south by Frankfurt. Got front line flak at Prum. The group ahead of us lost two ships here.

* * *

Commentary

Chemnitz was a city of approximately 400,000 people roughly 40 miles southwest of Dresden. It was the industrial center of Saxony with heavy industry and armaments plants and production facilities. It was particularly a center for making tanks and tank engines such as the Siegmar Plant. The city was known as the "Manchester of Saxony." It would serve as the principal source of supplies for German military opposition to the approaching Soviet armies. However, the city was also, like Dresden, flooded with refugees who fled from the eastern territories now overrun by the Soviet forces. Many of the refugees had just fled from the bombing of Dresden the day before. The city was well-defended with 678 flak batteries and Luftwaffe bases ringing it.[176]

This daylight attack by the 3rd Division was intended to soften up the defenses and destroy as much as possible in preparation for the nighttime raids of RAF Bomber Command. The raid was also intended to disrupt evacuation from the Eastern Front and hinder or help prevent German reinforcements from moving east to fight the Russians. The 3rd Division bombed by H2X but only two-thirds of the 441 B-17s located the target. The remainder of the bombers hit secondary targets including Bamberg in northern Bavaria. In all, Chemnitz was relatively undamaged.

* * *

CLOSE CALL ON THE WAY TO CHEMNITZ

Pilot Gene Jensen's account of a near miss collision between two entire squadrons on Mission #25 to Chemnitz.

> For a half hour the RAF Lanc's had been roaring over; It sounded especially nice to me because I thought it was our mission taking off. Then the inevitable happened and the lights snapped on. Sgt. Miner came in to wake up the crews. "breakfast now (0315), briefing at 0415. "Yes, Lt. Jensen, you're flying 608, leading the sec. element, lead flight. Breakfast was satisfying. I had fresh eggs, cereal, fruit juice and a couple of slices of nice warm toast and plenty of butter. Then to briefing. My God. Its almost to the Russian lines. Chemnitz to be exact.
>
> Take off time, weather, flight cover, take off order, radio call signs. A little talk by Col. Sutherlin to the first pilots...
>
> Take notes and then we're off. Check out our flying gear, joke with "Jimmy": in the equipment room. Take your time dressing, we've got over two hours to start engines. Finally 3 or 4 of us ride out in the trucks. Check the oxygen pressure; need plenty today; no loose brackets in the turbos, no cuts in the tires. Really no need to check it. We've an "On the ball ground crew."
>
> Just makes me feel better... Hell, we've got an hour delay. Everyone is asleep in the tent, 15 minutes before start engines, get dressed and wind her up.
>
> Good take off. Dick (Ayesh) flies it until we are assembled and then J.J. (Millet) and I take over for the long haul, in and back. Uneventful going in. Lot of clouds and we have to fly thru 'em. 25 missions have helped a lot and clouds aren't our primary worry. Hell, we're at the I.P., bomb bay doors come open and we fan out. We're leading 2nd element so we slide over to the left and J.J.(Millet) flies it cause he can see better, a solid cloud bank lies ahead of us. hope we won't have to fly into that. Yes, there goes the group ahead of us into it.

This will be plenty rough. Now we're in it, My God! There's a group coming straight at us(!). Guess we'll clear but that group ahead of us will have it close. And then we hit it, a solid wall of "propwash" from 13 forts ahead of us. Full controls have almost no effect. The formation scatters all over the sky. By "bombs away" we're almost back in formation but then turn to the right to the rally point and we can't quite make the formation so we swing in behind the form(ation). First time in our history a whole element has traded "spots." Call up Johnny for an ETA on France. Almost 2 hours... Oh my poor ... Soooo we drive on and on and on, Its more or less visual now and we're almost to the front lines before we hit a flak area. So for about 10 minutes we do evasive action and no hits are scored in our squadron. A Fort spins down out of the formation ahead of us and then we're over the lines and its strictly driving home.

Let down to 1500 ft. and fly home, J.J. (Millet) brings it in to a very uneventful landing. 8:30 minutes and I'm in no mood at all to sit anymore...10 more to go...over and out.

In the approach to the IP the three units were in their proper order. Apparently Element Two missed the turn at the Initial Point, and then made a long sweeping turn arriving over the target area at the same time as Element Three. After reassembly the order of the three units had changed from One-Two-Three to One-Three-Two. It was a very dangerous maneuver on part of the Lead Pilot in Element Two, and could have led to the loss of many aircraft. Air Crews were very unhappy with the Command pilot in Element Two. I have no information on what disciplinary actions, if any, were taken against the Element Commander!

* * *

#25—February 15, 1945

Mission—Cottbus M/Y
Load—10-500# G.P. RDX

Bomb Alt.—23,000ft

The synthetic oil plant at Rhuland was the visual target but we encountered a solid layer of clouds so we bombed the city of Cottbus, just 10 miles from the Russian lines. We made a run on Rhuland anyway but went round it and hit Cottbus. We must have hit something down there because after we dropped our bombs we saw a column of brown smoke come up to an altitude of 18,000 ft. (We also felt the explosion on the bomb run.) Here was very little flak. The route in was over he Zeider Zee-towards Leipzig, to Dresden then up to target. Back out as west to Frankfurt. We got a little front line flak on the way out. Take off 0700 and landed 1700.

* * *

#26—February 19, 1945

Mission—Osnabruck, but we bombed Munster M/Y
Load—12-500# G.P. RDX
  2500 Gals. of Gas
Bomb Alt.—26,000 ft

Breifing was to be at 0730 with take off at 1030. As I was checking ind. lites before take off, a bomb fell off the top station. Everyone jumped out of the ship for fear that it would go off but we put it back up and took off. Left coast at 20,000 ft and climbed to 26,000, just above the cloud layers. Over target cloud cover was 10/10 at 18,000 I only got rid of ten bombs as bomb rel. fuse burned out. I cranked doors up. I defused bombs and we brought them back as there is a shortage of them. Flak at the target was moderate tracking. Landed at 1600. Route in was over Zeider Zee and out the same. Fighter escort was good. After landing I learned two men had been wounded in our Sq.

* * *

#27—February 23, 1945

Mission—Truechtlingen, Germ. M/Y
Load—12-500# G.P. RDX and Max.
Gas load. (2780 gs.)
Bomb Alt.—15,000 ft

Route in was over Zeider Zee-towards Leipzig-south to tgt.-out by Colmar and Metz. Took off by instruments and assembled at 17,000 ft as a front was in the area. We were flying #3 of the Hi fit of the Hi sq. We lead 3rd Div which was leading the 8th AF. Col Price comm. pilot. We had lo/lo undercast till we got to the IP then CAVU. We went in at 19,000 and out. We missed tgt because lead bombardier [Name Deleted] left his extended vision in his bombsight therefore hitting short of the yards. Our other 2 sqs. hit it with perfect patterns in the yards. Yards were full with 6 locomotives. We started huge fires. After we dropped our bombs we circled to the left and watched other groups bomb. We could see their smoke bombs and bombs hit very plainly. Later P-51's went down and strafed everything in the area. Saw an airfield with 6 German planes. I saw Colmar and at Metz I could see 2 huge cemeteries which were very well kept where possibly Joe Stoddard might have been buried. Also saw Chateau-Salions; Mannes Canal. Countryside was green for a change. Return weather was terrible. Peeled of at buncher and approached at 500ft. Rain in the clouds. Good landing. I saw a deserted B-17 in France and a B-24 on a road in Ostend, Belgium. Also saw wreckage of 2 Forts which had collided earlier in the morning. Flying time-9hr and 30 min.

* * *

#28—February 24, 1945

Mission—Railroad Bridge in the heart of Bremen.
Load—2-1000#G.P. RDX

2-2000#G.P. and 2780gs. of gas
Bomb Alt.—25,500ft.

We flew #3 in lead fl. of Lead Sq. Our group was last over the target. Blanding with Belimow as Bobdr. 1st Div was going to Hamburg and 2nd Div near Hanover. Cloud cover in target area was 5/10 patchy. There were 300 Flak Guns in the City. We were Briefed for visual run. Wild bomb run with a rat race for the target. We made a steep right turn and avoided the flak in the city park. The flak was a very heavy barrage but I didn't see anyone go down. Talmage finished. I believe all 3 sqds. missed bridge with a few possible bombs on it and the rest in the city of Bremen.

* * *

#29—February 25, 1945

Mission—Munich M/Y
Load—6-500# G.P. RDX and 6-500#
M-17 Incendiary clusters, Max. gas load (2780)
Bomb Alt.—27,000ft.

1st and 3rd Div were going to Munich and 2nd Div. was hitting a flak free tgt. again. We were to follow 1st Div. Route in was Ostend to Colmar, east to Augsburg then NE to a point north of Munich as the IP then to tgt and out over the Alps and reverse of way in. We were #5 in the Low Sq.

We climbed steadily over France where it broke CAVU. Flak was very heavy accurate and intense tracking fire. I saw a ship get a direct hit and blow up taking another down with it, in the grp. ahead of us. It was the biggest ball of flame I have ever seen, with heavy black smoke. We made our Rally point over the Alps. They were very pretty with their snow covered peaks and green valleys. Flew close to Lake Constantine. We encountered a little flak from the front lines. Adair finished. Take off at 0730 landed at 1630.

* * *

March 15, 1945

On this date I found out that Johnson (whom I went to CTD with) was shot up and had to land in Switzerland—stayed there 9 days and now is on his way back to the States. That was his first mission.

* * *

#30—February 26, 1945

Mission—Berlin
Load—6-500#G.P. RDX and 6-500#
M-17 Incendiary clus. 2780 gals of gas.
Bomb Alt.—27,000ft

All 3 Div's were going to Berlin. We were leading the low element-flying in the high sqd. of the 95th Bo Grp. We aborted at 6 degrees because turbo supercharger burned out. 2 fighters escorted us out. We got credit for this mission because we were passed the sortie line. Landed with all the bombs.

* * *

#31—March 2, 1945

Mission—Rhuland-visual only Dresden-secondary and H2X
Load—20-250# G.P. RDX
Max. Gas (278
Bomb Alt.—23,500ft

We bomb Dresden because Rhuland was covered by clouds. 1st Div. were going to Bohlon before us and 2nd Div to Magdeburg after us. Flak over Zeider Zee. Jet jobs and enemy fighters hit us just before IP. I saw terrific dog fight. Several enemy fighters going down in flames. They shot down 2 Forts in grp. ahead of us. E/A attacked out of sun at 12 hi. Our ball turret gunner fired at him and scared him away before he got too close. 5/10 coverage in tgt. area. and 10/10 over tgt. Bomb by instr. No flak over tgt. but we saw flak from Brux, Czechoslavakia.

* * *

Commentary

Dresden had earlier been devastated with huge civilian loss, on February 13–14, 1944, by the RAF and USAAF.

* * *

#32—March 3, 1945

Mission—Brunswick(small arms plant) Last resort was
large Hermann Goering Steel Plant.
Load—12-260# Fragmentations Max. gas load.
Bomb Alt.—24,000ft.

We were flying lead of the second element of Chaff formation. 100Bo Grp. was leading the Div. therefore we had to put up Chaff ships. Thrasher was leading us. Col Wallace was leading the 100th. Route in over North Sea thru Cruxhaven-south to Brunswick then out over the Zeider Zee. We couldn't contact our fighters so we broke off ahead and went in alone. 4 P-51's passed us overhead then a few seconds later 6 ME 262's came around from 12 to 6 and came in from 6 level in pairs. 2 of them were very determined and came on in thru our formation. Our tail gunner opened fire on them causing them to pass us by and go after the lead (Thrasher). One of them shot the lead down then they both left with our escort chasing them. Thrasher dived down and the last we saw of him his wing broke off and his bombs were spewing out. I could see the red flashes from the E/A wings as he was firing. Believed to be firing 37mm. cannon. The jerries were all over. Flak was intense and very accurate. We could hear another group calling for fighters as they were being attacked. When we arrived at the barracks they were moving Thrash., Remil, Bott, and McGuires clothes out. They slept next to me. I was talking to Bott early in the morning and he remarked that he hated to kill all those people. Our fighters really took care of the enemy fighters. They were chasing them all over the sky. British anti-aircraft were alerted because the night before Nazi U-boats had attacked channel convoy.

* * *

LT. GENE JENSEN'S ACCOUNT OF MISSION #32

The 100th Bomb Group was responsible for leading a mission against a steel mill in Germany. Three of the 100th aircraft, including ours, were to fly ahead of the main bomber stream and drop chaff (aluminum strips) to fool German radar. They were supposed to have a P-51 fighter escort, but they were grounded by bad weather. As they reached the target area they sighted what appeared to be a lone P-51. Wrong! It was a German ME-262 jet powered fighter. The pilot flew through our three ship formation passing so close that we could see the rivets in the skin and the ejected cannon shells. His fire literally cut the left wing off the lead aircraft which then 'fell out of the sky.' He made a sweeping turn back to rejoin the main bomber stream but his timing was terrible. He arrived under the bomber stream just as their bomb bay doors opened and they were looking up at full bomb loads ready for release!"

* * *

Commentary

The jets usually made their attacks from threes to six o'clock low or level because from this angle they looked like P-51's with wing tanks. Therefore the gunners are afraid to shoot until they get in real close. They would coast in formation with their jets off, open fire, turn on their jets and vanish with terrific speed. They were armed with 30mm cannon. The P-51s and P-47s did not have a chance of catching an Me-262 in the air. Only if they came upon one with its jets off or if they happened to come out of a cloud directly on top of one.

In the Chapel at the Mighty Eighth Air Museum in Savannah, Georgia, there is a stained glass window dedicated to Lt. Jack Thrasher. It shows a benevolent Christ with His arms uplifted over an airman surrounded by Angels, The inscription reads, "No greater love hath any man than to give up his life for others."

* * *

March 4 (1945)

Learned today we destroyed 103 Jerry fighters yesterday.

* * *

#33—March 4, 1945

Mission—ME 262 component plant at Kempton. (Primary)
  Ulm M/Y (Secondary)
Load—6-500# G.P. RDX and 6-500# M-17 Incendiary clus.
  Gas 2600 gals.
Bomb Alt.—23,000ft.

Plan was to take off here and go over singularly and we were to assemble at 20,000 ft. 60 miles this side of the lines near Trier. We wre #2 of lead of Low Sq. Crossing the Channel we saw lots of tracers which we learned later was enemy aircraft firing at different ships. Earlier in the nite 70 German raiders had strafed and bombed East Anglia. They did no damage nor caused any casualties. We flew in the soup all the way. After forming we went into target Ulm M/Y. Heavy dense persistent contrails and the dense weather obscured everything. We could hardly see the other planes in our formation and nearly lost them several times. Some of the grps were recalled because of the bad weather. We bombed Ulm, saw no flak. Take off 0600 and landed 1500. Learned later the Jerries killed a couple people.

* * *

#34—March 8, 1945

Mission—Langendreer (Ruhr Valley)
Load—14-500# G.P. RDX 2600 gas
Bomb Alt.—24,000ft

Our target was a coking plant between Dortmund and Essen. Produced Benzol. We had a 10/10 cloud cover all the way. Briefed at 0730 and took off at 1000. We were #2 in the lead of the High Sq. We had no fighter escort. Encountered meagre flak. One bomb exploded just after it cleared the bomb bay of one of our ships and we got a few pieces of shrapnel in the ship. Route in over the Zeider Zee and out by Coblenz. This was a good mission to finish up on which is just what I did.

* * *

Commentary

As pilot Lt. Jensen recounted, "This mission completed our combat tour, and presented a difficult problem for me and the rest of the crew. I had a high temperature and felt terrible. I discussed my problem with the crew and told them that I thought I could make the trip, if the copilot or bombardier could fly most of the time. Dick Ayesh, our bombardier officer, was a born pilot and I'd let him fly the aircraft, even make takeoffs on several occasions. The crew decision was 'GO.' Thankfully it was an uneventful mission. (On completion of the mission I had logged a total of 855 hours of flight time.)"

19

THE LUCKY BASTARDS CLUB HEADING HOME

Following the completion of Dick's 34th combat mission, his actual combat duty came to an end. He always thought he would get totally smashed when done, and kept a bottle of Three Feathers Blended bourbon whiskey next to his cot. But he never opened it. There was plenty of partying going on at the Officers Club. He was assigned to work in intelligence at Thorpe Abbotts for six weeks until receiving his orders to return to the States.

While he could have extended his duty in Europe for two months and been promoted to Captain, he was exhausted mentally and physically. He didn't know anyone who wanted to stay longer. Everyone he knew wanted to get home. It was at this time that he was ordered to become a bombardier instructor at Midland Air Force Base in Texas. He knew that once he put in three months as a bombardier instructor, he would be transferred to fight against the Japanese in the Pacific. Of course, he wanted to go to Randolph Air Base for pilot's training school but that would have to wait. He made preparations to ship out from Liverpool to his next post at Fort Dix, New Jersey. As an officer, he was assigned responsibility for the transport of eight enlisted men from Liverpool to Fort Dix. He had to make sure they got to their separation points. His departure date from England was April 9, 1945. The war had not yet ended and the crossing was precarious as U-boats still prowled the Atlantic. He boarded the troop ship in a convoy which was escorted by several destroyers with anti-submarine armaments. He was looking forward to a naval officer's stateroom with all the amenities, including refined white bread and officer's mess.

On board with Dick were 3,800 American soldiers, including many wounded from the Battle of the Bulge. These wounded men were understandably given the best deck on the ship that officers would normally have occupied. Due to the Bulge wounded, Dick and other officers, including his crewmate, co-pilot Jim Millet, were given accommodations on the "C" deck in four-tiered bunks below the water.

Adding to the difficulty of the voyage was the news that arrived during the crossing that President Franklin Delano Roosevelt had died. A profound sadness pervaded everyone on board. Making things even worse, on the way back, they were under U-boat attack. Down in the "C" deck he could hear the "click-click" muffled sound of depth charges detonating. The North Atlantic was very rough and ships were tossed up so high that the propellers could be seen out of the water.

When he returned to Kansas, his wife, who had taken a job in Kansas City, met him at the train station in Kansas City. After a short stay, he took the train to Wichita and arrived at the Union Railroad Station, where his brother Fred met him there and drove him home in the family car. Everything looked and seemed smaller—the town, the family home, everything. Dick had a three-week leave before he had to be in Midland.

It was a time of great joy to be back with loved ones and friends from childhood. For anyone who was in uniform it was also a time to be spoiled by the many kindnesses shown to returning GIs. Lots of freebies were given to the GIs and, in Wichita, even traffic tickets were forgiven without fines. Like almost every vet who returned from the European theater, he fully expected to be transferred to the Pacific for further duty. But first he had to serve his three months in Texas. To get to Midland, he drove the family car, a maroon 4-door 1940 Ford. The only problem was it would overheat every 100 miles or so, requiring him to stop and add water. While at Midland, awaiting orders to either go to Randolph for pilot's training or to the Pacific, word arrived of the atomic bombs having been dropped on Hiroshima and Nagasaki and of the Japanese surrender.

Huge celebrations took place, but the problem was that Midland was dry. Anyone who really wanted to party had to go to nearby

Odessa to celebrate V-J Day, and what a party it was! Dick had passed everything for Randolph and was still awaiting orders to go to pilot's school there, but now the war was over. Those with 85 or more points (determined by how many medals at 5 points each, and length of service) could elect to be discharged. All Dick was interested in was to fly military aircraft in wartime. With the war over, he, like many, elected to be discharged.

He was back in Wichita trying to figure out what he should do. The Federal government had established a fund for returning veterans who had any problems finding jobs. The so-called 52/20 (because it provided $20/week for up to a full year) was available to help vets get back on their feet. He had ambition, but did not know how to harness it. Trying to survive and earn money was the first priority. He wanted to get a good job as soon as possible.

The war had really changed him. He'd seen too many things, horrible things that were difficult to forget. He never talked about the war with anyone, but it had aged him and matured him. He was plagued like so many others with battle dreams. In his recurring nightmares, he would often see guys hitting the ground and bouncing like tennis balls, or a plane breaking up or exploding in mid-air. He had a really tough time adjusting and figuring out what to do. His college courses taken during his college training detachment in cadet school at Oshkosh, Wisconsin counted for one year of transferred credit at Wichita University. He enrolled as a freshman, but at 23 he was older than the other students and didn't feel comfortable with the college kids in their saddle oxfords and campus pranks. It seemed like their interests were so childish and trivial.

He completed his first year at the University and took stock of his situation. He wanted to earn money as quickly as possible. He visited the Veterans Employment Bureau in Wichita and was sent for interviews with Proctor and Gamble and Firestone, and even considered joining the FBI. But an opportunity opened through a boyhood friend who had a California fruit market near a Federal housing tract called Planeview, located close to the giant Boeing aircraft plant. He began to dabble in business with his brother Fred (who with their brother Bill served with the USAAF on Guam during the war). Eventually Dick became an independent oil operator in partnership with Fred, opened a retail liquor store after Kansas went wet in 1949, and took up real estate investing.

He met a fellow veteran, Paul Hauser, who told Dick he was going to fly a B-26 to Dayton, Ohio and needed a navigator. Dick happily offered his help. They flew to Dayton and then Dick took a train to Atlantic City, New Jersey to visit his sister Rae, her husband Mike (who had served in the Aleutians campaign) and their one-year-old son. In 1950 Dick received his private pilot's license. Since then, aviation has been his life-long hobby and he has flown his own planes everywhere ever since.

Dick and Mary Kay struggled to put their lives back together after their long separation while Dick was in the service. But like many wartime marriages, the stresses of financial hardships, marital infidelity, and being separated for long periods of times led to divorce.

Such was the case with Dick and Mary Kay. Studies of marriage and divorce during World War II have shown that the divorce rate spiked sharply during the war years and that, in general, wartime marriages were less stable. Indeed, immediately following the war, the divorce rate fell sharply.[177] In 1955 he married Mildred (Mid) Lewis and they had three children, Jeff, Kevin and Susan. Over the years, Dick never attended reunions of the 100th Bomb Group until he was in his early eighties. However, he did keep in touch with crewmates, pilot Gene Jensen and co-pilot Jim Millet, over the many years since the war.

Dick is a Founding Member of the new American Air Museum at Duxford, about 40 miles north of London. The dedication was attended by Prince Charles and other British officials. In front of the building is a transparent wall dedicated to all of the air groups that fought from England. Inside the building there is a thick book of the founding members. Dick's name is in there with a memoriam to one of his best friends, school classmate Bob Tate, with whom he grew up and who was killed in the South Pacific flying P-38 fighters.

20

THE IMPACT OF STRATEGIC BOMBING ON FINAL VICTORY

The degree of success of the USAAF strategic precision bombing campaign can be measured in a number of ways. First, while much German war production was destroyed by heavy bombing, the production of tanks, aircraft, artillery, ammunition and other war materials seemed to continue unabated and in some months actually increased. Indeed, more tonnage of bombs was dropped in the year 1944 than all of the previous years combined, yet the German armaments industry increased output by nearly 300% above its output in the early part of 1942. This was due in large part to the genius of Albert Speer in maximizing the efficiency of production while at the same time uniquely having essentially carte blanche backing from Hitler to do whatever was necessary.[178]

Furthermore, the heavy bombing of principal ball bearing factories (particularly at Schweinfurt), which should have disrupted everything from weapons manufacture to typewriters, had only a moderate impact on the operations of the Third Reich. Many of their factories were dispersed or hidden, and major German resources were committed to repairing damaged plants and resuming production. Of course, while armaments production increased despite heavy bombing, every kind of German armament that was destroyed in the bombing was unavailable to inflict casualties on Allied forces. Moreover, it is sobering to consider what the war production figures would have been had the Allied bombing not taken place at all.

The German tank industry illustrates the above points. In tank production alone, the Allied bombing pounded tank building facilities at Kassel (Henschel), Stuttgart (Porsche), Essen (Krupp), and Berlin (Daimler-Benz). German tank production was crippled but not permanently knocked out. For example, in 1943 alone, 13,657 tanks of all models were produced, while during 1944 when Allied bombing was the heaviest, 18,956 tanks were built, including 1,069 of the most advanced, heavily armored and deadly Panzer VI, King Tiger 1 and 2 tanks with their 88mm guns. The production of the Tigers finally dropped to 140 in 1945.[179]

Intensified bombing of tank and armored vehicle facilities in the fall of 1944 was designed to prevent the Wehrmacht from strengthening its ground forces on both fronts against the Allied onslaught. In the words of the key Tiger tank manufacturer, Oscar Henschel himself, "Bombing caused our production figures to drop considerably. The Henschel factories produced only 42 Tiger Tanks (Royal Tiger) in February 1945 instead of the 120 they had been ordered to build. Allied (air) attacks of September 1944 were the most effective, I believe. If the bombers had kept up their attacks on my plants for two or three successive days, they would have been put out of commission for months."[180]

However, repeated bombing over successive days on the same war production target was the exception rather than the rule. As a result, German war factories were either repaired or rebuilt almost as fast as they were damaged. It also became harder to knock out an entire industry because factories were dispersed around the country or in many cases moved underground to reduce their vulnerability. The direct effect of Allied bombing on the German air industry further illustrates the point. During the last week of February 1944, German aircraft plants were struck across the country. Yet German aircraft production delivered to the Luftwaffe 39,807 aircraft of all types (but mostly Me-109s and FW-190s) in 1944, whereas in 1942, before any air attacks, production delivered 15,596 planes.[181]

Aircraft production had more than doubled despite the bombing. In fact, aircraft production reached a peak of 3,375 aircraft in September 1944 when Dick's crew was just arriving at Thorpe Abbotts. This amazing statistic is due in large measure to the transfer of the responsibility for production from the Luftwaffe to Armament Minister Speer's overall command. By January 1945, after a delivery of 3,155 aircraft in December 1944, production of conventional aircraft ceased due primarily to fuel shortages, and all efforts were placed on building the jet fighter, the Me-262. By May 1945, 1,200 Me-262s had been built.

It is worth considering the frightening prospect expressed here in the words of Hermann Goering, who in captivity stated, "We then knew we must develop the jet planes. Our plan for their early development was unsuccessful only because of your bombing attacks. Allied attacks greatly affected our training program, too. For instance, the attacks on oil retarded the training because our new pilots couldn't get sufficient training before they were put into the air. I am convinced that the jet planes would have won the war for us if we had had only four or five months' more time. Our underground installations were all ready. The factory at Kahla had a capacity of 1,000 to 1,200 jet airplanes a month. Now with 5,000 to 6,000 jets, the outcome would have been quite different. We could have trained sufficient pilots for the jet planes despite oil shortage, because we would have had underground factories for oil, producing a sufficient quantity for the jets. The transition to jets was very easy in training. The jet-pilot output was always ahead of the jet-aircraft production."[182]

It is even more disturbing to consider the consequences to the war effort if time had not been lost by Hitler's costly decision to convert the Me-262 from a fighter to a fighter-bomber.

At the same time, the nighttime area terror bombings on German civilians by the RAF were relatively ineffective, did little to lower German morale, and only served to strengthen their resolve to resist collapse. Even though the air directives were to attack oil refineries, Harris and the RAF still found ways to attack cities and try to ignore the "oily boys," as Harris called them. Harris wanted to defeat Germany from the air before the Allied armies crossed its frontiers. Yet 45 German cities had already been destroyed and the war had not ended.

Bombing civilian populations, notwithstanding Nazi government control, only stiffens defiance and resistance. People get very angry, hate-filled and revenge-seeking. This was the general feeling of vengefulness after the fire-bombing of Hamburg. According to Goering, "After the British attacked Hamburg our people were angry and I was ordered to attack indiscriminately." Harris opposed the oil plan virtually all the way to the end. The RAF night bombing became more effective only with the development of better radars—GEE, H2S and OBOE.

As a further, presumably more effective, implementation of area bombing, Operation Thunderclap had been proposed by the British. They wanted the Eighth Air Force to drop 5,000 tons of bombs on the center of Berlin in a couple of hours, followed by British night bombing. The idea was to inflict 275,000 casualties and have those who were not killed spend hours in bomb shelters full of anguish and fear, which together, the planners maintained, would convince the Germans to surrender.

The USAAF entirely rejected this plan. Eventually Berlin was hit by the Eighth in a February 1945 attack on marshalling yards (see Dick's diary) which caused 25,000 deaths. Yet this was a "precision" bomb run. Daylight precision bombing was officially maintained (i.e. attacking specific military and industrial targets) and this accuracy is confirmed by German sources and intelligence post-mission follow up. The strategic US bomber force was never, thrown at civilians deliberately. Blind (radar) bombing by the USAAF was not intentional area bombing but only necessitated by the weather. The British intentionally area bombed cities regardless of the weather, but targeted sectors of a city were marked by pathfinder aircraft dropping flares. As Dick recalled, "Early in the war there were bomb jettison areas in the North Sea if secondary targets were not hit. Rarely did we release bombs indiscriminately. Later in the war, if the bomb load had not been released on the primary or secondary targets, you simply landed with a full bomb load."

In total, Allied air forces in Europe had flown 1,440,000 bomber sorties, dropping 2,700,000 tons of bombs.[183] The tonnage of explosives dropped in the year 1944 alone exceeded the total dropped in all three previous years of the war.

Overall, the Allied attacks had devastated 79 German cities and reduced the majority of them to rubble. In terms of the total number of bombing raids per city by the USAAF and the RAF, Berlin was attacked 45 separate times, Hamburg 24 times, Essen was hit 22 times, Cologne was struck 20 times, Duisberg-Dusseldorf was hit 26 times and Stuttgart bombed 13 times. But these statistics are only the tip of the iceberg. The number of bombing raids on other German cities are given as follows: Bremen (10 raids), Dortmund (11), Hanover (8), Mannheim (7), Frankfurt (10), Kiel (11), Munich (12), Wilhelmshaven (8), Nurenburg (8), Regensburg-Schweinfurt (7). A total of 63 other German cities and towns suffered between one and five bombing attacks.

The human cost to Germany in terms of civilian lives was estimated to be 300,000 civilians killed and 780,000 wounded with the number of homeless exceeding 7,500,000 from an estimated 3,600,000 housing units destroyed or heavily damaged.[184] Of the 300,000 civilians estimated to have perished, a large fraction were killed in the two firebombings at Hamburg and Dresden and the heavy bombing raids on Berlin. These numbers are staggering and point to wartime civilian suffering unprecedented in Western history.

It was also clear that despite these crushing German civilian losses and cities destroyed, the most intense nighttime area (city) bombings (e.g. Berlin, Hamburg, Dresden) by the RAF could never bring the Reich to its knees even when followed successively by American daylight strategic bombing.

Overall, however, one must look elsewhere to identify the major successes of the strategic bombing. It seems clear that the major successes were four-fold and I list them here with my assessment of their order of importance to ending the war and preventing catastrophe.

(1) The bombing destruction of synthetic oil facilities denied the Nazi war machine of desperately needed petroleum products and fuel, and made mechanized combat operations on the ground and in the air all but impossible as documented in an earlier chapter on the synthetic oil attacks. To quote the immediate post-war observation of the manager of the giant Leuna Works, Christian Schneider: "Up until a week ago [middle of April 1945], the Leuna plant was still operating, turning out a pitifully thin trickle of fuel. The output was so small compared with its capacity potential that production officials had difficulty plotting it on a chart. The Eighth Air Force twice knocked out the plant so that the production was nil for a period of 15 days, and once the RAF did the same. Once after the attacks started, the plant got back to 70 percent capacity production for a period of

10 days. Another attack, and the plant got back to 50 percent. But from then on it never got more than a mere drop in comparison to its capacity."[185]

A further indication of the potency of the war on synthetic oil was provided by Generaleutnant Adolf Galland, Chief of Fighters and a Luftwaffe war ace who remarked, "In my opinion, it was the Allied bombing of our oil industries that had the greatest effect on the German war potential. Even our supplies for training new airmen were severely curtailed—we had plenty of planes from the autumn of 1944 on, and there were enough pilots up to the end of that year, but lack of petrol didn't permit the expansion of proper training to the air force as a whole."[186]

(2) The diversion of vast Luftwaffe resources and homeland defense forces and labor to repair bomb-damaged factories and plants and to resist the bombing and strafing attacks. This inevitably weakened German capabilities for devoting maximum resources in men and material to the two-front war the Reich was fighting. This included tying down over two million soldiers and civilians, many of whom could have been contributing to the ground war effort on the Eastern or Western Fronts. The flak defenses alone tied down a million men, with thousands of artillery pieces and millions of tons of ammunition, who would otherwise have been part of the war machine fighting on two fronts.

(3) The bombing (and fighter strafing) of railroads, marshalling yards, bridges and canals disabled the German transportation system, thereby impeding the transport of men, battle supplies, spare parts, tools and machines to the Eastern and Western Fronts. These points are brought home by none other than General Feldmarschall Karl Gerd von Rundstedt, Commander-in-Chief in the West before the German surrender, who stated: "Three factors defeated us in the West where I was in command. First, it was the unheard of superiority of your air force, which made all movement in daytime impossible. Second, the lack of motor fuel oil and gas so that the Panzers and even the remaining Luftwaffe were unable to move. Third the systematic destruction of all railway communications so that it was impossible to bring one single railroad train across the Rhine. This made impossible the reshuffling of troops and robbed us of all mobility. Our produc-

tion was also greatly interfered with by the loss of Silesia and bombardments of Saxony, as well as by the loss of oil reserves in Romania."[187] This conclusion is well supported by the analysis of captured documents analyzed by the US Strategic Bombing Survey right after the war.

A further expression of the critical role of attacks on transportation and their impact on the Reich is succinctly described by Alfred Krupp von Bohlen und Halbach, the leading German armaments maker: "Allied air attacks left only 40 percent of the Krupp works able to operate now. These plants of mine, and German industry as a whole, were more hampered by lack of speedy and adequate transportation facilities since the beginning of 1943 than by anything else.

The Allies, from their point of view, made a great mistake in failing to bomb rail lines and canals much earlier. Transport was the greatest bottleneck in production. Plants can be and were dispersed, but the Reichsbahn (the German railroad) couldn't put its lines underground." Other statements about the effects of attacks on transportation and related war industry included this assessment by the head of the German steel combine who said, "If you had started bombing a year later, the Westwall (Siegfreid Line) would never have been pierced. The virtual flattening of the great steel city of Dusseldorf, Germany's Pittsburgh, contributed at least 50 percent to the collapse of the German war effort."[188]

(4) The fourth and final important effect of Allied bombing is hypothetical and indirect—that is, the role of the air war in shortening the war. By greatly facilitating the collapse of the Third Reich and bringing a decisive end to the war through strategic bombing of synthetic oil especially, but also transportation and war production facilities, the German war machine was denied more time for technological development. This almost certainly would have included atomic weapons, more advanced offensive missiles than the V-2, the full implementation of the Me-262 jet fighter, and "miracle" weapons that Germans of ingenuity, prodigies of production and engineering, were capable of bringing to bear with only more time. This last factor was always a wild card lurking in the background.

To accomplish these four most critical triumphs, the Eighth Air Force suffered the highest casualty rate of all of the branches of the US armed forces. A total of 26,000 Eighth airmen were killed, which comprised 7.42% of personnel, compared with the branch having the next highest mortality rate, the US Marines at 3.29%. All together, the Eighth Air Force lost 6,537 bomber aircraft with a typical B-17 having an average service lifetime out of England of only 147 days.[189]

Half of the US Army Air Force's casualties in WWII were suffered by Eighth Air Force (more than 47,000 casualties, with more than 26,000 dead). Seventeen Medals of Honor went to Eighth Air Force personnel during the war. By war's end, they had been awarded a number of other medals, including 220 Distinguished Service Crosses and 442,000 Air Medals. Many more awards were made to Eighth Air Force veterans after the war that remain uncounted. There were 261 fighter aces in the Eighth Air Force during World War II. Thirty-one of these had 15 or more aircraft kills apiece. Another 305 enlisted gunners were also recognized as aces.[190]

One who has not been there can only imagine the gut check and raw courage it took to enter the claustrophobic confines of a heavy bomber day after day facing hazards during takeoff and assembly in the crowded skies of East Anglia, usually in awful weather, even before reaching the continent. Then, they endured the nerve shattering wait all the way to the IP, then having to fly absolutely straight and level to the target at a slow 160 mph without wavering as the heavy bomber, loaded with high explosives and 2,800 gallons of highly flammable fuel, shuddered from the impact of flak explosions all around, while being peppered with machine gun and cannon fire from pouncing enemy aircraft battering the ship, while they witness other bombers and buddies in their own squadrons and groups shot out of the sky. And if they were lucky enough to survive reaching the target and releasing the bomb load, they often faced the same beating on the way out.

It is therefore only with a complete sense of awe and admiration that we honor the courageous B-17 and B-24 bombers crews who carried out their duties on behalf of us all and helped save the world sixty years ago.

21

20TH CENTURY MORAL ISSUES AND 21ST CENTURY IMPLICATIONS

It is difficult to see a conflict through the eyes of those who really suffered its losses and deprivations. The tendency is always to revisit and revise history through fresh eyes at a later time. But for a world at war in which one is either the victorious, the vanquished or the victim, the conflict is seen through a unique prism in time and space that is difficult to replicate later by others. Through a British prism, with the horrors of the Blitz still fresh in their minds, few would shed any tears over the obliteration of 77 German cities, far in excess of what the British endured in 1940–41. Through an American prism, the deep anger and bitterness at the Japanese sneak attack on Pearl Harbor unleashed a limitless desire for revenge. Documented depravities committed by the Germans and Japanese, starting early in the war, only added to the public fervor for retribution in the Allied countries. In such cases however, one must ask how much "payback" should be considered proportionate.

There is also the question of where to draw the line between legitimate strategic objectives on the one hand, and actions which may be beyond the standards of civilized warfare on the other. To many it may seem absurd to even think of the Germans or Japanese as the victims of a war which they started, and, indeed, others may feel they got what they deserved. It was far less than the damage they inflicted on other countries and peoples, including, for example, the genocide against the Jews and others by the Germans and the documented depravities and cruelty inflicted upon the Chinese, the Koreans and other subjugated peoples by the Japanese military. But controversies exist on questions surrounding the morality of bombing city centers where civilian populations were most heavily concentrated late in the war at a time when defeat of the Axis foes seemed inevitable and imminent.

A consideration of this issue should first begin with a comparison of the bombing campaigns carried out against Germany and Japan. The United States adopted a strict policy of daylight precision bombing in Europe, and officially stuck by it throughout the war. Intentional, deliberate, area bombing in Europe was never carried out by the USAAF, unlike the RAF, which bombed cities at night using pathfinder aircraft to mark target areas with flares for the bombers but without much regard for civilian casualties. The American attitude toward this was quite different from the attitude of many in the British public. Americans had not been bombed by the Germans in their homeland. Of course, chief among the reasons for British night bombing was the avoidance of unacceptable daytime losses due to formidable German radar-directed, anti-aircraft defenses, the lack of long-range fighter escorts (the same reason that the Luftwaffe turned to night bombing) and because of their lack of a bombsight as accurate as the Norden.

For the US, when overcast conditions prevented the targets from being seen visually, US bombing was done by pathfinder forces and radar, which had a two-mile error circle about the target. But without radar bombing, the number of US strategic bombing missions would have been severely limited to only a few missions per month due to the generally poor and highly variable weather over northern Europe. Radar bombing inaccuracy almost certainly resulted in huge civilian casualties, but the important point is that for the USAAF, it was NOT intentional area bombing even if it was unavoidable.

However, US bombing policy toward Japan appeared quite different than toward Germany. For one thing, the USAAF had to be based within 1,500 nautical miles in order to be able to bomb the Japanese mainland. Once Japan was within the range of US bombers after the fall of Saipan and Guam, the Japanese home islands, of Hokkaida, Honshu (the largest, including Tokyo and Kyoto), Shikoku and Kyushu (the southernmost island) were accessible. B-29s dropped

147,000 tons of bombs on the home islands of Japan versus 1,360,000 tons dropped within the borders of Germany. Yet, the greater bomb loads of the B-29s, the smaller territory of the Japanese mainland compared with Germany and the concentration of heavy bombing over Japan in a shorter span of time served to concentrate more destructive power per unit area than against Germany. Not only were the Japanese defenses against bombers weaker than Germany's and more easily overwhelmed, Japan's capacity for repair, reconstruction, and dispersal were less than in the Reich. The destruction was generally more complete than in Germany.

The bombing of the Japanese home islands began with daylight strategic bombing using B-29s with the Norden bombsight from high altitude (~30,000 ft.) but these efforts proved to be largely inaccurate, due in large part to drift imposed by the high winds. While numerous aircraft engine factories were destroyed, the overall effect on Japanese war production fell short of expectations. In fact, US naval air and submarine interdiction of the Japanese merchant fleet, intercepting he Empire's import and sea transport of raw materials, had far more effect on Japanese war production than high altitude, daylight, strategic bombing by the USAAF.

Thus, on March 9, 1945, the decision was made to adopt low level (~7,000 feet) incendiary (not high explosive) bombing at night because most of the structures in Japanese cities were made of wood and paper, Japanese air defenses against night attacks lacked an effective night fighter force, there was relatively weak anti-aircraft artillery capability, and at lower altitude, the bombing accuracy would be greatly enhanced. By the time the decision of March 9 was made, much of Japan's war production had been dispersed and moved underground. It had to be inescapable to anticipate that these firebombings would destroy the congested population centers of Japanese cities with massive civilian casualties. In total, 66 Japanese cities were attacked with the built-up city centers destroyed in forty of them.[191]

The horrors of firebombing were visited upon far fewer German cities, but the enormity and cruelty of the destruction, especially to Dresden and Hamburg, was no less than in Japan. Dresden was regarded as having been spared through most of the war, due in part to its being a gem of international cultural heritage, "Florence on the

Elbe," the finest example in Europe of Baroque Humanism. By the final weeks of the war the city had also been choked with refugees from the Eastern Front fleeing the rapidly advancing Red Army, then only 80 miles away.

On the 13th of February, 1945, 773 Avro Lancasters bombed Dresden. During the next two days the USAAF sent over 527 heavy bombers to follow up the RAF attack.[192] Dresden was nearly totally destroyed. As a result of the firestorm it was afterwards impossible to count the number of victims. Recent research suggests that 35,000 were killed, but some German sources have argued that it was over 100,000.

In a fire bombing, the bombers release their incendiary bombs at relatively low altitudes with the subsequent intense fires superheating the air to ~1,800 degrees F. This creates massive updrafts of heated air which intensify when many separate scattered fires merge. The heated air lifted in the updraft is replaced by cooler surface air moving laterally inward from the outside to replace the risen heated air. The resulting very large horizontal difference in temperature and pressure causes rapid winds and suction which create tornadoes of fire sweeping everything in their path, yanking up trees, melting asphalt streets (many died when their footwear became glued to the molten asphalt as they fled), and sucking people from buildings into its vortex, as well as incinerating humans alive in their bomb shelters or causing them to die of smoke inhalation or asphyxiation due to carbon monoxide. The massive fires depleted the air of oxygen, thereby suffocating people, while the high temperatures caused the lungs to burst. At the extremely high temperatures of 1,800F to 5,000F, buildings collapse.

Against German cities, the effects of relentless day and night bombing had still not produced outward signs that German morale was collapsing. By contrast, the highest bombing priorities of synthetic oil and the German transportation sector were indeed achieving great success. When word (unintentionally via a press leak) reached the US homeland about Operation Thunderclap and Thunderclap-scale bombings of German cities, there was an outcry against terror bombing that reached all the way to the White House.[193]

Moreover, a number of USAAF Generals such as James Doolittle and Laurence Kuter spoke out consistently against area and terror bombing as not being the American way.[194]

In stark contrast, no such reservations were as strongly expressed regarding the decimation of Japanese city centers. The fire bombings of the largest Japanese cities took place late in the war when many expected Japan to capitulate without the need for an invasion of the Japanese mainland. It was when Tojo and his hawkish clique had been removed after the fall of Saipan, when the Japanese social fabric was disintegrating, and while transport and importation by sea—Japan's very lifeline—was being nearly totally disrupted by US naval air and submarine assets.

It must also be noted that there was no large population of Japanese ancestry in the US. If one steps beyond the confines of political correctness, it is possible that the difference arose from racial considerations. The Germans were a Caucasian population whereas the Japanese were not. This may have been one factor in explaining the difference in attitude, together with the lingering bitterness and anger about the Japanese attack on Pearl Harbor. There is little doubt that some retribution bombing, or calls for it, occurred in World War II.

In the final analysis, target selection in Japan had to be dictated by the assumption that a ground force invasion of the Japanese homeland would be necessary to force capitulation.

It should be stated that defending a possible Allied war crime by saying the Nazis or the Japanese committed, say, 100 times more crimes is the troubling and classic example of moral relativism. It is equivalent to saying that one war crime by the Allies is not a crime when compared with 100-fold war crimes by Japan or the Nazis. The other troubling argument justifying area bombing is that the civilian populations were just as guilty for giving support to their regimes. Sadly, a large fraction of the civilian populations in Germany and Japan were children who were not responsible for anything that transpired. These victims played no part in supporting the war machines of their countries or, in the case of Germany, the persecution of the Jews.

For example, even if one holds the entire German people as being responsible for the Holocaust, this would not justify the deaths of the estimated 75,000 German children (40,000 boys and 35,000 girls) who were killed in the Allied bombing.[195] As Jorge Friedrich points out in "Der Brand," these children did not run the gas chambers, did not gas the Jews, did not attack Poland or invade Russia. In any case, even for the Allied forces who were so nobly freeing a suffering humanity in Europe and Asia, there is no place in any meaningful sense of morality for defending immoral behavior by reference to another's immorality. Losing the moral high ground in a conflict by matching an enemy's barbarity with the same sullies the national honor and sacrifices of the victorious.

If city bombing, viewed as a part of total war, was a means of bringing a conflict to a swifter conclusion, thus actually saving lives that otherwise would have been lost in a lengthened war, then it was not a crime. Consider General William Tecumseh Sherman's campaign in Georgia in 1864, just after the fall of Atlanta during the Civil War. His intention was to bring total war to the South, to impress upon the civilian population the heavy cost and futility of supporting the rebellion. There was little loss of civilian life during the sweep of Georgia by Sherman's armies, but widespread destruction of food, agricultural output, infrastructure and property. The March to the Sea is often considered a "war-winning" move, as the entire conflict ended less than four months later. If bringing the war to the quickest conclusion is the more moral act, then the bombing of Dresden and other population centers in Germany and Japan would be justified.

It is well known that this moral logic certainly applied to the decision to use nuclear fission bombs against Nagasaki and Hiroshima, Japan. There were reasonable estimates that an invasion of the Japanese mainland would have resulted in 500,000 US casualties, not to mention hundreds of thousands of Japanese lives, both military and civilian. One questions, however, if the bombing of Dresden shortened the war to the extent that the German civilian lives lost were less in number than the number of Allied lives that were saved if the war was shortened as a result of the bombing. This remains a highly debatable question. Many believe that the bombing of Dresden did not shorten the war by a single day.

Credible arguments have also been made (e.g. in the United States Strategic Bombing Survey, Pacific War) just after World War II that an invasion of the Japanese homeland would never have occurred even without the use of the atomic bombs because the Japanese homeland had been so decimated already, Japanese war production had been halted, Tojo and much of his hawkish clique were gone, and the social fabric of Japanese society and civilian support for the war was rapidly deteriorating.

At the same time, the uncertainties of how much more sacrifice would be needed to end the suffering on all sides impelled the Allies to abandon all reservations and moral considerations of civilian suffering and death. From the perspective of a dispassionate observer, militarily it is easier for warring powers to inflict casualties on civilians, the people who are most vulnerable to attack. The firebombing of German and Japanese cities like Hamburg, Dresden and Tokyo through the intentional use of incendiary bombs led to massive civilian deaths due to burned lungs and inability to breathe. In a sense, is this any different than using chemical weapons to achieve the same effect? Some see little difference between the two.

In a larger sense, the war criminals are rarely the airmen, sailors or soldiers executing questionable operations. They were compelled to follow their orders strictly. In some cases the war criminals are those in the highest level of power and authority who gave the orders or influenced the policy and left others to do the dirty work.

It is very likely that a global conflagration on the scale of World War II will never happen again because of increasingly precise weaponry, advanced technology, nuclear deterrence and the overwhelming strength of the US armed forces. However, the moral issues raised in warfare, especially today when guerilla insurgencies mingle with civilian populations, will not go away. A war crime must be judged so by all sides, with evidence supporting the charge of a crime far outweighing evidence to the contrary. In Vietnam, for example, it was the Americans themselves who investigated and prosecuted the soldiers behind the My Lai Massacre. In the Iraq War launched in 2003, the US military has investigated a similar case of alleged civilian deaths at the town of Haditha. It seems clear that US forces in Iraq and Afghanistan spare no effort to avoid civilian casualties, even among civilians who are sympthetic to the insurgents. This is the American way and always has been.

NOTES

1. O'Connor, P.J., *Delano: Stories of the Neighborhood* (Wichita, KS: Rowfant), 2001.
2. Astor, Gerald, *The Mighty Eighth: The Air War in Europe as Told by the Men Who Fought It* (New York: Dell Books), 1997.
3. Jablonski, Edward, *Flying Fortress: The Illustrated Biography of the Flying Fortress and the Men Who Flew Them* (Garden City, NY: Doubleday), 1965.
4. Jablonski, Edward, *Flying Fortress: The Illustrated Biography of the Flying Fortress and the Men Who Flew Them* (Garden City, NY: Doubleday), 1965.
5. Piekalkiewicz, Janusz, *The Air War: 1939–1945* (London: Blandford Press), 1985.
6. Piekalkiewicz, Janusz, *The Air War: 1939–1945* (London: Blandford Press), 1985.
7. Piekalkiewicz, Janusz, *The Air War: 1939–1945* (London: Blandford Press), 1985.
8. Astor, Gerald, *The Mighty Eighth: The Air War in Europe as Told by the Men Who Fought It* (New York: Dell Books), 1997.
9. Neillands, R., *The Bomber War: The Allied Air Offensive Against Nazi Germany* (Woodstock, NY: Overlook Press), 2001.
10. Parsch, Andreas, unpublished historical essay.
11. Parsch, Andreas, unpublished historical essay.
12. Parsch, Andreas, unpublished historical essay.
13. Parsch, Andreas, unpublished historical essay.
14. Miller, Donald, *Masters of the Air: America's Bomber Boys Who Fought the Air War Against Nazi Germany* (New York: Simon and Schuster), 2006.
15. Neillands, R., *The Bomber War: The Allied Air Offensive Against Nazi Germany* (Woodstock, NY: Overlook Press), 2001.

16. Neillands, R., *The Bomber War: The Allied Air Offensive Against Nazi Germany* (Woodstock, NY: Overlook Press), 2001.
17. Freeman, Roger A., *B-17 Fortress at War* (New York: Charles Scribner), 1977.
18. Astor, Gerald, *The Mighty Eighth: The Air War in Europe as Told by the Men Who Fought It* (New York: Dell Books), 1997.
19. Neillands, R., *The Bomber War: The Allied Air Offensive Against Nazi Germany* (Woodstock, NY: Overlook Press), 2001.
20. Jablonski, Edward, *Flying Fortress: The Illustrated Biography of the Flying Fortress and the Men Who Flew Them* (Garden City, NY: Doubleday), 1965.
21. Seal, Jon, "Escorting and Attacking USAAF Heavy Bomber Formations," in World War II Europe Series, Microsoft Combat Flight Simulator article, 2006.
22. Boyne, Walter J., "Reconnaissance on the Wing," Journal of the Air Force Association, Vol. 82, No. 10, October, 1999.
23. O'Leary, Michael, *United States Army Air force Fighters of World War II* (Harrisburg, PA: Historical Times Press), 1996.
24. O'Leary, Michael, *United States Army Air force Fighters of World War II* (Harrisburg, PA: Historical Times Press), 1996.
25. Boyne, Walter J., "Reconnaissance on the Wing," Journal of the Air Force Association, Vol. 82, No. 10, October, 1999.
26. Cross, Roy, *The Fighter Aircraft Pocketbook* (New York: Sports Car Press), 1962.
27. O'Leary, Michael, *United States Army Air Force Fighters of World War II* (Harrisburg, PA: Historical Times Press), 1996.
28. Boyne, Walter J. "Reconnaissance on the Wing," Journal of the Air Force Association, Vol. 82, No. 10, October, 1999.
29. Cross, Roy, *The Fighter Aircraft Pocketbook* (New York: Sports Car Press), 1962.
30. Fortier, N., *An Ace of the Eighth: An American Fighter Pilot's Air War in Europe* (New York: Presidio Press/Ballantine Books), 2003
31. O'Leary, Michael, *United States Army Airforce Fighters of World War II* (Harrisburg, PA: Historical Times Press), 1996.
32. Boyne, Walter J., "Reconnaissance on the Wing," Journal of the Air Force Association, Vol. 82, No. 10, October, 1999.
33. Cross, Roy, *The Fighter Aircraft Pocketbook* (New York: Sports Car Press), 1962.
34. Seal, Jon, "Escorting and Attacking USAAF Heavy Bomber Formations," in World War II Europe Series, Microsoft Combat Flight Simulator article, 2006.

35. Seal, Jon, "Escorting and Attacking USAAF Heavy Bomber Formations," in World War II Europe Series, Microsoft Combat Flight Simulator article, 2006.
36. Doolittle, James H., *I'll Never Be So Lucky Again* (New York: Bantam), 1991.
37. 38. Seal, Jon, "Escorting and Attacking USAAF Heavy Bomber Formations," in World War II Europe Series, Microsoft Combat Flight Simulator article, 2006.
39. Seal, Jon, "Escorting and Attacking USAAF Heavy Bomber Formations," in World War II Europe Series, Microsoft Combat Flight Simulator article, 2006.
40. Spick, Mike, *Luftwaffe Fighter Aces* (London: Greenhill Books), 1996.
41. Seal, Jon, "Escorting and Attacking USAAF Heavy Bomber Formations," In World War II Europe Series, Microsoft Combat Flight Simulator article, 2006.
42. Spick, Mike, *Luftwaffe Fighter Aces* (London: Greenhill Books), 1996.
43. Spick, Mike, *Luftwaffe Fighter Aces* (London: Greenhill Books), 1996.
44. Spick, Mike, *Luftwaffe Fighter Aces* (London: Greenhill Books), 1996.
45. Alling, Charles A., *A Mighty Fortress: Lead Bomber Over Europe* (Havertown, PA: Casemate), 2004.
46. Freeman, Roger A., *B-17 Fortress at War* (New York: Charles Scribner): 1977.
47. Piekalkiewicz, Janusz, *The Air War: 1939–1945* (London: Blandford Press), 1985.
48. Neillands, R., *The Bomber War: The Allied Air Offensive Against Nazi Germany* (Woodstock, NY: Overlook Press), 2001.
49. Howland, John W., "Through the Cloud Bombing," *The Navigator,* 381st Bomb Group, 2002.
50. Neillands, R., *The Bomber War: The Allied Air Offensive Against Nazi Germany* (Woodstock, NY: Overlook Press), 2001.
51. Neillands, R., *The Bomber War: The Allied Air Offensive Against Nazi Germany* (Woodstock, NY: Overlook Press), 2001.
52. Neillands, R., *The Bomber War: The Allied Air Offensive Against Nazi Germany* (Woodstock, NY: Overlook Press), 2001.
53. Miller, Donald, *Masters of the Air* (New York: Simon and Schuster), 2006.
54. Morrison, Wilbur H., *Fortress Without a Roof* (New York: St. Martin's Press), 1982.
55. Parton, James, *Impact: Taking the War to the Foe, The Army Air Force Confidential Picture History of World War II* (Harrisburg, PA: National Historical Press), 1989.

56. Howland, John W., "Through the Cloud Bombing," *The Navigator,* 381st Bomb Group, 2002.
57. Doolittle, James H., *I'll Never Be So Lucky Again* (New York: Bantam), 1991.
58. Doolittle, James H., *I'll Never Be So Lucky Again* (New York: Bantam), 1991.
59. Piekalkiewicz, Janusz, *The Air War: 1939–1945* (London: Blandford Press), 1985.
60. Neillands, R., *The Bomber War: The Allied Air Offensive Against Nazi Germany* (Woodstock, NY: Overlook Press), 2001.
61. Piekalkiewicz, Janusz, *The Air War: 1939–1945* (London: Blandford Press), 1985.
62. Neillands, R., *The Bomber War: The Allied Air Offensive Against Nazi Germany* (Woodstock, NY: Overlook Press), 2001.
63. Hepcke, Gerhard, *The Radar War: 1930–1945* (Martin Hollmann), 2007.
64. Piekalkiewicz, Janusz, *The Air War: 1939–1945* (London: Blandford Press), 1985.
65. Neillands, R., *The Bomber War: The Allied Air Offensive Against Nazi Germany* (Woodstock, NY: Overlook Press), 2001.
66. Piekalkiewicz, Janusz, *The Air War: 1939–1945* (London: Blandford Press), 1985.
67. Neillands, R., *The Bomber War: The Allied Air Offensive Against Nazi Germany* (Woodstock, NY: Overlook Press), 2001.
68. Piekalkiewicz, Janusz, *The Air War: 1939–1945* (London: Blandford Press), 1985.
69. Neillands, R., *The Bomber War: The Allied Air Offensive Against Nazi Germany* (Woodstock, NY: Overlook Press), 2001.
70. Piekalkiewicz, Janusz, *The Air War: 1939–1945* (London: Blandford Press), 1985.
71. Jensen, Gene, *Part III: The War Years* (Unpublished Memoirs), 1998.
72. 100th Bomb Group Museum Archive, Thorpe Abbotts, private communication, 2005
73. 100th Bomb Group Museum Archive, Thorpe Abbotts, private communication, 2005
74. Jensen, Gene, *Part III: The War Years* (Unpublished Memoirs), 1998.
75. Jensen, Gene, *Part III: The War Years* (Unpublished Memoirs), 1998.
76. Freeman, Roger A., *The Mighthy Eighth: A History of the U.S. Eighth Army Corps* (New York: Doubleday), 1978.
77. Riddling, Jan, Archivist/Historian for the 100th Bombardment Group, 2007.

78. Bailey, Ronald H., *The Air War in Europe* (New York: Time-Life Books), 1979.
79. Bailey, Ronald H., *The Air War in Europe* (New York: Time-Life Books), 1979.
80. Miller, Donald, *Masters of the Air: America's Bomber Boys Who Fought the Air War Against Nazi Germany* (New York: Simon and Schuster), 2006.
81. Freeman, Roger A., *The Mighty Eighth War Manual* (New York: Cassell), 2002.
82. Freeman, Roger A., *The Mighty Eighth War Manual* (New York: Cassell), 2002.
83. Freeman, Roger A., *The Mighty Eighth War Manual* (New York: Cassell), 2002.
84. Astor, Gerald, *The Mighty Eighth: The Air War in Europe as Told by the Men Who Fought It* (New York: Dell Books), 1997.
85. Astor, Gerald, *The Mighty Eighth: The Air War in Europe as Told by the Men Who Fought It* (New York: Dell Books), 1997.
86. Hoyt, Edwin P., *The Airmen: The Story of American Fliers in World War II* (New York: McGraw-Hill), 1990.
87. Astor, Gerald, *The Mighty Eighth: The Air War in Europe as Told by the Men Who Fought It* (New York: Dell Books), 1997.
88. Craven, W.F., and Cates, J.L., *The US Army Air Forces in World War II, Vol. III: Argument to VE-Day* (Chicago: Univ. of Chicago Press), 1951.
89. Whitten, Christopher, *European Theater, World War II History* (United States Army Center of Military History), 2006.
90. Whitten, Christopher, *European Theater, World War II History* (United States Army Center of Military History), 2006.
91. Hastings, Max, *Armageddon: The Battles for Germany 1944–45* (New York: Knopf), 2004.
92. Short, Neil, *Germany's West Wall* (Oxford, UK: Osprey Publishing Co.), 2004.
93. Short, Neil, *Germany's West Wall* (Oxford, UK: Osprey Publishing Co.), 2004.
94. Craven, W.F., and Cates, J.L., *The US Army Air Forces in World War II, Vol. III: Argument to VE-Day* (Chicago: Univ. of Chicago Press), 1951.
95. Whitten, Christopher, *European Theater, World War II History* (United States Army Center of Military History), 2006.
96. Whitten, Christopher, *European Theater, World War II History* (United States Army Center of Military History), 2006.
97. Craven, W.F., and Cates, J.L., *The US Army Air Forces in World War II, Vol. III: Argument to VE-Day* (Chicago: Univ. of Chicago Press), 1951.

98. Craven, W.F., and Cates, J.L., *The US Army Air Forces in World War II, Vol. III: Argument to VE-Day* (Chicago: Univ. of Chicago Press), 1951.
99. Hastings, Max, *Armageddon: The Battles for Germany 1944–45* (New York: Knopf), 2004.
100. Hastings, Max, *Armageddon: The Battles for Germany 1944–45* (New York: Knopf), 2004.
101. Hastings, Max, *Armageddon: The Battles for Germany 1944–45* (New York: Knopf), 2004.
102. Hastings, Max, *Armageddon: The Battles for Germany 1944–45* (New York: Knopf), 2004.
103. Craven, W.F., and Cates, J.L., *The US Army Air Forces in World War II, Vol. I: Plans and Early Operations* (Chicago: Univ. of Chicago Press), 1948.
104. Esposito, Vincent J., *The West Point Atlas of American Wars, Vol. II* (New York: Praeger Publishers), 1959.
105. Craven, W.F., and Cates, J.L., *The US Army Air Forces in World War II, Vol. III: Argument to VE-Day* (Chicago: Univ. of Chicago Press), 1951.
106. Craven, W.F., and Cates, J.L., *The US Army Air Forces in World War II, Vol. III: Argument to VE-Day* (Chicago: Univ. of Chicago Press), 1951.
107. *After the Battle*, "High Wycombe Air HQs," Issue No. 87, (London: Battle of Britain International Ltd.), 36–41.
108. Doolittle, James H., *I'll Never Be So Lucky Again* (New York: Bantam), 1991.
109. Hastings, Max, *Armageddon: The Battles for Germany 1944–45* (New York: Knopf), 2004.
110. *After the Battle*, "High Wycombe Air HQs," Issue No. 87, (London: Battle of Britain International Ltd.), 36–41.
111. Doolittle, James H., *I'll Never Be So Lucky Again* (New York: Bantam), 1991.
112. Doolittle, James H., *I'll Never Be So Lucky Again* (New York: Bantam), 1991.
113. Price, A., *Targetting the Reich: Allied Photographic Reconnaissance over Europe, 1939–1945* (London: Greenhill Books), 2003.
114. Price, A., *Targetting the Reich: Allied Photographic Reconnaissance over Europe, 1939–1945* (London: Greenhill Books), 2003.
115. Price, A., *Targetting the Reich: Allied Photographic Reconnaissance over Europe, 1939–1945* (London: Greenhill Books), 2003.
116. Boyne, Walter J. "Reconnaissance on the Wing," Journal of the Air Force Association, Vol. 82, No. 10, October, 1999.
117. Parton, James, *Impact: Taking the War to the Foe, The Army Air Force Confidential Picture History of World War II* (Harrisburg: National

Historical Press), 1989.
118. Piekalkiewicz, Janusz, *The Air War: 1939–1945* (London: Blandford Press), 1985.
119. Rostow, Walter W., "Enemy Objectives Unit, Recollections of the Bombing," in *Discovery*, Univ. of Texas at Austin, Vol. 14, No. 2, 1997.
120. Rostow, Walter W., "Enemy Objectives Unit, Recollections of the Bombing," in *Discovery*, Univ. of Texas at Austin, Vol. 14, No. 2, 1997.
121. Rostow, Walter W., "Enemy Objectives Unit, Recollections of the Bombing," in *Discovery*, Univ. of Texas at Austin, Vol. 14, No. 2, 1997.
122. Rostow, Walter W., "Enemy Objectives Unit, Recollections of the Bombing," in *Discovery*, Univ. of Texas at Austin, Vol. 14, No. 2, 1997.
123. Rostow, Walter W., "Enemy Objectives Unit, Recollections of the Bombing," in *Discovery*, Univ. of Texas at Austin, Vol. 14, No. 2, 1997.
124. Rostow, Walter W., "Enemy Objectives Unit, Recollections of the Bombing," in *Discovery*, Univ. of Texas at Austin, Vol. 14, No. 2, 1997.
125. Rostow, Walter W., "Enemy Objectives Unit, Recollections of the Bombing," in *Discovery*, Univ. of Texas at Austin, Vol. 14, No. 2, 1997.
126. Rostow, Walter W., "Enemy Objectives Unit, Recollections of the Bombing," in *Discovery*, Univ. of Texas at Austin, Vol. 14, No. 2, 1997.
127. Rostow, Walter W., "Enemy Objectives Unit, Recollections of the Bombing," in *Discovery*, Univ. of Texas at Austin, Vol. 14, No. 2, 1997.
128. Rostow, Walter W., "Enemy Objectives Unit, Recollections of the Bombing," in *Discovery*, Univ. of Texas at Austin, Vol. 14, No. 2, 1997.
129. Ludmer, Henry, *Oil in Germany* (Univ. of Toledo Press), 1947.
130. Ludmer, Henry, *Oil in Germany* (Univ. of Toledo Press), 1947.
131. Chemlin Chemistry Library, *The Return of a Classic to Fuel Production* (Essays on the Bergius and Fischer Tropsch Processes), 2007.
132. Chemlin Chemistry Library, *The Return of a Classic to Fuel Production* (Essays on the Bergius and Fischer Tropsch Processes), 2007.
133. Ludmer, Henry, *Oil in Germany* (Univ. of Toledo Press), 1947.
134. United States Strategic Bombing Survey, US Government Printing Office, September 30, 1945.
135. United States Strategic Bombing Survey, US Government Printing Office, September 30, 1945.
136. United States Strategic Bombing Survey, US Government Printing Office, September 30, 1945.
137. United States Strategic Bombing Survey, US Government Printing Office, September 30, 1945.
138. Speer, Albert, *Inside the Third Reich* (New York: Macmillan), 1970.
139. United States Strategic Bombing Survey, US Government Printing Office, September 30, 1945.

140. United States Strategic Bombing Survey, US Government Printing Office, September 30, 1945.
141. Hogg, Ian, *German Artillery of World War II* (London: Greenhill Books), 2002.
142. Hogg, Ian, *German Artillery of World War II* (London: Greenhill Books), 2002.
143. Hogg, Ian, *German Artillery of World War II* (London: Greenhill Books), 2002.
144. Piekalkiewicz, Janusz, *The Air War: 1939–1945* (London: Blandford Press), 1985.
145. "German 88mm Anti-Aircraft Artillery During World War II," Wikipedia, 25 Nov. 2005.
146. Astor, Gerald, *The Mighty Eighth: The Air War in Europe as Told by the Men Who Fought It* (New York: Dell Books), 1997.
147. "German 88 mm Anti-Aircraft Artillery During World War II," Wikipedia, 25 Nov. 2005.
148. "German 88mm Anti-Aircraft Artillery During World War II," Wikipedia, 25 Nov. 2005.
149. Jablonski, Edward, *Flying Fortress: The Illustrated Biography of the Flying Fortress and the Men Who Flew Them* (Garden City, NY: Doubleday), 1965.
150. Halpert, Sam, *A Real Good War* (London: Cassell Military Press), 2001.
151. Halpert, Sam, *A Real Good War* (London: Cassell Military Press), 2001.
152. Cross, Roy, *The Fighter Aircraft Pocketbook* (New York: Sports Car Press), 1962.
153. Boyne, Walter J., "Reconnaissance on the Wing," Journal of the Air Force Association, Vol. 82, No. 10, October, 1999.
154. Cross, Roy, *The Fighter Aircraft Pocketbook* (New York: Sports Car Press), 1962.
155. Cross, Roy, *The Fighter Aircraft Pocketbook* (New York: Sports Car Press), 1962.
156. Boyne, Walter J., "Reconnaissance on the Wing," Journal of the Air Force Association, Vol. 82, No. 10, October, 1999.
157. Cross, Roy, *The Fighter Aircraft Pocketbook* (New York: Sports Car Press), 1962.
158. Boyne, Walter J., "Reconnaissance on the Wing," Journal of the Air Force Association, Vol. 82, No. 10, October, 1999.
159. Cross, Roy, *The Fighter Aircraft Pocketbook* (New York: Sports Car Press), 1962.

160. Cross, Roy, *The Fighter Aircraft Pocketbook* (New York: Sports Car Press), 1962.
161. Boyne, Walter J., "Reconnaissance on the Wing," Journal of the Air Force Association, Vol. 82, No. 10, October, 1999.
162. Boyne, Walter J., "Reconnaissance on the Wing," Journal of the Air Force Association, Vol. 82, No. 10, October, 1999.
163. Cross, Roy, *The Fighter Aircraft Pocketbook* (New York: Sports Car Press), 1962.
164. Lay, Beirne, from the *Saturday Evening Post.*
165. Lay, Beirne, from the *Saturday Evening Post.*
166. Astor, Gerald, *The Mighty Eighth: The Air War in Europe as Told by the Men Who Fought It* (New York: Dell Books), 1997.
167. Miller, Donald, *Masters of the Air: America's Bomber Boys Who Fought the Air War Against Nazi Germany* (New York: Simon and Schuster), 2006.
168. Esposito, Vincent J., *The West Point Atlas of American Wars, Vol. II* (New York: Praeger Publishers), 1959. (USMA)
169. Jensen, Gene, *Part III: The War Years* (Unpublished Memoirs), 1998.
170. Jensen, Gene, *Part III: The War Years* (Unpublished Memoirs), 1998.
171. Miller, Donald, *Masters of the Air* (New York: Simon and Schuster), 2006.
172. Ogley, Robert, *Doodlebugs & Rockets: The Battle of the Flying Bombs* (Westerham Kent: Froglets Publications), 2002.
173. Ogley, Robert, *Doodlebugs & Rockets: The Battle of the Flying Bombs* (Westerham Kent: Froglets Publications), 2002.
174. Davis, Richard G., *Carl A. Spaatz and the Air War in Europe* (Washington DC: Smithsonian Institution Press), 1992.
175. Miller, Donald, *Masters of the Air: America's Bomber Boys Who Fought the Air War Against Nazi Germany* (New York: Simon and Schuster), 2006.
176. Taylor, Frederick, *Dresden* (Perennial: New York), 2005.
177. Pavalko, E.K., and Elder, G.H., "World War II and Divorce: A Lifr Course Perspective," *American Journal of Sociology*, Vol. 95, No. 5, pp. 1213–34. 1990.
178. Speer, Albert, *Inside the Third Reich* (New York: Macmillan), 1970.
179. United States Strategic Bombing Survey, US Government Printing Office, September 30, 1945.
180. Parton, J., *Impact: Victory in Europe* (Harrisburg: NHS) Vol. 3, No. 7 (July, 1945).
181. Parton, J., *Impact: Victory in Europe* (Harrisburg: NHS) Vol. 3, No. 7 (July, 1945).

182. Parton, J., *Impact: Victory in Europe* (Harrisburg: NHS) Vol. 3, No. 7 (July, 1945).
183. United States Strategic Bombing Survey, US Government Printing Office, September 30, 1945.
184. United States Strategic Bombing Survey, US Government Printing Office, September 30, 1945.
185. Parton, J., *Impact: Victory in Europe* (Harrisburg: NHS) Vol. 3, No. 7 (July, 1945).
186. Parton, J., *Impact: Victory in Europe* (Harrisburg: NHS) Vol. 3, No. 7 (July, 1945).
187. Parton, J., *Impact: Victory in Europe* (Harrisburg: NHS) Vol. 3, No. 7 (July, 1945).
188. Parton, J., *Impact: Victory in Europe* (Harrisburg: NHS) Vol. 3, No. 7 (July, 1945).
189. Astor, Gerald, *The Mighty Eighth: The Air War in Europe as Told by the Men Who Fought It* (New York: Dell Books), 1997.
190. Astor, Gerald, *The Mighty Eighth: The Air War in Europe as Told by the Men Who Fought It* (New York: Dell Books), 1997.
191. United States Strategic Bombing Survey (Pacific War), US Government Printing Office, July 1, 1946.
192. Taylor, Frederick, *Dresden* (New York: Perrennial), 2005.
193. Neillands, R., *The Bomber War: The Allied Air Offensive Against Nazi Germany* (Woodstock, NY: Overlook Press), 2001.
194. Davis, Richard G., *Carl A. Spaatz and the Air War in Europe* (Washington, DC: Smithsonian Institution Press), 1992.
195. Freidrich, Jorge, *Der Brand: Deutschland im Bombenkrieg* (Propylaeen-Verlag: Berlin), 2002.

BIBLIOGRAPHY

Addison, Paul, and Crang, Jeremy, *Firestorm: The Bombing of Dresden, 1945* (Chicago: Irvin R. Dee), 2006.

"High Wycombe Air HQs," in *After the Battle*, Issue No. 87 (London: Battle of Britain International Ltd.), 1998.

Alling, Charles A., *A Mighty Fortress: Lead Bomber Over Europe* (Havertown, PA: Casemate), 2004.

Andrews, Paul, *We're Poor Little Lambs: The Story of the Piccadilly Lily* (Springfield, VA: Foxfall Press), 1995.

Astor, Gerald, *The Mighty Eighth: The Air War in Europe as Told by the Men Who Fought It* (New York: Dell Books), 1997.

Bailey, Ronald H., *The Air War in Europe* (New York: Time-Life Books), 1979.

Bowman, Martin, *B-17 Flying Fortress Units of the Eighth Air Force, Part 1* (Oxford: Osprey Publishing), 2000.

Boyne, Walter J., "Reconnaissance on the Wing," in *Journal of the Air Force Association*, Vol. 82, No. 10, October 1999.

Boyne, Walter J., *Clash of Wings: Air Power in World War II* (New York: Simon and Schuster), 1998.

Chemlin Chemistry Library, "The Return of a Classic to Fuel Production" (Essays on the Bergius and Fischer Tropsch Processes), 2007

Craven, W.F., and Cates, J.L., *The US Army Air Forces in World War II, Volume I: Plans and Early Operations* (Chicago: Univ. Chicago Press), 1948.

Craven, W.F., and Cates, J.L., *The US Army Air Forces in World War II, Volume II: Torch to Pointblank* (Chicago: Univ. Chicago Press), 1949.

Craven, W.F., and Cates, J.L., *The US Army Air Forces in World War II,*

Volume III: Argument to VE-Day (Chicago: Univ. Chicago Press), 1951.

Crosby, Harry, *A Wing and a Prayer* (New York: Harper Collins), 1993.

Cross, Roy, *The Fighter Aircraft Pocketbook* (New York: Sports Car Press), 1962.

Davis, Richard G., *Carl A. Spaatz and the Air War in Europe* (Washington DC: Smithsonian Institution Press), 1992

Doolittle, James H., "Daylight Precision Bombing" in *Impact: Pounding the Axis* (Harrisburg, PA: National Historical Society), 1989.

Doolittle, James H., *I'll Never Be So Lucky Again* (New York: Bantam), 1991.

Esposito, Vincent J., *The West Point Atlas of American Wars, Volume II* (New York: Praeger Publishers), 1959.

Fortier, N., *An Ace of the Eighth* (New York: Ballantine), 2003.

Freeman, Roger A., *The Mighty Eighth War Manual* (New York: Cassell), 2002.

Freeman, Roger A., *The Mighthy Eighth: A History of the U.S. Eighth Army Air Corps* (New York: Doubleday), 1978.

Freeman, Roger A., *B-17 Fortress at War* (New York: Charles Scribner), 1977.

Freidrich, Jorge, *Der Brand: Deutschland im Bombenkrieg* (Berlin: Propylaeen-Verlag), 2002.

"German 88mm Anti-Aircraft Artillery During World War II," from Wikipedia, 25 Nov. 2005.

Halpert, Sam, *A Real Good War* (New York: Cassell Military Press), 2001.

Hardy, M.J., *The North American P-51 Mustang: The Story of the Perfect Pursuit Plane* (New York: Arco Publishing Company), 1979.

Harvey, Maurice, *The Allied Bomber War, 1939–45* (Tunbridge Wells, UK Spellmount Publishers), 1992.

Hastings, Max, *Armageddon: The Battles for Germany 1944–45* (New York: Knopf), 2004.

Hogg, Ian, *German Artillery of World War II* (London: Greenhill Books), 2002.

Hepcke, Gerhard, *The Radar War: 1930–1945* (Monterey, CA: Martin Hollmann), 2007.

Howland, John W., "Through the Cloud Bombing," *The Navigator,* 381st Bomb Group, 2002.

Hoyt, Edwin P., *The Airmen: The Story of American Fliers in World War II* (New York: McGraw-Hill), 1990.

Irving, David, *The Destruction of Dresden* (New York: Ballantine), 1963.

Jablonski, Edward, *Flying Fortress: The Illustrated Biography of the Flying Fortress and the Men Who Flew Them* (Garden City, NY: Doubleday), 1965.

Jablonski, Edward, *America in the Air War* (Alexandria, VA: Time-Life Books), 1982.

Jensen, Gene, *The Chronicles of Gene, Part III: The War Years* (Unpublished Memoirs), 1998.

Kuter, Laurence S., *Airman at Yalta* (New York: Duell, Sloan, and Pearce), 1955.

Lay, Beirne, "I Saw Regensburg Destroyed," in *The Saturday Evening Post*, November 6, 1943.

Ludmer, Henry, *Oil in Germany* (Toledo, OH: Univ. of Toledo Press), 1947.

Merseberg, in *Columbia Encyclopedia*, 6th Edition (Ann Arbor, MI: Arbortext), 2005.

McClane, John W., *31 Missions from a Navigator's Viewpoint* (Unpublished Memoirs), 1985.

McCullough, David G., *American Heritage History of World War II* (New York: American Heritage Publishing), 1966.

McKee, Alexander, *Dresden 1945: The Devil's Tinderbox* (New York: Barnes and Noble Books), 2000.

Miller, Donald, *Masters of the Air: America's Bomber Boys Who Fought the Air War Against Nazi Germany* (New York: Simon and Schuster), 2006.

Morrison, Wilbur H., *Fortress Without a Roof* (New York: St. Martin's Press), 1982.

Neillands, R., *The Bomber War: The Allied Air Offensive Against Nazi Germany* (Woodstock, NY: Overlook Press), 2001.

Oakley, Thomas, 100th Bomb Group Museum Thorpe Abbotts, private communication, 2005.

O'Connor, P.J., *Delano: Stories of the Neighborhood* (Wichita, KS: Rowfant), 2001.

Ogley, Robert, *Doodlebugs & Rockets: The Battle of the Flying Bombs* (Westerham, Kent: Froglets Publications), 2002.

O'Leary, Michael, *United States Army Air Force Fighters of World War II* (Harrisburg, PA: Historical Times Press), 1986.

Parsch, Andreas, unpublished historical essay, 2007.

Parton, James, *Impact: Pounding the Axis* (Harrisburg, PA: National Historical Society), 1989.

Parton, James, "Impact: Victory in Europe" (Harrisburg, PA: National Historical Press), Vol. 3, No. 7, July, 1945.

Parton, James, *Impact: Taking the War to the Foe, The Army Air Force Confidential Picture History of World War II* (Harrisburg, PA: National Historical Press), 1989.

Pavalko, E.K., and Elder, G.H., "World War II and Divorce: A Lifr Course Perspective," in *American Journal of Sociology*, Vol. 95, No. 5, pp. 1213–1234, 1990.

Peifer, Douglas, *Air and Space Power Journal*, Vol. 18, p. 121, 2003.

Piekalkiewicz, Janusz, *The Air War: 1939–1945* (London: Blandford Press), 1985.

Price, A., *Targetting the Reich: Allied Photographic Reconnaissance over Europe, 1939–1945* (London: Greenhill Books), 2003.

Price, Jay M., *Images of America: Wichita, 1860–1930* (Chicago: Arcadia), 2003.

Riddling, Jan, Archivist and Historian for the 100th Bombardment Group, private communications, 2007.

Rostow, Walter W., "Recollections of the Bombing," in *Discovery: Research and Scholarship at the University of Texas at Austin*, Vol. 14, No. 2, 1997.

Schaffer, Ronald, *Wings of Judgment: American Bombing in World War II* (Oxford: Oxford University Press), 1980.

Seal, Jon, "Escorting and Attacking USAAF Heavy Bomber Formations," in World War II Europe Series, Microsoft Combat Flight Simulator article, 2007.

Short, Neil, *Germany's West Wall* (London: Osprey Publishing), 2004.

Smith, W. Griswold, "Five Missions Over Germany," in *The Bloody Hundredth*, edited by Horace L. Varian (100th Bomb Group Committee), 1979.

Speer, Albert, *Inside the Third Reich* (New York: Galahad), 1995.

Spick, Mike, *Luftwaffe Fighter Aces* (London: Greenhill Books), 1996.

Sullivan, Gordon R., *Rhineland* (US Army Center of Military History), CMH Pub 72-25, 2003.

Tanner, Stephen, *Refuge from the Reich: American Airmen and Switzerland During World War II* (Rockville Centre, NY: Sarpedon), 2000.

Taylor, Frederick, *Dresden* (New York: Perennial), 2005.

United States Strategic Bombing Survey (War in Europe), US Government Printing Office, September 30, 1945.

United States Strategic Bombing Survey (Pacific War), US Government Printing Office, July 1, 1946.

National Museum of the US Air Force Fact Sheet, "P-47 Thunderbolt," Wright Patterson Air Force Base, 2007.

Wasserstein, Bernard, *Britain and the Jews of Europe 1939–1945* (Oxford: Clarendon Press), 1999.

Varian, H., *The Bloody Hundredth: Missions and Memories of a World War II Bomb Group* (100th Bomb Group Committee), 1979.

Whitten, Christopher, *European Theater,* World War II History Essay (US Army Center of Military History), 2006.

INDEX

Aachen, Germany, 71, 73, 124, 132–133
Adams, Elmer, 49
Agfa Concentration Camp, 130
Air Medal, 186
Aircraft, Allied military: AT-11, 10; Avro Lancaster, 190; B-17 Flying Fortress, 11, 17, 23–24, 27–30, 32–35, 39–41, 49–50, 53–54, 57–58, 65–67, 80, 88, 104, 109, 117–120, 124–126, 136, 138–140, 152–153, 164, 168, 186; B-17F, 18, 89; B-17G, 11, 27, 33, 50, 89; B-24 Liberator, 10, 17–18, 61, 168, 186; B-26, 152, 178; B-29, 188–189; BQ-7, 17; BQ-8, 18; C-47, 138; F-9A, 88; F-9B, 88–89; F-9C, 89; Mosquito, 87–88, 115; P-38 Lightning, 3, 17–18, 29, 88, 178; P-47 Thunderbolt, 29–30, 50, 81, 139, 173; P-51 Mustang, 3, 24, 29–30, 32, 42, 81, 92, 95, 135–137, 161, 163, 168, 171–173; Pathfinder, 40; PB4Y-1, 18; Spitfire, 87–88, 113–114
Aircraft, civilian: Beech, 5, Boeing, 5, Cessna, 5, Ford Tri-Motor, 3, Stearman, 5
Aircraft, German: Bf-109, 93, 112–113; Do 200 (Dornier), 35, Do-17 (Dornier), 45, 93; Do-217, 45; FW-189, 93; FW-190, 34, 93, 112, 114, 119, 132, 161, 180; FW-190A, 114; FW-190A-5, 115; FW-190A-8, 115; FW-190D, 115; He-111, 93; Heinkel 219, 45; Ju-87, 93; Junkers-88, 43, 45–46, 112; Me-109, 34, 45, 65, 93, 113, 119, 180; Me-109D, 113; Me-109E, 113; Me-109F, 113; Me-109G, 114; Me-110, 34, 43; Me-262, 45, 112, 115–116, 163, 171–173, 181, 185; Me-410, 43
Allied Expeditionary Air Force, 92
Alling, Lt. Charles, 35
Allison Junior High School, 2
American Air Museum, Duxford, England, 178
anti-aircraft weapons: 12.7mm,

108; 20mm, 108; 37mm, 108; 88mm, 107; 109–110, 112, 125, 180; 128mm, 109; barrage balloon, 108; flak, 109, 111, 123, 125–129, 132, 138–139, 152–154, 157, 161–164, 167, 169–171, 172, 174, 184; searchlights, 109; surface-to-air missile, 108
Antwerp, Belgium, 73–74, 151, 153
Aphrodite project, 17–18
Ardennes Offensive, 73, 105, 124, 141, 151–152
Argentan-Falaise pocket, 74
Augsburg, Germany, 169
Auschwitz Concentration Camp, 130
Auschwitz-Birkenau, 102
Aviation Cadet Training Center, Santa Ana, California, 8
Ayesh, Bill, 2
Ayesh, Lt. Dick, 1–3, 5–7, 9, 11, 13, 15, 22, 24, 31, 35, 49–51, 54, 56–57, 59, 61, 63, 65–66, 69, 85, 102, 104, 112, 117–120, 122–124, 126, 129, 133, 136–137, 139–140, 143–144, 146–149, 152–154, 165, 174–178, 180, 182
Ayesh, Mary Kay, 5, 154, 178
Ayesh, Rae, 2, 178
Ayesh, Ralph, 2
Ayesh, Sam and Mabel, 1–2

Bagramyan, Marshal I. K., 77
Baltic Sea, 43, 77
Bamberg, Germany, 164
Baroque Humanism, 190
Bastogne, Belgium, 156
Battle of Britain, 39, 113
Beech, Walter, 2
Beechcraft Aircraft Co., 10
Bergius hydrogenation process, 98–99, 101
Bergius, Friedrich, 97–98
Berlin, Germany, 43, 66, 77–78, 80, 101, 103, 109, 125, 138, 159, 161–163, 170, 180, 182–183
Berlin-Tokyo-Rome Tripartite Axis, 5
Bird, Bob, 49
Bitterfeld Concentration Camp, 130
Blaskowitz, General Johannes (German), 70
Boeing Aircraft Co., 11
Bohlen und Halbach, Alfred Krupp von, 185
Bohlen-Rotha, Germany, 101
Bonaparte, Napoleon, 97
Bosch, Carl, 97
Bradley, Gen. Omar, 70, 73, 94
Brandenburger, Gen. Erich, 70
Bremen, Germany, 63, 66, 80, 168–169, 183
Brest, France, 73–74
British Air Ministry, 92
British Army Units: 1st Army, 70; 2nd Army, 70; 21st Army Group, 70, 73, 151
Bruneval, France, 44
Brunswick, Germany, 171
Brux, Czechoslovakia, 171
Buchenwald Concentration Camp, 130
Bulge, Battle of the, 105, 128, 154, 176
Bury St. Edmunds, England, 54

Caen, France, 69
Calais, France, 133
Cambrai, France, 136
Casablanca Conference, 80
"Castor" project, 18–19
Cessna Aircraft Co., 5–7
Cessna, Clyde, 2
chaff, 44, 46, 125, 171–172
Chemnitz, Germany, 163–165
Cherbourg, France, 73
Clark, Gen. Mark, 74
Coblenz, Germany, 136, 140, 156, 174
Cohlmia, Father George, 120, 150
College Training Detachment, 8
Colmar, Germany, 168–169
Cologne, Germany, 63, 80, 112, 122–124, 182
Combined Bomber Offensive, 70
Combined Chiefs of Staff (Allied), 70
Congress of Vienna, 97
Congressional Medal of Honor, 10, 186
Cottbus, Germany, 166–167
Cotton, Sidney, 87
Crerar, Gen. Harry, 70
Crosby, Harry, 67
Cruxhaven, Germany, 161, 171
Curzon, Lord, 98

Danube River, 101
Darmstadt, Germany, 138
Dayton, Ohio, 178
D-Day, 80–81, 91–92, 94, 124
Delano, Columbus, 1
Deming, New Mexico, 10, 49, 157
Dempsey, Gen. Sir Miles, 70
Department of Defense, 17
Derben, Germany, 161
Devers, Gen. Jacob L., 74
Diss, England, 51, 53, 150
Distinguished Flying Cross, 137
Distinguished Service Cross, 186
The Domesday Book, 53
Donoua, Charlie, 157
Doolittle, Gen. James, 2, 32, 42, 80–81, 84–86, 190
Dortmund, Germany, 39, 99, 134, 174, 183
Dresden, Germany, 14, 80, 164, 167, 170–171, 183, 189–190, 192–193
Dunch, Judi, 149
Duren, Geermany, 133
Dusseldorf, Germany, 80, 99, 182, 185
Duxford, England, 178

Eaker, Gen. Ira, 80, 84
Earhart, Amelia, 2
Earp, Wyatt, 1
East Anglia, 60–61, 126, 139, 173, 186
East Prussia, 75, 77, 97
Eastern Front, 75, 77, 164, 184, 190
Economic Warfare Division, 91
Eisenhower, Gen. Dwight D., 70, 73, 89, 93–94, 146
Elvden, Suffolk, 54
Emmerich, Germany, 99
Enemy Objectives Unit (EOU), 91–95
Episcopal See, 97
Eremenko, Gen. Andrei, 77
Erfurt, Germany, 80
Essen, Germany, 39, 80, 174, 180, 182

Firestone, 177
Fischer, Franz, 98
Fischer-Tropsch process, 98–99
Foch, Marshal, 98
Foggia, Italy, 74
Ford, Henry, 6
Formations: combat box, 32–33; combat wing, 27, 86; Group Javelin Down, 27; squadron formation, 27
Fort Dix, New Jersey, 175
Frankfurt, Germany, 112, 139, 157, 164, 167, 183
French Army, 1st Army, 74
Friedrich, Jorge, 191
Friessner, Gen. Johannes, 77
Ft. Leavenworth, Kansas, 7
Fulda, Germany, 160
Furth, Germany, 80

Galland, Gen. Adolf, 95,184
Geilenberg, Edmund, 103
Gelsenkirchen, Germany, 39, 101
German Army: 1st Panzer Army, 70, 124, 134; 1st Parachute Army, 70; 5th Panzer Army, 70; 7th Panzer Army, 70, 124; 10th Army, 75; 11th Panzer Division, 74; 14th Army, 75; 15th Panzer Army, 70, 124; 19th Panzer Army, 71, 74; Army Group B, 70, 124; Army Group Center, 77; Army Group E, 77; Army Group G, 70; Army Group North, 77; Army Group South, 77; Army Group Vistula, 77; Hermann Goering Panzer Division, 75; Southwest Army Group, 75
Goddard, George W., 88
Godonov, Marshal Leonid, 77
Goering, Hermann, 181
Gonda, John, 49, 138
Goose Bay, Labrador, 50
Gothic Line, 75
Greek Orthodox Church, 2
Greenland, 51
Grenier Field, 50
Ground Electronic Equipment (GEE), 37–39, 42, 126, 182
Guam, 188
Gulf of Finland, 77

Haditha, Iraq, 193
Hamburg, Germany, 14, 80, 99, 128, 157, 169, 181–183, 189, 193
Hamm, Germany, 134
Hanover, Germany, 80, 99, 127, 161, 169, 183
Harpe, Gen. Josef, 77
Harris, Sir Arthur, 83, 95, 181–182
Hauser, Paul, 178
Heinrici, Gen. Gotthard, 77
Heligoland, 161
Henry I, King, 97
Henschel, Oscar, 180
Hermann Goering Steel Plant, 171
High Wycombe, England, 79, 83–86
Himmelbet defense system, 43, 45–46
Himmler, Heinrich, 77
Hiroshima, Japan, 176, 192
Hitler, Adolf, 5–6, 73, 75–76, 93, 102–103, 115, 128, 130, 136, 141, 144, 151, 179, 181
Hodges, Gen. Courtney H., 70, 75, 124, 133

Hoechst Concentration Camp, 130
Holland, 43, 126
Holocaust, 191
Horham, England, 54
Hoskins, Bob, 149
Hudson, Lt. Charles, 22
Hughes, Howard, 2
Hungary, 77, 98, 101

I.G. Farben, 99, 129–130
I.G. Farben Chemical Plant, 102, 130
Iceland, 51
Inman Brothers Flying Circus, 3
Iraq War, 193

Jabara, Col. Jimmy, 3
jamming devices, 44
Japan, 188–189, 191
Jefferson Barracks, 7
Jeffrey, Col. (-), 56
Jensen, Lt. Gene, 49, 61, 63, 131, 137, 139, 141, 165, 172, 174, 178
Jones, R. V., 44
Jordan, 35

Kaiser Wilhelm Institute for Coal Research, 98
Kaiserslautern, Germany, 153
Kammhuber Line, 43–44
Kammhuber, Lt. Gen. Josef, 43
Kansas City, Missouri, 176
Karlsruhe, Germany, 71
Kassel, Germany, 80, 157, 180
Kempton, Germany, 173
Kennedy, Joe Jr., 18
Kennedy, President John F., 18
Kesselring, Field Marshal Albrecht, 75
Kiel Canal, 161, 183
Kiel, Germany, 132
Kingman, Arizona, 9
Kleve, the Netherlands, 71
Knobelsdorff, Gen. Otto von, 71
Knox, Robert, 66
Koniev, Marshal Ivan, 78
Korean war, 3
Krupp AG, 39, 185
Kuter, Laurence, 190
Kyoto, Japan, 188

La Havre, France, 74
Landon, Alf, 6
Langendreer, Germany, 174
Latiolait, Joe, 49
Lay, Beirne, 118, 120
Leige, Belgium, 151
Leipzig, Germany, 80, 93, 103, 135, 164, 167–168
LeMay, Col. Curtis E., 27
Lemelsen, Gen. Joachim, 75
Leuna (Merseberg) Germany, 94, 98, 101
Leuna Synthetic Oil Refinery, 102–104, 127, 129, 135, 157, 183
Lewis, Mildred, 178
Lincoln, Nebraska, 49–50
Lindbergh, Charles, 2, 6
Lippe River, 134
Liverpool, England, 175
Lohr, Gen. Alexander, 77
London, England, 51, 53, 144–146, 148–150, 178
Ludwigshafen Concentration Camp, 130
Ludwigshaven, Germany, 129–130
Luftwaffe, 27, 31–35, 51, 59, 66,

80–81, 85, 87, 91, 93, 95, 98, 102–105, 112–113, 115, 119, 121, 128, 136, 144, 164, 180, 184, 188
Luftwaffe Units, I/KG 200, 35
Luneback, Germany, 156
Lutzendorf, Germany, 101
Luxembourg, 71, 152

Magdeburg, Germany, 101, 170
Maginot Line, 71
Mainz, Germany, 140, 160
Malinovsky, Marshal Rodion, 78
Manchester, New Hampshire, 50
Manhattan Project, 21
Mannheim, Germany, 183
Manteuffel, Gen. Hasso von, 70
Marjayoun, Lebanon, 1
Maslennikov, Gen. Andrei, 77
Masters of the Air, 122, 143
Mathis, Lt. Jack, 10
McConnell Air Force Base, 3
McConnell, Tommy, 3
McCormick Elementary School, 2
McNair, Gen. Lesley, 134
Merseberg, Germany, 80, 97, 103–104, 109, 118, 127–129, 135, 157
Messerschmitt factory, 93, 98
Messerschmitt, Willy, 113
Metz, Germany, 168
Meuse River, 151
Midland Air Force Base, Texas, 175–176
Miller, Donald, 122, 143
Millet, Jim, 49, 141, 165–166, 176, 178
Miner, Sgt. (-), 165
Model, Field Marshal Walter, 70, 124
Montgomery, Sir Bernard L., 70, 73–74, 94
Mrs. Henderson Presents, 149
Munich, Germany, 80, 115, 169, 183
munitions: "block buster", 14–15; Fragmentation bombs, 13; General Purpose bombs, 13–14, 123–124, 126–127, 129, 132, 134–135, 138– 140, 152–153, 156–157, 160, 169; General Purpose RDX, 161–163, 166–171, 173–174; High Capacity bomb, 15; incendiary bombs, 13–15; M-17 cluster bomb, 15–16; M-17 Incendiary, 123–124, 126, 134, 139–140, 153, 160, 169–170, 173; M-19 incendiary bomb, 16; M-47A1 phosphorus, 15; M-50 magnesium, 15; M-50A1 bomblets, 16; M-52 magnesium, 15; M-64 GP bomb, 14; M-69 incendiary, 15–16; Medium Capacity bomb, 15; napalm, 15; "smart bombs", 17; Torpex, 18; V-1 buzz bomb, 30, 144–146; V-2 rocket, 144–147, 185
Munster, Germany, 66, 124, 126, 167
My Lai Massacre, 193

Nagasaki, Japan, 176, 192
Nazi Party, 5–6
Neillands, Robin, 22
New Guinea, 3
Nijmegen, the Netherlands, 71
Nilsson, John, 53
Nobel Prize, 97

Norden bombsight, 10, 21–25, 45, 136, 188, 189
Norden, C.L., 21
Normandy, invasion at, 69, 80, 89, 94, 133
North African Campaign, 79
Nuemunster, Germany, 132
Nurenburg, Germany, 183

Oakley, Tom, 145
Odessa, Texas, 177
Operation Barbarossa, 76
Operation Cobra, 133
Operation Crossbow, 146
Operation Dragoon, 74
Operation Octopus, 91
Operation Overlord, 69–70, 74, 81, 89
Operation Pointblank, 146
Operation Thunderclap, 163, 182, 190
Oshkosh State Teachers College, 8
Oshkosh, Wisconsin, 177
Osnabruck, Germany, 161, 167
Ostend, Belgium, 168–169
Otto I, Emperor, 97
Oxford, England, 149

Paris, France, 136
Patch, Gen. Alexander, 74
Patton, Gen. George S., 70, 73–74, 129, 133, 151
Pearl Harbor, attack on, 5–7, 187, 191
Peasants' War, 97
Peaslee, Col. Budd, 42
"Perilous" project, 18
Petrov, Gen. I. Y., 78
photo-reconnaissance, 87–88
Piccadilly Circus, 147–148
Ploesti, Romania, 75, 94, 98, 101
Po Valley, 75
Poland, 75–76
Politz, Germany, 101
Portal, Air Chief Marshal Charles, 163
Posen, Poland, 93
Price, Col. (-), 168
Proctor and Gamble, 177
Protestant Reformation, 97

radar, Allied: Boozer, 47; Buncher, 62–63, 127, 168; Fishpond, 47; H2S, 38, 40, 44–47, 124, 126, 182; H2X, 40–42, 44, 46, 124, 126, 128, 134, 140–141, 156, 164, 170; Monica, 47; OBOE, 38–39, 182; Splasher, 62, 127
radar, German: Flensburg, 46; Freya, 41–45; FuG-20, 46; Himmelbet defense system, 43; Knickebein, 39; Lichtenstein, 38, 44, 46; Naxos (FuG-227), 46; Naxos (FuG-350), 46; Spanner, 45; Wassermann, 41, 43; Wurzburg-Reissen, 38, 41–45
Randolph Air Base, 175–177
Red Cross, 55, 59, 136, 148, 150
Regan, James, 66
Regensburg, Germany, 65–66, 80, 99, 120
Regensburg-Schweinfurt, Germany, 183
Reinhardt, Gen. Hans, 77
Republic Aviation Company, 30
Rhine River, 91, 184
Rhuland, Germany, 167, 170
Rhur Valley, Germany, 39

Rickenbacker, Eddie, 2
Roberts, Jim, 49, 128
Roer River, 133
Rokossovsky, Marshal Konstantin, 78
Romania, 77, 101
Rome, Italy, 74
Rooney, Andy, 121
Roosevelt, President Franklin, 6, 176
Rosenthal, Maj. (-), 162
Rostow, Walter, 92–94
Royal Air Force, 6–7, 15, 37–39, 44, 55–56, 69, 79, 83, 87, 92–93, 104, 109–110, 114, 129, 131–133, 144, 146, 171, 181–183, 188, 190
Royal Air Force Bomber Command, 95, 163–164
Royal Canadian Air Force, 3, 6–7
Ruhr Valley, 73, 102, 112
Rundstedt, Field Marshal Gerd von, 70, 73, 184
Russian Army: First Belorussian Front, 78; First Ukrainian Front, 78; Fourth Baltic Front, 77; Fourth Ukrainian Front, 78; Leningrad Front, 77; Second Baltic Front, 77; Second Ukrainian Front, 78; Third Baltic Front, 77; Third Belorussian Front, 77; Third Ukrainian Front, 78

Saale River, 97
Saarbrucken, Germany, 71, 80
Saipan, 188
Salerno, Italy, 74
Santa Ana, California, 148
Savannah, Georgia, 173
Saxe-Merseburg, 97
Saxony, Germany, 97
Schelde Estuary, 74
Schmidt, Hermann, 137
Schneider, Christian, 183
Scholven, Germany, 101
Schweinfurt, Germany, 80, 179, 183
Seine River, 70
Selective Service System, 6
Selective Training and Service Act of 1940, 6
Sherman, Gen. William T., 192
Siegfried Line, 71, 73, 75, 124, 133–134, 185
Silesia, Poland, 77, 185
Simpson, Gen. William, 70, 74
Sioux City, Iowa, 49–50
Smith, W. Griswold, 118
Snetterton Heath, England, 54
Spaatz, Gen. Carl, 80–81, 93, 146, 163
Speer, Albert, 179–180
Spick, Michael, 33
St. Lo, France, 70, 80, 133
Stalin, Josef, 76–77
Standard Oil Company of New Jersey, 99, 131
Standard Oil Development Co., 15
Stearman, Lloyd, 2
Stoddard, Joe, 168
Story of the Century, 53
Strasbourg, 71
Student, Gen. Kurt, 70, 134
Stuttgart, Germany, 80, 180, 183
Sublett, Henry, 49
Supreme Headquarters Allied Expeditionary Force (SHAEF), 70, 74, 92
Sutherlin, Col. (-), 165

Switzerland, 43, 160, 170

Tassigny, Gen. Jean de Lattre de, 74
Tate, Bob, 3, 7, 178
Tedder, Air Marshal Arthur, 93–94, 146
Tegli Munitions Plant, 138
Telefunken Company, 46
Thirty Years' war, 97
Thomasson, Floyd, 49
Thorpe Abbotts, England, 51, 53–54, 57, 63, 65–66, 69, 117, 127, 131, 153, 175, 180
Thrasher, Lt. Jack, 171–173
Three Feathers Bourbon, 56, 175
Tokyo, Japan, 188, 193
Tolbukbin, Marshal Fydor, 78
Trasimene Line, 74
Trier, Germany, 173
Troglitz, German, 101
Tropsch, Hans, 98
Truechtlingen, Germany, 168

Ulm, Germany, 80
ULTRA, 94, 151
United States Army Military Units: 1st Army, 70, 73, 75, 124, 129, 133, 151; 3rd Army, 70, 73–74, 133, 151; 4th Infantry Division, 80; 5th Army, 74; 5th Infantry Division, 133; 6th Army Group, 74; 7th Army, 74; 7th Infantry Division, 133; 9th Army, 70, 74, 151; 12th Army Group, 70, 73, 92; 19th Infantry Division, 133
United States Army Air Corps, 1, 7–8, 147
United States Army Air Force (USAAF), 3, 15, 21, 29, 31, 34–35, 39, 91, 110, 133, 179, 188, 190
United States Army Air Force Military Units: VIII Bomber Command, (see Eighth Air Force); 1st Bomb Division, 93, 28, 162, 169; 1st Scouting Force, 42; 2nd Bomb Division, 93, 169; 3rd Bomb Division, 93, 162, 164, 168; 4th Combat Bombardment Wing, 54; 13th Combat Bombardment Wing, 54, 161; 15th Air Force, 74, 80, 92, 94; 34th Bomb Group, 35; 45th Combat Bombardment Wing, 54; 95th Bomb Group, 54, 135, 139, 161, 170; 100th Bomb Group, 18, 51, 53–56, 63, 65–67, 85, 104, 118, 153, 159, 161, 171–172, 178; 303rd Bomb Group, 10; 348th Bomb Group, 42; 349th Bomb Group, 54; 350th Bomb Group, 54, 124; 351st Bomb Group, 54; 390th Bomb Group, 54, 66; 418th Bomb Group, 54, 161; Third Air Division, 54; Eighth Air Force, 10, 14–16, 21, 28–29, 32, 34, 40, 44, 54, 66–67, 69, 75, 79–81, 83–85, 91–92, 94, 103–104, 121–122, 125–126, 128, 132–134, 148–149, 157, 168, 173, 182–183, 185–186
United States Strategic Air Forces (USSTAF), 80–81, 87, 146
United States Strategic Bomb Survey, 129

Veterans Employment Bureau, 177
Vietinghoff, Gen. Heinrich Goffried von, 75
Vistual River, 76, 105
V-J Day, 177

Walfen Concentration Camp, 130
Wallace, Col. (-), 171
Warsaw, Poland, 77
Waterloo, Battle of, 97
Weichs, Gen. Maximilian von, 77
Weimer, Germany, 163
Welheim, Germany, 101
Wesseling, Germany, 101
West Wall, the, 71, 73–74, 124, 185
Western Front, 76, 128, 184
Wichita, 5
Wichita Eagle, 6
Wichita North High School, 2, 5
Wichita University, 177
Wichita, Kansas, 1–3, 51, 120, 150, 176–177
Wiese, Gen. Friedrich, 71
Wilhelmshaven, Germany, 40, 183
William the Conqueror, 53
Women's Land Army Base, 131
World War I, 2, 98, 130–131
Wycombe Abbey Girls School, 83

Yugoslavia, 77

Zangen, Gen. Gustav-Adolf von, 70
Zeider Zee, 126–128, 164, 167–168, 170–171, 174
Zeitz, Germany, 135
Zhukov, Marshal Georgi, 78
Zuckerman, Solly, 93–94
Zyklon B, 130